The 20th Century Quizbook

The 20th Century Quizbook

Compiled and introduced by

David Self

This edition published by Limited Editions 1994

First published by Thorsons
An Imprint of HarperCollins*Publishers*
77–85 Fulham Palace Road
Hammersmith, London W6 8JB

Published by Thorsons 1992
3 5 7 9 10 8 6 4

A catalogue record for this book
is available from the British Library

ISBN 0 583 31860 6

Typeset by Harper Phototypesetters Ltd,
Northampton, England
Printed and bound in Great Britain by
HarperCollinsManufacturing, Glasgow

Contents

Introduction	7
Theme Quiz (Number 1): *20th-century Speak*	13
General Knowledge Quizzes (Numbers 2–10)	15
Theme Quiz (Number 11): *What's Your Sport?*	33
General Knowledge Quizzes (Numbers 12–20)	35
Theme Quiz (Number 21): *Capital Cities*	53
General Knowledge Quizzes (Numbers 22–30)	55
Theme Quiz (Number 31): *Soap Sagas*	73
General Knowledge Quizzes (Numbers 32–40)	75
Theme Quiz (Number 41): *Hits from the Shows*	93
General Knowledge Quizzes (Numbers 42–50)	95
Theme Quiz (Number 51): *One Language, Two Nations*	113
General Knowledge Quizzes (Numbers 52–60)	115
Theme Quiz (Number 61): *Top of the Pops*	133
General Knowledge Quizzes (Numbers 62–70)	135
Theme Quiz (Number 71): *Modern Abbreviations*	153
General Knowledge Quizzes (Numbers 72–80)	155
Theme Quiz (Number 81): *Do You Speak the Language?*	173
General Knowledge Quizzes (Numbers 82–90)	175
Theme Quiz (Number 91): *The First World War*	193
General Knowledge Quizzes (Numbers 92–100)	195
Theme Quiz (Number 101): *More Modern Lingo*	213
General Knowledge Quizzes (Numbers 102–10)	215
Theme Quiz (Number 111): *A la Carte*	233
General Knowledge Quizzes (Numbers 112–20)	235
Theme Quiz (Number 121): *Famous Buildings*	253
General Knowledge Quizzes (Numbers 122–30)	255
Theme Quiz (Number 131): *More Capitals*	273
General Knowledge Quizzes (Numbers 132–40)	275
Theme Quiz (Number 141): *Who Wrote That?*	293
General Knowledge Quizzes (Numbers 142–50)	295
Theme Quiz (Number 151): *Singles*	313
General Knowledge Quizzes (Numbers 152–60)	315
Theme Quiz (Number 161): *Curtain Up!*	333
General Knowledge Quizzes (Numbers 162–70)	335

Theme Quiz (Number 171): *The Second World War*   353
General Knowledge Quizzes (Numbers 172–80)   355
Theme Quiz (Number 181): *Sports Kit*   373
General Knowledge Quizzes (Numbers 182–90)   375
Theme Quiz (Number 191): *Brand Names*   393
General Knowledge Quizzes (Numbers 192–99)   395
Number 200: *Answers to Follow!*   411

Introduction

In 1900, millions of men and women laboured for long hours at dangerous jobs in mines, quarries and factories.

In 1900, long-distance travel was by rail or ship. The streets of our towns were crowded with trams and horse-drawn carriages.

In 1900, communication with those living any distance away had to be by letter.

But, since then, the world has changed more than in any other century. Since the beginning of the twentieth century, we have conquered air travel and begun to explore space. Radio and television have made instant communication possible around the world – as have the telephone and the fax machine. Many previously fatal diseases have been brought under control.

Today, provided you can afford such things, you can get a meal out of your freezer, cook it in a couple of minutes in your microwave and (when you've eaten it) put your plate in the dishwasher.

In 1900, America was a week away from Europe by ship; Australia was a five-week journey. Now the peoples of all five continents are bound closely together by speedy travel and instant communication. We have become one global village.

And in this global village, new nations have come into being and ancient ones have regained their independence. We have seen the rise and fall of Communism and the spread of democracy to many countries where people previously did not have the freedom to vote.

But not everything has been for the good during this century. We have seen two devastating World Wars which have caused more suffering, misery and death than any previous wars. The century has also seen the period of fear and distrust known as the 'Cold War' – and also the invention and use of nuclear weapons. There are still millions of people who are homeless or living in poverty and we have yet to conquer famine and many diseases (some of them new and frighteningly deadly).

This unique century (which has brought with it the concept of 'leisure') has also seen one particularly strange invention: the quiz. The word itself is an old one. Originally it meant an odd or eccentric person. Then it came to mean a practical joke. Its first use (in its meaning of a question-and-answer game) seems to have occurred in the United States in 1891. The word gradually came into general use, on both sides of the Atlantic, in the early years of this century. The new 'popular' newspapers began to carry puzzles and 'quiz corners' – but it was not until the invention of radio (and later, television) that the activity (and the word) became as well known as they are today.

The first radio quizzes to attract large audiences in Britain were broadcast on continental stations; one of the earliest quizzes seems to have been broadcast by Radio Luxembourg in 1934. It was called *The Symington's Soups Film Star Competition Programme*. Listeners had to collect entry forms from grocers' shops, fill in the answers while listening to the programme – and then post off the completed form. Winners won vouchers for powdered soup!

In Britain, before the Second World War, all domestic broadcasting was controlled by the BBC – and the BBC was suspicious of quizzes! As early as 1926, it decided that 'the broadcasting of competitions should be carefully considered . . .and under no circumstances is more than one a month to be held.'

In fact the first British radio quiz is believed to have been on the *Children's Hour* programme in November 1937. It was an inter-regional quiz called 'Regional Round'. Very soon after this, the first quiz for adults was broadcast. It was called *Transatlantic Quiz*.

Broadcast quizzes became really popular during the Second World War. On Christmas day in 1939, the BBC broadcast one live from northern France, with British soldiers answering questions put to them by a question-master in London. It very nearly had to be taken off the air when the servicemen's answers threatened to reveal their location to any enemy who might have been listening!

As the war went on, the broadcast quiz grew in popularity and, following the war, many new versions rapidly gained popularity – especially with the spread of television. Some involved personalities answering questions; others involved the general public.

While we obviously enjoy watching other people showing off their knowledge (and ignorance) on television, the quiz is also a very popular participant sport. In recent years it has become a frequent entertainment in village halls, social clubs and (especially) in pubs. In some pubs, Monday night is quiz night. So too are Tuesday, Wednesday, Thursday, Friday and Saturday!

These competitions may involve serious matches between teams arranged in leagues – or more friendly, unofficial quizzes. In either case they provide much fun and entertainment for both participants and spectators. But all such quizzes require a steady supply of questions – as do the most informal family competitions. It is to fill this need that this bumper book of 5,000 questions has been specially compiled – a considerably larger number than is found in most quiz books!

All the questions in this book have been thoroughly researched – and, at this point, I must express my extreme gratitude to Monica Dorrington for her considerable help in word-processing the text.

'Topical' questions and ones to which answers are likely to alter have been omitted and (while no guarantee can be given that a fact will not alter, say when a scientist makes a new discovery) it is hoped that quizmasters can rely on the answers supplied!

The book is intended for all those responsible for running quizzes in clubs, village halls, and pubs – and in hospitals and schools, the services and the social sections of large firms. It is also hoped that it will provide many hours of entertainment as a family 'run-your-own-quiz' guide, and as a 'keep-the-family-happy-in-the-back-of-the-car' book!

It is in fact a book of quizzes for all occasions. It can provide plenty of fun for the family, amongst friends or as a basis for school or 'public' contests, or when you just want to test your own knowledge.

The 200 quizzes in this book include many general knowledge quizzes, and also more specialized 'thematic' quizzes. (Numbers 1, 11, 21, 31, etc.). You will find the answers on the page following each quiz. This means that you can refer to them easily, but you can also avoid any temptation to cheat! There is space on each page, which you can use either for filling in the answers or for keeping the scores – and if you do this lightly in pencil, you can use the book again and again.

It has often been said that an 'easy' question is one to which everyone knows the answer and a 'difficult' one is one to which *you* don't know the answer. An 'unfair' one is a question to which only one person happens to know the answer – and that's a fluke!

However, my experience adjudicating television and radio quiz shows has taught me a lot about which questions most people are *likely* to know the answers to and which questions may cause more problems. With this in mind, the questions in each quiz have been arranged in ascending order of difficulty and the quizzes are also arranged in order of increasing difficulty.

There are 24 questions per quiz (plus a tie-breaker) arranged in two groups of 12 – so the quizzes are suitable for two teams, (Team A and Team B) each of 3, 4, or 6 contestants.

- The questions are graded within each game – a pair of 'matched' easier ones for the first team-member, then getting progressively harder.

- The questionmaster can select from the 24 questions depending on the number of team-members and the degree of difficulty required.

- Phonetic pronunciations are given for tricky words; and, as well as the required answer, 'acceptable' variants are also included to eliminate argument and reinforce the questionmaster's authority!

- A tie-breaker question is provided for all games, to make 25 questions in all. These vary from the light-hearted to the trivial, and from the moderately difficult to *Mastermind* finalist standard!

- The questions appear on the right-hand pages, with the solutions (and the tie-breaker) on the following (left-hand) page.

- In short, the intention is to provide quiz organizers with 200 quizzes ready for use 'straight from the book' without further sorting, checking, verifying etc.

- All the questions relate to the events of the twentieth century – but include, for example, geographical questions about places which have been in the news at some time since 1900.

In serious or public competitions, it is always wise to formulate the rules quite precisely and to publish these rules in advance of the competition.

A basic decision facing any quiz organizer is whether each question is 'open' to any competitor who can offer an answer, or whether questions will be posed to contestants (or teams) in turn. The advantage of the first style is that it generates much more pace and excitement. For it to function efficiently, each individual contestant (or, in the case of team quizzes, each team) should have a buzzer or light which will indicate quite clearly who was first to offer an answer. In this type of quiz, a person should be required to answer as soon as he or she buzzes, otherwise he or she merely handicaps his or her opponents.

While quizzes in which questions are posed to contestants in turn may lack pace, they do provide a longer entertainment. They also allow each contestant to participate equally rather than favouring the fastest thinkers. This form may be more suitable when contestants are of different ages – but even here you can bring in a timing element or impose time limits for individual questions or sequences of questions. You can add variety by letting your teams confer in some rounds but not in others.

How you score is again up to you. You may want to award two points for a correct answer, one point for a 'half-correct' answer, one point for a corrected answer from the opposing team if a question is passed over, and nothing for a wrong answer. Or you may like to give a sequence of, say, six questions to one team (or person), and then to award a bonus for getting them all right.

In most quizzes an unanswered question or one answered incorrectly is usually offered to the opposing team or to the other individual contestants. Because they have had longer to think and possibly because their recollection has been helped by the previous attempt, the question will normally be easier for them than it was for the first person to answer. It may therefore be decided not to award as many points for answering someone else's question, or for answering second, as for answering your own question or for answering first.

In any quiz, the quizmaster needs to be able to decide immediately whether he or she can accept a particular answer or not. For this reason, questions must be precise and unambiguous. They must be phrased carefully so as to elicit brief and concise answers which are clearly either right or wrong and not matters for debate. It is hoped that the questions in this book will satisfy these demands and will therefore be helpful in running quizzes that are not interrupted by delays, arguments or confusion! You should not therefore need an adjudicator, because the questions are deliberately straightforward, the answers short and to the point, and any alternative answers are supplied: but you may need a scorer, or at least someone to check the quizmaster's scoring!

The quizmaster should always make it clear whether he or she has accepted an answer or not. From an audience's point of view, it is also more interesting if they can see the score and not rely on the scorer's announcement at the end of each round. A simple scoreboard can be made in the style of the old-fashioned cricket scoreboard where the score was shown by numbers hung on nails.

And finally, you can make up other kinds of rounds to go with the quizzes here. You can show slides, photographs, or newspaper cuttings, for example of famous landmarks, famous people, or important recent or current events; you can play brief excerpts from records, or a pianist can play snatches of tunes; you can invent questions about current pop groups, radio and television series, or local personalities; and you can ask questions about current events. And if you look closely at the questions in this book, you will not only have the material for 200 ready-made quizzes, but also the ideas for many, many more.

Remember, a quiz is always great fun for both contestants and audience, provided it is well-organized and fair!

When it comes to setting the questions for television and radio quizzes I always have to bear in mind the producer's instructions: all the questions must be of reasonable general knowledge and they must be about everyday subjects the average person might fairly be expected to know about. This seems to me to be one of the attractive features of general knowledge quizzes, whether they take place on television, in village halls, pubs, schools or the home: in fair competition, they encourage us to show that we are informed about the world around us. Such information can be only for the good.

No. 1: 20th-century Speak

To begin with, a round of questions to test whether you understand some of the words and expressions that have recently come into our language! What is meant by the following?

a1   Acid house
b1   An airhead
a2   Aromatherapy
b2   Body-popping
a3   A Barbour
b3   The brat-pack
a4   A Brixton briefcase
b4   Cardboard city
a5   A 'cat' (on a motor car)
b5   To cold call
a6   A couch potato
b6   Crucial
a7   E-numbers
b7   The F-Plan
a8   A Mexican wave
b8   Glasnost
a9   A Scud
b9   Semtex
a10 The glitterati
b10 The leading edge
a11 Friendly fire
b11 A human shield
a12 The Third Age
b12 The grey economy

No. 1 Answers

a1 A style of popular music (with a fast beat); also a youth cult associated with the music and (sometimes) with drug-taking

b1 *An empty-headed person; someone who talks nonsense*

a2 A form of health or beauty therapy that uses natural oils

b2 *A type of jerky, robot-like dancing*

a3 A waxed, outdoor jacket

b3 *Young Hollywood stars; any group of young, spoiled people*

a4 A large, portable stereo radio/cassette player (a ghetto blaster)

b4 *An area of a town or city where the homeless congregate*

a5 A catalytic converter (filters pollutants from vehicle exhaust)

b5 *To visit or telephone (without an invitation) in the hope of selling something*

a6 A lazy person (who may spend a lot of time watching television)

b6 *Very good, important, fantastic*

a7 A code number describing a food additive

b7 *A high-fibre diet*

a8 A cheer in a sports stadium, which 'ripples' round the crowd

b8 *Openness; greater freedom of information*

a9 A long-range missile (surface to surface)

b9 *A (colourless, odourless) plastic explosive*

a10 Celebrities or 'glittering stars'

b10 *Most advanced, the 'latest'*

a11 Fire or shooting from one's own side, during a war

b11 *A person or group of people used to fend off a hostile attack*

a12 Old age; the age of retirement

b12 *Money not accounted for officially; unofficial earnings*

Tie-breaker

Q What is head-hunting?

A *Seeking skilled employees or managers with a view to persuading them to change jobs – to join the organization the 'headhunter' works for or represents*

No. 2

a1   Which vegetable is an emblem of Wales?

b1   *Which flower is the emblem of Scotland?*

a2   Mathematics: what is the square of 12?

b2   *More mental arithmetic: what is the square of 8?*

a3   In which English county is the holiday resort of Ilfracombe?

b3   *In which English county is the holiday resort of Skegness?*

a4   What would you do with a John Collins?

b4   *What would you be drinking if you were drinking 'Earl Grey'?*

a5   For what do the letters STD stand?

b5   *In transport, for what do the letters HGV stand?*

a6   What colour do conventional traffic lights show, after they've shown amber alone?

b6   *What colour do traffic lights show, after they've shown green?*

a7   Ultramarine is a shade of what colour?

b7   *Sienna is a shade of what colour?*

a8   Cos, Webb's Wonderful, Winter Density are all types of what?

b8   *Globe and Jerusalem are both types of which vegetable?*

a9   With which group are or were Roger Daltrey, Keith Moon and Pete Townshend all associated?

b9   *Which is the home city of the eighties rock group, U2?*

a10   Which South African word means 'separate development' or segregation?

b10   *In which country is* Pravda *a newspaper?*

a11   In rugby union, what colour jerseys are worn by the Welsh team?

b11   *Which sport is played by the Washington Redskins?*

a12   Which war was said to be 'the war to end all wars'?

b12   *In which year was the Battle of Britain fought in the skies over Britain?*

No. 2 Answers

a1 The leek
b1 *Thistle*
a2 144
b2 *64*
a3 Devon
b3 *Lincolnshire*
a4 Drink it (it consists of gin, lemon or lime, soda and sugar)
b4 *Tea*
a5 Subscriber Trunk Dialling
b5 *Heavy Goods Vehicle*
a6 Red
b6 *Amber (yellow)*
a7 Blue
b7 *Brown (with some red)*
a8 Lettuce
b8 *Artichoke*
a9 The Who
b9 *Dublin, Ireland*
a10 Apartheid
b10 *Russia*
a11 Red
b11 *American football*
a12 The First World War
b12 *1940*

Tie-breaker

Q Which were the six original members of the European
Economic Community?
A *France, West Germany, Italy, Belgium, Netherlands, Luxembourg*

No. 3

a1   With which part of the body is a chiropodist concerned?

b1   *What do we call a doctor's 'listening instrument'?*

a2   Apart from possibly being a Communist sailor, what is a Red Admiral?

b2   *What is bladder wrack?*

a3   What would you be most likely to test in a wind tunnel?

b3   *What do we call a factory in which oil is processed?*

a4   What does a jaywalker do?

b4   *In Britain nowadays, what is a 'giro'?*

a5   Of which Scottish region is Inverness the capital?

b5   *Which Scottish loch has become especially famous for its monster?*

a6   What is measured in 'decibels'?

b6   *Which country launched 'Sputniks'?*

a7   With which sport do you associate Steve Davis?

b7   *In which sport did Frank Bruno become famous?*

a8   What would you expect to find in a WPB?

b8   *What do we call a container of liquid and gas which squirts out the liquid as mist?*

a9   What is tabasco?

b9   *What do we call the meat we get from a deer?*

a10   Which Irish pop star promoted the charity pop concert called 'Live Aid'?

b10   *Which kind of music is especially associated with Bob Marley?*

a11   In weight, how many pounds make a stone?

b11   *How many square feet are there in a square yard?*

a12   For what does the abbreviation CBI stand?

b12   *For what does the abbreviation FBI stand?*

No. 3 Answers

a1 Hands and/or feet
b1 *Stethoscope*
a2 A butterfly
b2 *Seaweed*
a3 Aircraft
b3 *Refinery*
a4 Crosses the road without proper regard for traffic signals
b4 *A cheque or money order; especially for payment of Social Security Benefit*
a5 Highland
b5 *Loch Ness*
a6 Noise
b6 *Soviet Union (Russia)*
a7 Snooker
b7 *Boxing (heavyweight)*
a8 Waste paper, etc.
b8 *Aerosol*
a9 (Hot, peppery) sauce
b9 *Venison*
a10 Bob Geldof
b10 *Reggae*
a11 14
b11 *9*
a12 Confederation of British Industry
b12 *Federal Bureau of Investigation*

Tie-breaker

Q Which profession did Ove Arup follow?
A *Architect (and civil engineer). He designed the Sydney Opera House, Penguin Pool at London Zoo and the Snape Maltings (near Aldeburgh in Suffolk)*

No. 4

a1   Which flower is the emblem of Holland?

b1   *The white rose is the emblem of which English county?*

a2   Colloquially speaking, what do we mean when we talk about a fish out of water?

b2   *What do we mean when we say we're at a loose end?*

a3   What is measured by a pedometer?

b3   *In which product would you be most likely to find fluoride?*

a4   In which country is the holiday resort of Estoril?

b4   *In which country is the holiday resort of Sorrento?*

a5   Mental arithmetic: How many items are there in a gross and a half?

b5   *If you add together half a dozen and half a gross, what do you get?*

a6   What is kept in a portfolio?

b6   *What is the purpose of a periscope?*

a7   What do the letters HB stand for on a pencil?

b7   *What is the word 'memo' short for?*

a8   What three colours are there on the flag of the Republic of Ireland?

b8   *What three colours are there on the national flag of the Netherlands?*

a9   From which part of a rubber tree is the rubber obtained?

b9   *What kind of vegetable is a marrowfat?*

a10   For which sport is Badminton House famous?

b10   *For which sport is Bisley famous?*

a11   Back in 1961, who was the first man to travel in space?

b11   *Which Briton made the first transatlantic flight by balloon (in 1987)?*

a12   In which city is the Brandenburg Gate?

b12   *Which of the following would you not find in Egypt: the Pyramids, Cleopatra's Needle, the Sphinx?*

No. 4 Answers

a1 Tulip
b1 *Yorkshire*
a2 A person out of place, someone ill at ease
b2 *We've nothing to do, we've got spare time, no work*
a3 How far you walk
b3 *Toothpaste*
a4 Portugal
b4 *Italy*
a5 216
b5 *78*
a6 Papers
b6 *To help you see above eye level (or round corners)*
a7 Hard black
b7 *Memorandum*
a8 Green, white and orange
b8 *Red, white and blue*
a9 The sap
b9 *Pea*
a10 Horse-riding, three-day eventing, horse trials
b10 *Shooting*
a11 Yuri Gagarin
b11 *Richard Branson*
a12 (East) Berlin
b12 *Cleopatra's Needle*

Tie-breaker

Q Which D. H. Lawrence novel was 'on trial' for obscenity in 1960?

A *Lady Chatterley's Lover*

No. 5

a1   What product's quality is measured by its octane rating?

b1   *On a car, for what would you use the dipstick?*

a2   If you're suffering from laryngitis, which part of your body is affected?

b2   *Which part of the body is primarily affected by conjunctivitis?*

a3   Is talcum powder animal, vegetable or mineral?

b3   *What useful ingredient do broad bean plants put into their soil?*

a4   Sussex, Cocker and clumber are all types of which kind of dog?

b4   *What kind of dogs are: Lakelands, Airedales and Sealyhams?*

a5   In which American city is the Golden Gate Bridge?

b5   *In which city is the Brooklyn Bridge?*

a6   How many centimetres are there in five metres?

b6   *How many metres are there in a kilometre?*

a7   From 1959, of which English football club was Bill Shankly manager?

b7   *Who was Jayne Torvill's ice-skating partner?*

a8   In which country is the Brecon Beacons National Park?

b8   *Which island is separated from the mainland by the Menai Straits?*

a9   In America, what kind of drink is bourbon?

b9   *For what drink was chicory a wartime substitute?*

a10   To help which country was the song 'Do They Know it's Christmas?' recorded by many stars in 1984?

b10   *'Magic Moments', 'Catch a Falling Star' and 'Delaware' were all hits for which American star?*

a11   By what abbreviation is the Organization of Petroleum Exporting Countries known?

b11   *Which organization is known as the PLO?*

a12   Which cross was the symbol of the Free French during the Second World War?

b12   *In the Second World War, what were Gold, Juno and Sword?*

No. 5 Answers

a1 Petrol
b1 *To measure the engine oil*
a2 Throat
b2 *The eye*
a3 Mineral (magnesium silicate)
b3 *Nitrogen*
a4 Spaniel
b4 *Terriers*
a5 San Francisco
b5 *New York*
a6 500
b6 *1,000*
a7 Liverpool
b7 *(Christopher) Dean*
a8 Wales
b8 *Anglesey*
a9 Type of whisky (made from corn or rye, not barley)
b9 *Coffee*
a10 Ethiopia
b10 *Perry Como*
a11 OPEC
b11 *Palestine Liberation Organization*
a12 Cross of Lorraine
b12 *The British Invasion beaches in Normandy*

Tie-breaker

Q What is or was the profession of Lindsay Anderson?
A *Film director*

No. 6

a1   By what other name is a viper known?

b1   With which mammal is the disease rabies usually associated?

a2   Colloquially speaking, what do we mean when we talk about a cat-and-dog life?

b2   What is a fool's paradise?

a3   In which English county is the holiday resort of St Ives?

b3   In which English county is the holiday resort of Margate?

a4   In which sport might you have competed in the Refuge Assurance League?

b4   In which sport is the Davis Cup played for?

a5   If an artist was using burnt umber, what colour they be using?

b5   Which is the colour of jealousy?

a6   What name do we give to the polluted weather phenomenon that kills plants and forests and erodes buildings and statues?

b6   What is the usual name for the trapping of the sun's rays in the lower atmosphere, due to pollutants in the atmosphere?

a7   What is sometimes called a 'rubberneck-wagon'?

b7.   What does an Australian mean when he talks about a 'sheila'?

a8   In 1906, what food was first manufactured by William Kellogg?

b8   According to some people, which part of the edible frog is a delicacy?

a9   Every autumn, there are illuminations along which holiday resort's Golden Mile?

b9   On the second Sunday in November, where in London is the nation's Remembrance Day service held?

a10   For what are the letters ARP an abbreviation?

b10   For what do the initials WRVS stand?

a11   Until 1960, which coin was a quarter of one penny?

b11   Is the obverse side of a coin heads or tails?

a12   Nicknamed 'the Boss', he had a major hit with the album 'Born in the USA'. Who was this pop or rock star?

b12   Which blind pop star led the campaign to turn Martin Luther King's birthday into an American national holiday?

No. 6 Answers

a1 Adder
b1 *Dogs*
a2 A life of quarrelling
b2 *A state of happiness or success which may change at any moment; an insecure situation*
a3 Cornwall
b3 *Kent*
a4 Cricket
b4 *Lawn Tennis*
a5 (Dark) brown
b5 *Green or yellow*
a6 Acid rain
b6 *Greenhouse effect*
a7 Tourist coach, bus; sightseeing-bus
b7 *A girl, woman*
a8 Corn flakes
b8 *The legs*
a9 Blackpool
b9 *At the Cenotaph in Whitehall*
a10 Air Raid Precautions
b10 *Women's Royal Voluntary Service*
a11 Farthing
b11 *Heads*
a12 Bruce Springsteen
b12 *Stevie Wonder*

Tie-breaker

Q Which British male tennis star won Wimbledon in 1934, 1935 and 1936?
A *Fred Perry*

No. 7

a1 What do you worry about if you are a hypochondriac?

b1 *What is amnesia?*

a2 Which motor manufacturing company was started by Lord Nuffield?

b2 *Cars: what colour were all the early Model 'T' Fords?*

a3 By what abbreviation is the American space agency known?

b3 *What do the initials NATO stand for?*

a4 Barbel, chubb and tench are all types of . . . what?

b4 *What kind of animals are Cheviots, Southdowns and Shropshires?*

a5 In which sport was Rocky Marciano a champion?

b5 *In which sport did Giant Haystacks become well known?*

a6 What is the county town of Cumbria?

b6 *What is the county town of Hampshire?*

a7 In which month does the Lord Mayor's Show take place in London?

b7 *What do we call the annual ceremony on the River Thames when all the new-born cygnets are marked?*

a8 Who first said, 'Never in the field of human conflict was so much owed by so many to so few'?

b8 *Which British prime minister told the nation, 'I have to say, no such undertaking has been received'?*

a9 Of which chemical element is the symbol C?

b9 *Of which chemical element is the symbol the letter N?*

a10 'Bye Bye Love' and 'Wake Up Little Susie' were hits for which pop duo?

b10 *Robert Zimmerman (who wrote and sang the pop ballad 'Blowin' in the Wind') was better known by what name?*

a11 Which is the smallest of the following: hundredweight, stone, ton?

b11 *Which is the smallest of the following: furlong, foot, chain?*

a12 Who first reached the South Pole in December 1911?

b12 *Apart from Sherpa Tenzing, who reached the summit of Mount Everest in 1953?*

No. 7 Answers

a1   Your health
b1   *Loss of memory*
a2   Morris (he was born William Richard Morris)
b2   *Black*
a3   NASA (National Aeronautics and Space Administration)
b3   *North Atlantic Treaty Organization*
a4   Fish
b4   *Sheep*
a5   Boxing
b5   *Wrestling*
a6   Carlisle
b6   *Winchester*
a7   November
b7   *Swan-upping*
a8   Sir Winston Churchill
b8   *Neville Chamberlain*
a9   Carbon
b9   *Nitrogen*
a10   The Everly Brothers
b10   *Bob Dylan*
a11   Stone
b11   *Foot*
a12   Roald Amundsen
b12   *(Sir Edmund) Hillary (Sir John Hunt was expedition leader: he did not reach the summit)*

Tie-breaker

Q Which Belfast musician issued albums titled 'Astral Weeks' and 'Moondance'?
A *Van Morrison*

No. 8

a1   Colloquially speaking, what do we mean when we talk about a wet blanket?

b1   What is a golden handshake?

a2   In which country is the holiday resort of Torremolinos?

b2   In which country is the Algarve?

a3   Which British breed of cat is famous for not having a tail?

b3   In which part of England were coypus (say: coy-pews) found in the wild?

a4   For what are the letters TSB an abbreviation?

b4   For what do the initials PAYE stand?

a5   From which European country does *paella* come?

b5   From which country does the food lasagne originate?

a6   What is a juggernaut?

b6   Usually, what kind of transport is a 'funicular'?

a7   In which sport would you use a spoon, a brassie or a niblick?

b7   With which sport do you connect Fastnet?

a8   'Let It Be' was the last album released by which pop group?

b8   Which young pop guitarist died in 1970, having had a hit with 'Hey Joe'?

a9   Which university city stands on the river Isis?

b9   Which university is situated at Canterbury?

a10   Who led the unsuccessful British expedition to the South Pole in 1901–4?

b10   To which high position was Karol Wojtyla (say: voy-ti-wa) elected in 1978?

a11   Which metal is extracted from bauxite?

b11   What is the everyday name for sodium carbonate?

a12   In 1990, in which country were free, democratic elections held for the first time in 70 years?

b12   Who is King of Jordan?

No. 8 Answers

a1   A depressing person, a person who always fears the worst
b1   A leaving present
a2   Spain
b2   Portugal
a3   Manx
b3   East Anglia
a4   Trustee Savings Bank
b4   Pay As You Earn
a5   Spain
b5   Italy
a6   Heavy lorry
b6   (Mountain) railway
a7   Golf
b7   Yachting, sailing
a8   The Beatles (1970)
b8   Jimi Hendrix
a9   Oxford
b9   Kent
a10   Captain (Robert F.) Scott
b10   Pope
a11   Aluminium
b11   Washing soda
a12   Soviet Union
b12   Hussein

Tie-breaker

Q Who was Francis Bacon?
A (Irish) painter

No. 9

a1   What happens when there's an epidemic?

b1   *What is flatulence?*

a2   What was the bunny hug?

b2   *What kind of transport is a 'whirlybird'?*

a3   Can you name a drink which usually contains the stimulant caffeine?

b3   *On a menu, what is meant by 'petits pois' (say: pu-tee pwa)?*

a4   What is meant by 'perestroika'?

b4   *Which politician was nicknamed 'The Iron Lady'?*

a5   What kind of mammal is a bighorn?

b5   *What kind of animal is a merino?*

a6   In which sport did Billie Jean King become famous?

b6   *In which sport did Mike Gatting captain England?*

a7   How many angles has a decagon?

b7   *How many sides has a heptagon?*

a8   In the 1920s, who or what was a flapper?

b8   *In which country would you be most likely to meet a geisha girl?*

a9   For what do the initials BMA stand?

b9   *For what do the initials PhD stand?*

a10   From which London railway station would you leave if you were travelling to Cardiff?

b10   *In which town or city would you be if you were driving along the Royal Mile?*

a11   What is an alloy?

b11   *What is bitumen?*

a12   Digital watches use changing numbers to show the time. What do we call a watch that uses hands and a dial?

b12   *On the top row of a typewriter, which four letters follow Q W E R T Y?*

No. 9 Answers

a1 A disease is caught by lots of people
b1 *Wind ('too much gas in the stomach')*
a2 A dance
b2 *Helicopter*
a3 Tea or coffee (some colas)
b3 *Peas*
a4 Restructuring
b4 *Margaret Thatcher*
a5 Sheep (Rocky Mountain sheep)
b5 *A sheep (Also a sheep pasture inspector)*
a6 Tennis
b6 *Cricket*
a7 Ten
b7 *Seven*
a8 Bold young lady
b8 *Japan*
a9 British Medical Association
b9 *Doctor of Philosophy*
a10 Paddington
b10 *Edinburgh*
a11 A mixture of two (or more) metals
b11 *An oil or 'pitch' (accept: tar)*
a12 Analogue
b12 *U I O P*

Tie-breaker

Q Writers Virginia Woolf, Lytton Strachey, Clive Bell and Duncan Grant all lived in the same district of London and were known by the name of that district. What was the group's name?

A *The Bloomsbury Group*

No. 10

a1   Which large bird is said to bury its head in the sand, when it's afraid?

b1   *For which flightless bird is New Zealand famous?*

a2   Colloquially speaking, what do we mean when we talk about a rough diamond?

b2   *What is meant by 'gob-smacked'?*

a3   What is 'fromage frais' (say: fro-marge fray)?

b3   *From what is macaroni chiefly made?*

a4   In which country is the holiday resort of Tangier?

b4   *If you were having a holiday on the island of Rhodes, in which country would you be?*

a5   In sport, what is the LTA?

b5   *Which body frames the rules by which horse-racing is organized?*

a6   With which city do you associate the comedian Billy Connolly?

b6   *What invention by Percy Shaw in 1934 has been a great help to motorists?*

a7   As what did Sir Stanley Spencer achieve fame?

b7   *Which painter had a 'blue period'?*

a8   Who became leader of the Soviet Union in 1985?

b8   *In which country was Adolf Hitler born?*

a9   For what did the initials BAOR stand?

b9   *On VE Day 1945, what did VE mean?*

a10   Of which university are Corpus Christi, Queens and Emmanuel all colleges?

b10   *Charing Cross and Guy's are both medical schools of which university?*

a11   Which film featured Bill Haley's hit song, 'Rock Around the Clock'?

b11   *Whose album, called 'True Blue', topped the charts in 28 countries in 1986?*

a12   What is the chemical formula for carbon dioxide?

b12   *Which scientist first formulated the important equation, $E = mc^2$?*

No. 10 Answers

a1 Ostrich
b1 *Kiwi*
a2 A good-hearted person who has rough manners
b2 *You are astounded, rendered speechless or incoherent*
a3 Low-fat curd cheese; dessert based on sweetened cheese (accept: quark)
b3 *Flour, flour paste (accept: pasta)*
a4 Morocco
b4 *Greece*
a5 Lawn Tennis Association
b5 *Jockey Club*
a6 Glasgow
b6 *Cat's eyes*
a7 Artist/painter
b7 *Picasso*
a8 Mikhail Gorbachev
b8 *Austria*
a9 British Army of the Rhine
b9 *Victory in Europe*
a10 Cambridge
b10 *London*
a11 *Blackboard Jungle*
b11 *Madonna*
a12 CO_2
b12 *Einstein*

Tie-breaker

Q Who wrote a book which begins, 'I shall tell you a tale of four little rabbits whose names were Flopsy, Mopsy, Cottontail and Peter'?
A Beatrix Potter

No. 11: What's Your Sport?

In which sport have each of the following men and women become famous?

a1   Jimmy Connors
b1   *Ray Reardon*
a2   Lee Trevino
b2   *Adrian Moorhouse*
a3   Viv Richards
b3   *J. P. R. Williams*
a4   Sharron Davies
b4   *Gary Player*
a5   Big Daddie
b5   *Steve Cauthen*
a6   Linda Ludgrove
b6   *Eddie Merckx*
a7   Dennis Lillee
b7   *Steve Perryman*
a8   Cliff Thorburn
b8   *Mick McManus*
a9   Arthur Ashe
b9   *Richard Meade*
a10   Chris Tavare (say: tav-a-ray)
b10   *Kirk Stevens*
a11   Carlos Reutemann (say: roy-tuh-man)
b11   *John Francome*
a12   René Arnoux
b12   *Reg Harris*

No. 11 Answers

a1	Tennis
b1	*Snooker*
a2	Golf
b2	*Swimming*
a3	Cricket
b3	*Rugby Union (Rugger; not Rugby League)*
a4	Swimming
b4	*Golf*
a5	Wrestling
b5	*Horse-racing*
a6	Swimming
b6	*Cycling*
a7	Cricket
b7	*Soccer*
a8	Snooker
b8	*Wrestling*
a9	Tennis
b9	*Three-day eventing (accept: showjumping)*
a10	Cricket
b10	*Snooker*
a11	Motor-racing
b11	*Horse-racing*
a12	Motor-racing
b12	*Cycling*

Tie-breaker

Q Which country led the boycott of the 1980 Summer Olympics?
A United States of America (the games were held in Moscow)

No. 12

a1   What would you do with 'winkle-pickers'?

b1   *What is the Red Duster?*

a2   What is the common name for a baby kangaroo?

b2   *What are gobies, dace and perch?*

a3   What is claustrophobia?

b3   *What is meant by the medical term, obesity?*

a4   In boxing, at what 'weight' do you fight, if you weigh just under eight stone?

b4   *With which famous steeplechase do you primarily associate 'Red Rum'?*

a5   In the world of pop, who was the drummer (replaced by Ringo Starr) who was part of the original Beatles line-up?

b5   *Which group was formed in 1955 to back the singer Buddy Holly?*

a6   By what abbreviation is the Oxford Committee for Famine Relief known?

b6   *By what abbreviation is the Navy, Army and Air Force Institutes known?*

a7   By which Christian name is the Queen's second son known?

b7   *Which member of the Royal Family was born in Greece?*

a8   In which art has Joan Sutherland achieved fame?

b8   *Who composed the music for* Phantom of the Opera?

a9   How is asbestos obtained?

b9   *In what do we find the sugary substance called lactose?*

a10   Which acid is used in car batteries and is used to make fertilizers and explosives?

b10   *Of which chemical element is the symbol the letters Cu?*

a11   Which geometrical figure has no beginning and no end?

b11   *What do we call half a sphere?*

a12   In which European capital were there student riots in 1968?

b12   *Which modern school subject is named after the Latin word meaning 'to know' or 'knowledge'?*

No. 12 Answers

a1	*Wear them: they are shoes with pointed toes*
b1	*A flag (The Red Ensign; flown on British merchant ships)*
a2	Joey
b2	*Fish*
a3	Fear of closed spaces, fear of being shut in
b3	*Fatness, being overweight*
a4	Flyweight
b4	*Grand National*
a5	Pete Best
b5	*The Crickets*
a6	OXFAM
b6	*NAAFI*
a7	Andrew
b7	*Prince Philip, Duke of Edinburgh*
a8	Opera (singing)
b8	*Andrew Lloyd Webber*
a9	It is mined from the earth
b9	*Milk*
a10	Sulphuric
b10	*Copper*
a11	Circle (or ellipse)
b11	*Hemisphere*
a12	Paris
b12	*Science*

Tie-breaker

Q For what product did 'Roses grow on you' become an advertising slogan in the sixties?

A *Cadbury's Roses Chocolates*

No. 13

a1   What would you usually do with a knickerbocker glory?
b1   *What is the Turkey Trot?*
a2   Of which two colours is turquoise a mixture?
b2   *Of what colour is emerald a shade?*
a3   Which pop singer starred in the films *The Young Ones* and *Summer Holiday?*
b3   *Whose home was a mansion called 'Graceland' in Memphis?*
a4   On which island is the holiday resort of Palma?
b4   *In which sea could you swim if you were on holiday on the east coast of Italy?*
a5   Which organization for children has as its motto, 'Lend a hand'?
b5   *What do we call an adult who runs a Brownie pack?*
a6   What does ACAS try to do?
b6   *For what do the initials TUC stand?*
a7   What is the proper name for the white of an egg?
b7   *Which bird is suggested by the word 'aquiline'?*
a8   Which Chinese leader became known for his 'little red books'?
b8   *Which peace-loving Indian leader was assassinated in 1948?*
a9   In Britain, how many pounds are there in a hundredweight?
b9   *How many acres are there in a square mile?*
a10   In which sport was Randolph Turpin a champion?
b10   *By what other name was the heavyweight boxer Muhammad Ali formerly known?*
a11   Which metal will flow without being heated?
b11   *Which of these is not an alloy: bronze, brass, pewter?*
a12   Which animal is a national emblem of India?
b12   *Which animal is the national emblem of South Africa?*

No. 13 Answers

a1   Eat it (it's an ice-cream sundae)
b1   *A dance*
a2   Blue and green
b2   *Green*
a3   Cliff Richard
b3   *Elvis Presley*
a4   Majorca
b4   *Adriatic*
a5   Brownies
b5   *Brown Owl (her assistants are called Tawny Owl and Snowy Owl)*
a6   Settle industrial disputes (strikes, etc.)
b6   *Trades Union Congress*
a7   Albumen
b7   *Eagle*
a8   Mao Zedong (also known as: Mao Tse-Tung)
b8   *Mahatma Gandhi*
a9   112 (100 in USA)
b9   *640*
a10   Boxing (light-heavyweight)
b10   *Cassius Clay*
a11   Mercury
b11   *None of them; all are alloys*
a12   Elephant
b12   *Springbok*

Tie-breaker

Q Which area of southern England became Britain's twelfth national park in 1992?
A *The New Forest*

No. 14

a1   In which sport do you 'kick for touch'?

b1   *In which sport might you win a Lonsdale Belt?*

a2   What does a Spaniard mean when he says, 'adios'?

b2   *What does a German mean when he says, 'Danke schön' (say: dan-ke shurn)?*

a3   Daisy wheel and dot matrix are both types of what?

b3   *In computing, what is a 'bit'?*

a4   What kind of shape of fish are flounders, dabs and plaice?

b4   *For which kind of fish is Dover especially famous?*

a5   What is induced by a narcotic?

b5   *What kind of drug is an amphetamine?*

a6   What is meadowsweet?

b6   *What is the Dartford Warbler?*

a7   In which House does the Queen speak at the State Opening of Parliament?

b7   *In Parliament, what is a 'back bencher'?*

a8   Of which university are Pembroke, Nuffield and All Souls colleges?

b8   *Which university is situated near Norwich?*

a9   Which pop drummer, singer and songwriter played with the group Genesis and had a hit with 'You Can't Hurry Love'?

b9   *'Rock 'n' Roll Music' and 'Sweet Little Sixteen' were major hits for which pop guitarist?*

a10   For what is OM an abbreviation?

b10   *For what does the abbreviation C-in-C stand?*

a11   What is ecology?

b11   *What do you study if you're a vulcanologist?*

a12   What is the least number of coins you can use to pay 91p exactly?

b12   *What is the least number of coins you can use to pay 35p exactly?*

No. 14 Answers

a1 Rugby Union or Rugby League
b1 *Boxing*
a2 Goodbye, farewell
b2 *Thank you very much*
a3 (Computer) printers
b3 *A digit, the smallest unit of information*
a4 Flat fish
b4 *Sole*
a5 Sleep; drowsiness
b5 *Pep pill; stimulant; induces 'well-being'*
a6 A (wild) flower
b6 *Bird*
a7 House of Lords
b7 *An ordinary MP; one without office*
a8 Oxford
b8 *University of East Anglia*
a9 Phil Collins
b9 *Chuck Berry*
a10 Order of Merit
b10 *Commander-in-Chief*
a11 The study of the environment (the relationship of plants and animals to their environment)
b11 *Volcanoes*
a12 Four (50p, 20p, 20p, 1p)
b12 *Three (20p, 10p, 5p)*

Tie-breaker

Q What colour beret is usually worn by United Nations peace-keeping troops?
A *Light blue*

No. 15

a1   What kind of animal is a marmoset?

b1   *What kind of dog is a Jack Russell?*

a2   Who led the 1960s all-girl pop group, the Supremes?

b2   *Johnny Rotten and Sid Vicious were members of which group?*

a3   What is meant by the phrase, 'à la mode'?

b3   *What is most likely to have a dust jacket?*

a4   Which game is unique to the public school, Eton?

b4   *Which former captain of the West Indies cricket team retired in 1974 (and was later knighted)?*

a5   Who was dictator of the Soviet Union from 1924 to 1953?

b5   *Which woman became prime minister of India in 1966?*

a6   In London, outside which building does the Changing of the Guard take place?

b6   *In what general direction does the Thames flow through London?*

a7   Which North American city is famous for its 'Mardi Gras' (say: mar-dee grah) carnival?

b7   *In which American city were there severe earthquakes in 1906 and 1989?*

a8   In science, what do we call a completely empty space in which there are no atoms?

b8   *Also in science, what do we call a substance which cannot be split into simpler substances?*

a9   Jerusalem, New English and Good News are all versions of which book?

b9   *On what subject would you find information in 'Burke's'?*

a10   In geometry, how many 'faces' has a square-based pyramid?

b10   *How many times does a tangent touch a circle?*

a11   By what abbreviation did we describe the Strategic Arms Limitation Talks?

b11   *By what abbreviation is the Australia and New Zealand Army Corps known?*

a12   Which planet in our solar system is nearest to the sun?

b12   *Of the planets in our solar system, which is the largest?*

No. 15 Answers

a1	Monkey (small)
b1	*Terrier*
a2	Diana Ross
b2	*The Sex Pistols*
a3	In fashion
b3	*Book*
a4	Eton Wall Game and/or Eton Fives
b4	*Sir Garry (Garfield) Sobers*
a5	Joseph Stalin
b5	*Indira Gandhi*
a6	Buckingham Palace
b6	*Eastwards*
a7	New Orleans
b7	*San Francisco*
a8	Vacuum
b8	*An element*
a9	The Bible
b9	*Peerage*
a10	Five
b10	*Once*
a11	SALT
b11	*ANZAC*
a12	Mercury
b12	*Jupiter*

Tie-breaker

Q On television, whose catch phrase was 'you dirty old man, you!'?

A *The younger Steptoe (Harold) (to his father)*

No. 16

a1 What work is done by a 'clippie'?

b1 *If you worked 'on the footplate', what would your job be?*

a2 According to the film and book title, how many dalmatians were there?

b2 *Which mammal's survival would be threatened by a bamboo shortage?*

a3 What does an American mean when he talks of a janitor?

b3 *In America, what is a billfold?*

a4 Whereabouts in your head are your adenoids?

b4 *Whereabouts in your body is your cerebrum?*

a5 By what name is Princess Anne's daughter known?

b5 *By what title was Princess Diana's father known?*

a6 What was distinctive about the daily paper, the *Daily Worker*?

b6 *Which Jewish girl became famous for the diary she kept while hiding from Nazi soldiers in the Netherlands?*

a7 In which sport might you obtain a Black Belt?

b7 *Which animals raced at White City?*

a8 What is RoSPA concerned with preventing?

b8 *In transport, for what did the initials LNER stand?*

a9 'It Might as Well Rain until September' was a hit in 1962 for which highly successful female songwriter?

b9 *'Only the Lonely', 'Running Scared' and 'Oh, Pretty Woman' were hits for which Texan male vocalist?*

a10 Which is the largest country (by land area) in Africa?

b10 *And which is the largest country (by population) in Africa?*

a11 In Britain, in 'old money' how much was a guinea worth?

b11 *How much was 40p in pre-decimal British money?*

a12 Which American spacecraft blew up, just after being launched in 1986?

b12 *Who was the first man to set foot on the Moon?*

No. 16 Answers

a1   Bus conductress

b1   *Engine driver (or fireman)*

a2   101

b2   *Panda*

a3   Caretaker or porter

b3   *Wallet*

a4   Between back of nose and throat

b4   *Brain*

a5   Zara

b5   *Earl Spencer (formerly Lord Althorp)*

a6   It was a Communist paper

b6   *Anne Frank*

a7   Judo

b7   *Greyhounds*

a8   Accidents (Royal Society for the Prevention of Accidents)

b8   *London and North Eastern Railway*

a9   Carole King

b9   *Roy Orbison*

a10   Sudan

b10   *Nigeria*

a11   21/- (21 shillings); £1-1/- (one pound, one shilling)

b11   *8/- (eight shillings)*

a12   Challenger

b12   *Neil Armstrong*

Tie-breaker

Q Which two countries are separated by the Shatt-al-Arab waterway?

A Iran and Iraq

No. 17

a1   In which industry can you win an Oscar?

b1   *What job would you have if you used a joy-stick in your work?*

a2   Has an earthworm either ears or eyes?

b2   *Do peanuts grow under the ground or above it?*

a3   In which American city did Al Capone head a gang controlling gambling, liquor and vice?

b3   *Which country refused to extradite train robber Ronald Biggs because he had a child in that country?*

a4   Does a convex lens curve inwards or outwards towards its centre?

b4   *In magnetism, do 'like' poles attract or repel?*

a5   On an account sheet, what is meant by the letters DR?

b5   *In the world of finance, for what is MLR an abbreviation?*

a6   Of which country was Pierre Trudeau prime minister?

b6   *Of which country was Sir Robert Menzies a statesman and premier?*

a7   What was the symbol of the German Nazi Party?

b7   *For what are the names Belsen, Buchenwald and Dachau remembered?*

a8   Which champion jockey went to prison in 1987?

b8   *The Brazilian soccer star, Edson Arantes do Nascimento, is better known by what nickname (of only four letters!)?*

a9   Which pop group had a hit with 'You Make Me Feel Brand New'?

b9   *Who sang the title song from the James Bond film, 'Moonraker'?*

a10   Of which American state is Montgomery the capital?

b10   *Of which American state is Salt Lake City the capital?*

a11   In chemistry, what is the opposite of an alkali?

b11   *Which scale measures the strength of acids and alkalis?*

a12   Which country lies immediately to the west of Afghanistan?

b12   *And which country lies to the west of Iran?*

No. 17 Answers

a1	Film industry
b1	*Pilot or aviator*
a2	No, neither
b2	*Under*
a3	Chicago
b3	*Brazil*
a4	Outwards
b4	*Repel*
a5	Debit (or debt)
b5	*Minimum lending rate*
a6	Canada
b6	*Australia*
a7	Swastika
b7	*Nazi concentration camps*
a8	Lester Piggott
b8	*Pelé (say: pell-ay)*
a9	The Stylistics
b9	*Shirley Bassey*
a10	Alabama
b10	*Utah*
a11	Acid
b11	*The pH scale*
a12	Iran
b12	*Iraq*

Tie-breaker

Q Can you name one of the British landing ships destroyed at Bluff Cove during the Falklands War?

A *Sir Tristram; Sir Galahad*

No. 18

a1   For what are the letters SWALK an abbreviation?
b1   *What kind of electricity is meant by the initials DC?*
a2   For what do the initials HMSO stand?
b2   *What is an ICBM?*
a3   In the world of medicine, for what do the initials SRN stand?
b3   *What international organization is known by the initials, WHO?*
a4   In which city is the Longchamps race course?
b4   *In athletics, what is the shortest track race?*
a5   In America, what is a faucet?
b5   *In America, what is meant by going 'downtown'?*
a6   What is the minimum school leaving age?
b6   *What is the youngest age you can vote?*
a7   What is Margaret Thatcher's middle name?
b7   *Of which political party was Clement Attlee once the leader?*
a8   Until 1970, which British fish was traditionally a royal fish?
b8   *With which city do we associate the liver bird?*
a9   Mental arithmetic: What is .25 of 300?
b9   *What is the fraction ⅔ expressed as a percentage?*
a10   Which pop group had hits with 'Let It Be' and 'Strawberry Fields Forever'?
b10   *Which pop group had a hit with 'Take a Chance on Me'?*
a11   In a lunar month, how many 'phases' of the Moon are there?
b11   *What is the Fahrenheit equivalent of 100° Centigrade?*
a12   In Africa, which country is immediately south of Egypt?
b12   *And which country lies to the south of Namibia and Botswana?*

No. 18 Answers

a1 Sealed/signed with a loving kiss
b1 *Direct Current*
a2 Her Majesty's Stationery Office
b2 *(Inter-Continental Ballistic) Missile*
a3 State Registered Nurse
b3 *World Health Organization*
a4 Paris
b4 *100 metres*
a5 Tap
b5 *Going to a city centre, business centre*
a6 16
b6 *18*
a7 Hilda
b7 *Labour*
a8 Sturgeon
b8 *Liverpool*
a9 75
b9 *66 ⅔% or 66.6% recurring*
a10 The Beatles
b10 *Abba*
a11 Four
b11 *212°*
a12 Sudan
b12 *South Africa*

Tie-breaker

Q In 1978, which two statesmen shared the Nobel Peace Prize for their efforts to bring peace to the Middle East?

A *President Sadat of Egypt, Prime Minister Begin of Israel*

No. 19

a1 For what did Mary Quant become famous in the sixties?
b1 And for what did the American Billy Graham become famous?
a2 At which school was Billy Bunter a pupil?
b2 In one of John Wyndham's books, what are the huge plants called that dominate the world?
a3 In which city is there a modern development called the Barbican?
b3 For what maximum period is a British parliament elected?
a4 From which animal do we get mohair?
b4 If an animal is said to be a predator, how does it live?
a5 From 1988 to 1992, who was vice-president of the United States of America?
b5 Who was the American black leader who won the Nobel Peace Prize in 1964?
a6 If you add together half a score and half a century, what do you get?
b6 What is the least number of coins you can use to pay 24p exactly?
a7 In the world of cinema, what is the job of the producer?
b7 And what is the role of the director?
a8 Which duo had hits with 'Welcome Home' 'Don't Stay Away Too Long' and 'Rainbow'?
b8 Who sang 'I'm the Leader of the Gang (I am!)'?
a9 By what three initial letters do we call the chemical substance in our bodies which determines what we look like?
b9 For which organization are the initials WWF an abbreviation?
a10 By what name do we normally call Light Amplification by Stimulated Emission of Radiation?
b10 Which theory was published in 1905 by Einstein?
a11 Which American black athlete won four gold medals in the 1936 Berlin Olympics?
b11 Which American golfer won the nickname, 'Golden Bear'?
a12 Which woman became prime minister of Pakistan in 1988?
b12 Who was the woman prime minister of Israel from 1969 to 1974?

No. 19 Answers

a1   Fashion, design
b1   *Preaching Christianity; evangelizing*
a2   Greyfriars
b2   *Triffids*
a3   London
b3   *5 years*
a4   (Angora) goat
b4   *By hunting, eating other animals*
a5   Dan Quayle
b5   *Martin Luther King*
a6   60
b6   *Three (20p, 2p, 2p)*
a7   He is the film's business organizer; he raises the money, hires the cast and director
b7   *He rehearses and directs the actors and cameras*
a8   Peters and Lee
b8   *Gary Glitter*
a9   DNA
b9   *World Wide Fund for Nature*
a10   Laser
b10   *Theory of Relativity*
a11   Jesse Owens
b11   *Jack Nicklaus*
a12   Benazir Bhutto
b12   *Golda Meir (say: may-ear)*

Tie-breaker

Q Which profession did Denys Lasdun and Edwin Lutyens both follow?
A *Architecture*

No. 20

a1 What does a Frenchman mean when he says, 'Service compris' (say: ser-vis kom-pree)?

b1 *What does a Frenchman mean when he says, 'Comment allez-vous' (say: kom-mon tallay voo)?*

a2 Tenon and Cross are both kinds of which tool?

b2 *What do we call a spoon sized between a tea- and a table-spoon?*

a3 On what date each year do the United States celebrate their independence?

b3 *By what name is Mardi Gras (say: mar-dee grah) generally known in Britain?*

a4 Which house became the Queen Mother's home when she left Buckingham Palace?

b4 *Who is president of the Save the Children Fund?*

a5 What is a euphemism?

b5 *What does a mnemonic device help you to do?*

a6 During the Second World War, what was a V2?

b6 *In the Second World War, who or what was a boffin?*

a7 What is alopecia?

b7 *What is hydrophobia?*

a8 If you drove north from Belgium, which country would you visit next?

b8 *If you drove west from Switzerland, which country would you enter next?*

a9 Which pop star created a character called Ziggi Stardust?

b9 *Which pop group had hits with 'Does Your Mother Know?', 'Mamma Mia' and 'Dancing Queen'?*

a10 In which sport is there a Prix de l'Arc de Triomphe?

b10 *In which sport was there a 'Brown Bomber'?*

a11 Which is larger, an American or British billion?

b11 *Which was the smallest of the following: florin, half-crown, or crown?*

a12 What did Major White and Alexei Leonov both do in 1965?

b12 *Who was the first woman in space?*

No. 20 Answers

a1   Service (tip) included
b1   *How are you? (How do you do?)*
a2   Saws
b2   *Dessert spoon*
a3   July 4th
b3   *Shrove Tuesday (accept: Pancake Day)*
a4   Clarence House
b4   *The Princess Royal (Princess Anne)*
a5   A polite or 'nice' way of saying something rude or unpleasant
b5   *Remember something*
a6   A missile/rocket
b6   *(Backroom) (research) scientist*
a7   Baldness
b7   *Fear of water*
a8   Holland
b8   *France*
a9   David Bowie
b9   *Abba*
a10   Horse-racing
b10   *Boxing (Joe Louis)*
a11   British (a million million) (American is only a thousand million)
b11   *Florin*
a12   Walked in space
b12   *Valentina Tereshkova*

Tie-breaker

Q Albert Campion was the fictional detective invented by which woman crime writer?
A *Margery Allingham*

No. 21: Capital Cities

The following countries and their capitals have all been in the news in recent years. Of which country is each of the following the capital city?

a1   Nicosia
b1   *Valletta*
a2   Addis Ababa
b2   *Tehran*
a3   Tirana
b3   *Freetown*
a4   Ankara
b4   *Katmandu*
a5   Riyadh
b5   *Phnom Penh*
a6   Rabat
b6   *Port au Prince*

And what is the capital city of these countries?

a7   Cuba
b7   *Indonesia*
a8   Sudan
b8   *Uganda*
a9   Peru
b9   *Vietnam*
a10   Jordan
b10   *Lebanon*
a11   Syria
b11   *Thailand*
a12   Chile
b12   *Uruguay*

No. 21 Answers

a1	Cyprus
b1	*Malta*
a2	Ethiopia
b2	*Iran*
a3	Albania
b3	*Sierra Leone*
a4	Turkey
b4	*Nepal*
a5	Saudi Arabia
b5	*Cambodia*
a6	Morocco
b6	*Haiti*
a7	Havana
b7	*Jakarta*
a8	Khartoum
b8	*Kampala*
a9	Lima
b9	*Hanoi*
a10	Amman
b10	*Beirut*
a11	Damascus
b11	*Bangkok*
a12	Santiago
b12	*Montevideo*

Tie-breaker

Q Into which capital city did the Soviet Union airlift troops on Christmas Eve, 1979?

A *Kabul (Afghanistan)*

No. 22

a1   With which country do you associate a Wiener Schnitzel?

b1   *In which kind of restaurant would you be most likely to eat a poppadom?*

a2   In which game might you be dealt a Royal Flush?

b2   *In the game of pitch and toss, what do you 'pitch'?*

a3   Where in your body is there an anvil, hammer and a stirrup?

b3   *What is a greenstick fracture?*

a4   Which male pop star featured in the films *Purple Rain* and *Under the Cherry Moon*?

b4   *Brian Jones, Mick Taylor and Ron Wood were all members of the same pop group – but never at the same time. Which group?*

a5   In 1963, Lester Pearson became prime minister of which country?

b5   *Of which country was Eamon de Valera a statesman?*

a6   In which novel is Winston Smith overcome by Big Brother?

b6   *What is the term used to describe an illustration facing the title page of a book?*

a7   Which artist draws the 'Peanuts' cartoon strips?

b7   *In which children's comic can you read about Dennis the Menace and Lord Snooty?*

a8   Where are Greenwich Village and Times Square?

b8   *Which city is the centre of the American car industry?*

a9   In maths, the denary system is based on the number ten. On which number is the binary system based?

b9   *What is the square root of 121?*

a10   In the Second World War, who was the Italian Fascist leader?

b10   *Who was the Commander of the Free French forces during the Second World War?*

a11   Celsius, Réaumur and Fahrenheit are all what?

b11   *On a map, what places are joined by isotherms?*

a12   Who said, 'My fellow Americans, ask not what your country can do for you, but what you can do for your country'?

b12   *Whose law was this: 'Work expands so as to fill the time available for its completion'?*

a1   Austria
b1   Indian
a2   Poker (five highest cards in one suit)
b2   Coins
a3   Ear
b3   A partly broken (or bent) bone (especially in children)
a4   Prince (Prince Rogers Nelson)
b4   The Rolling Stones
a5   Canada
b5   Eire, Republic of Ireland
a6   1984
b6   Frontispiece
a7   Charles Schulz
b7   The Beano
a8   New York
b8   Detroit
a9   2
b9   11
a10   Mussolini (Benito)
b10   General de Gaulle
a11   Temperature scales
b11   Places with the same temperature
a12   John F. Kennedy
b12   (C. Northcote) Parkinson

Tie-breaker

Q By the name of which London suburb are these films known:
Whisky Galore, Passport to Pimlico and *The Lavender Hill Mob?*

A *Ealing (The Ealing Comedies)*

No. 23

a1 In what type of needlework would you use a templet?

b1 *If you are ironing clothes, which require the greatest heat: wool, linen or nylon?*

a2 From which London railway station would you leave if you were travelling to Liverpool?

b2 *From which London station would you leave if you were travelling to Newcastle upon Tyne?*

a3 What does a journalist mean when he says he's got a 'scoop'?

b3 *In the sixties whose slogan was 'Make love, not war'?*

a4 What is the unit of currency in Switzerland?

b4 *Which economic/political system has been said to have an unacceptable face?*

a5 Which bear does Michael Bond write about?

b5 *Who owned the teddy bear called Winnie-the-Pooh?*

a6 In America, what is a derby (say: durby)?

b6 *In America, what is or was a rustler?*

a7 Which political party is called Plaid Cymru?

b7 *In the eighties, of which political party was Dr David Owen a leading figure?*

a8 In America, what was 'Prohibition' (from 1920 to 1933)?

b8 *And whom did Senator McCarthy seek in his 'witch hunts'?*

a9 Hausa and Yoruba are languages spoken in which part of Africa?

b9 *And what is the commonest language in East Africa?*

a10 What was the home country of the long-distance runner, Emil Zatopek?

b10 *From which country did the young gymnast Nadia Comeneci come?*

a11 In which country was the explorer Sir Edmund Hillary born?

b11 *What was the name of Sir Ernest Shackleton's ship (which was crushed in Antarctic ice)?*

a12 On which Caribbean island did steel bands originate?

b12 *Germany has a large number of immigrant 'guest workers'. From which country principally do they come?*

No. 23 Answers

a1 Patchwork
b1 Linen
a2 Euston
b2 King's Cross
a3 He's got a story no other journalist has
b3 Hippies/flower people/flower children
a4 (Swiss) Franc
b4 Capitalism
a5 Paddington
b5 Christopher Robin (Milne)
a6 (Bowler) hat
b6 Cattle thief
a7 Welsh Nationalists
b7 Social Democrat
a8 A ban on the manufacture and sale of alcoholic drinks
b8 Communists
a9 West Africa
b9 Swahili
a10 Czechoslovakia
b10 Romania
a11 New Zealand
b11 Endurance
a12 Trinidad
b12 Turkey

Tie-breaker

Q Which Yorkshire cricketer created a record by scoring 364 for England against Australia in 1938?
A Len Hutton

No. 24

a1   Which football team is known as The Gunners?
b1   *Which team plays at home at Ibrox Park?*
a2   What happens if you inhale chloroform?
b2   *In which of your organs is there a drum?*
a3   Of which country is Aer Lingus the national airline?
b3   *Of which country is Sabena the national airline?*
a4   Which television comedian was famous for his blood-donor show or sketch?
b4   *Which comedian was known as 'Big-Hearted Arthur'?*
a5   At the end of a game of snooker, which ball must be potted immediately before the black?
b5   *What is the usual number of pins in a game of skittles?*
a6   In 1963, which pop group had a hit with the song 'She Loves You'?
b6   *Which group sang 'Save All Your Kisses for Me'?*
a7   Before decimalization in Britain, how many old pennies were there in a half-crown?
b7   *What fraction of a metre is a centimetre?*
a8   For what sort of work are civil engineers responsible?
b8   *And for what are structural engineers responsible?*
a9   What is the official language of Uruguay?
b9   *What is the language of Monaco?*
a10   Of which country did Brian Mulroney become prime minister in 1984?
b10   *Of which country was Robert Muldoon prime minister from 1975 to 1984?*
a11   Of which American state is Little Rock the capital?
b11   *Of which American state is Denver the capital?*
a12   Of which country was Angola formerly a colony?
b12   *Luxor and Aswan are towns on which river?*

No. 24 Answers

a1 Arsenal
b1 *(Glasgow) Rangers*
a2 You become insensible (accept: become unconscious)
b2 *Ear*
a3 Ireland (Eire)
b3 *Belgium*
a4 Tony Hancock
b4 *Arthur Askey*
a5 The pink
b5 *9*
a6 The Beatles
b6 *Brotherhood of Man*
a7 30
b7 *One hundredth*
a8 Constructing roads, tunnels, bridges, dams, railways, etc.
b8 *Construction of steel and concrete buildings and bridges*
a9 Spanish
b9 *French*
a10 Canada
b10 *New Zealand*
a11 Arkansas
b11 *Colorado*
a12 Portugal
b12 *Nile*

Tie-breaker

Q Which rock group issued albums called 'Meaty, Beaty, Big and Bouncy', 'Tommy' and 'A Quick One'?
A *The Who*

No. 25

a1   Which television star has been famous for the phrase, 'Didn't he do well'?

b1   *With which comedian do you associate the catch phrase, 'Nikky, nokky, noo!'?*

a2   Who was the longest-serving British prime minister this century?

b2   *What was Margaret Thatcher's first Cabinet post?*

a3   Which American state is sometimes nicknamed 'The Last Frontier'?

b3   *Of which state is Nashville the capital?*   ·

a4   What is the official language of Malta?

b4   *In which country is Maori a native language?*

a5   For which comic strip did the Belgian artist Hergé (say: eyre-jay) become famous?

b5   *In cartoons, which animal has often been used to represent Russia?*

a6   In which country was the tennis player Martina Navratilova born?

b6   *In which sport did Gareth Edwards captain Wales?*

a7   Which part of the United Kingdom became a separate state in 1921?

b7   *The 1957 Treaty of Rome founded . . . what?*

a8   Where is the M8 motorway?

b8   *In which English county is the M2?*

a9   Which pop singer had a hit with 'Silver Lady'?

b9   *Which pop group first sang about 'The Combine Harvester'?*

a10   Who created the detective, Hercule Poirot?

b10   *Who wrote the children's book Charlie and the Chocolate Factory?*

a11   Chittagong is an important city in which country?

b11   *By what name is the Chinese city of Beijing (say: bay-jing) also known in the West?*

a12   Which politician became famous for the phrases, 'You've never had it so good' and 'The wind of change'?

b12   *Which member of the Royal Family once said, 'It's the biggest waste of water in the country by far. You spend half a pint and flush two gallons'?*

No. 25 Answers

a1	Bruce Forsyth
b1	*Ken Dodd*
a2	Margaret Thatcher
b2	*Secretary of State for Education*
a3	Alaska
b3	*Tennessee*
a4	Maltese or English
b4	*New Zealand*
a5	Tintin
b5	*A bear*
a6	Czechoslovakia
b6	*Rugby Union*
a7	Irish Free State, Eire
b7	*The European Economic Community (Common Market)*
a8	Scotland (Edinburgh to Glasgow)
b8	*Kent*
a9	David Soul
b9	*The Wurzels*
a10	Agatha Christie
b10	*Roald Dahl*
a11	Bangladesh
b11	*Peking*
a12	Harold Macmillan
b12	*Duke of Edinburgh*

Tie-breaker

Q Soft, flexible watches; strange bony figures; surreal shapes – in which Spanish painter's work would you find all these?

A Salvador Dali

No. 26

a1   When are you in your 'salad days'?

b1   *Who or what was a bobby-soxer?*

a2   In which city is there a railway station called Waverley?

b2   *In which English city is there a railway station called Lime Street?*

a3   What job would you probably have if you were a member of the NUT?

b3   *Which profession is governed by the Law Society?*

a4   In London, what have the Palace, the Phoenix and the Piccadilly in common?

b4   *What did the Clean Air Act in 1956 more or less do away with in London?*

a5   For what are Tarot cards now used?

b5   *What number plays a vital part in the game of Pontoon?*

a6   Of which American state is Atlanta the capital?

b6   *Of which American state is Denver the capital?*

a7   In 1928, which important drug was discovered by Professor Alexander Fleming?

b7   *Which doctor performed the first human heart transplant operation?*

a8   Who plays the father in the film, *Kramer versus Kramer*?

b8   *Who directed the 1941 film,* Citizen Kane?

a9   Of which country is Benfica a famous football team?

b9   *Name the two famous Glasgow soccer clubs.*

a10   Who wrote the novels *The War of the Worlds* and *Kipps*?

b10   *Who wrote the novel* Women in Love?

a11   With which country do you associate Jomo Kenyatta?

b11   *What was the title of the former 'King' of Iran?*

a12   For which kind of music has Ella Fitzgerald become famous?

b12   *'Bird' and 'Yardbird' were nicknames of which jazz musician?*

No. 26 Answers

a1	When you're young (and inexperienced)
b1	*Teenage fan (of pop music or of a film star)*
a2	Edinburgh
b2	*Liverpool*
a3	Teacher (National Union of Teachers)
b3	*Solicitors*
a4	All are theatres
b4	*Coal fires in central London, and (consequently) smog*
a5	Fortune-telling
b5	*21*
a6	Georgia
b6	*Colorado*
a7	Penicillin
b7	*Dr Christiaan Barnard*
a8	Dustin Hoffman
b8	*Orson Welles*
a9	Portugal
b9	*Celtic and Rangers*
a10	H. G. Wells
b10	*D. H. Lawrence*
a11	Kenya
b11	*Shah (of Persia)*
a12	Jazz (singer), especially 'scat singing'
b12	*Charlie Parker*

Tie-breaker

Q Which Argentine cruiser was sunk by the British submarine
'Conqueror' during the Falklands War?

A *General Belgrano*

No. 27

a1   Which Royal Prince served in the navy during the Falklands War?

b1   *Which member of the Royal Family was educated at Cheam, Gordonstoun and Geelong Grammar schools?*

a2   What is 'Alitalia'?

b2   *Of which country is El Al the national airline?*

a3   Which language is spoken in Austria?

b3   *What is the main language spoken in Argentina?*

a4   What kind of music is performed by Fairport Convention, Steeleye Span and the Dubliners?

b4   *Which jazz trumpeter and singer had hits with 'Hello Dolly' and 'What a Wonderful World'?*

a5   In which sport did Jahangir Khan achieve success and fame?

b5   *In which Olympic event did the athlete Daley Thompson excel?*

a6   Of which American state is Phoenix the capital?

b6   *What is the capital of the American state, Massachusetts?*

a7   Which film star's real name was Norma Jean Baker or Mortenson?

b7   *In the film* Singin' in the Rain, *which star was in fact singing in the rain?*

a8   On which day of the week is Maundy money distributed?

b8   *In Britain, in which month is the Winter Solstice?*

a9   By what name is the French Government which collaborated with the Germans in the Second World War known?

b9   *Which Frenchman led the liberation of France in 1944?*

a10   Who wrote the novel *Brave New World*?

b10   *Who wrote the novels* Decline and Fall *and* A Handful of Dust?

a11   Which is the largest lake in Africa?

b11   *In surface area, which is the largest natural lake in England?*

a12   In which year did Hitler invade Czechoslovakia?

b12   *In which year did Argentina invade the Falkland Islands?*

No. 27 Answers

a1	Andrew
b1	*Prince Charles*
a2	Airline (Italian)
b2	*Israel*
a3	German
b3	*Spanish*
a4	Folk
b4	*Louis Armstrong*
a5	Squash
b5	*Decathlon*
a6	Arizona
b6	*Boston*
a7	Marilyn Monroe
b7	*Gene Kelly*
a8	Thursday
b8	*December (approx. December 21st)*
a9	Vichy Government
b9	*General de Gaulle*
a10	Aldous Huxley
b10	*Evelyn Waugh*
a11	Lake Victoria
b11	*Lake Windermere*
a12	1939
b12	*1982*

Tie-breaker

Q In America, what was the job or profession of Frank Lloyd
Wright?
A *Architect*

No. 28

a1 Which leader was briefly deposed while on holiday in 1991?

b1 *By what name is Mikhail Gorbachev's wife known?*

a2 Which city is served by Stansted Airport?

b2 *In which country is Shannon airport?*

a3 Softball is a gentler version of which sport?

b3 *How often are the Olympic Games held?*

a4 What have the following in common: Thirlmere, Buttermere and Wastwater?

b4 *On which lake is Bowness situated?*

a5 Which pop star first sang about 'Space Oddity'?

b5 *Which is the singer Kiri Te Kanawa's home country?*

a6 Who wrote the book *Murder on the Orient Express*?

b6 *Which crime writer created the private eye, Philip Marlowe?*

a7 Which is the largest country (by population) in Asia?

b7 *Which country lies to the south of Mongolia?*

a8 Which American city is said to be the capital of country-and-western music?

b8 *Which record company is said to have developed 'the sound of young America' by featuring and controlling stars such as Diana Ross, Stevie Wonder and the Temptations?*

a9 Bengali, Urdu and Hindi are all native languages of which continent?

b9 *'Singhalese' refers to which country?*

a10 At the start of the century, was the school-leaving age in Britain 8, 12, or 14?

b10 *In Britain, was the school-leaving age raised to 16 in 1944, 1963, or 1973?*

a11 From which Asian country did Soviet troops withdraw in 1989?

b11 *In 1967, which country won the Six Day War?*

a12 What sort of world-wide epidemic killed about 20 million people immediately after the First World War?

b12 *Which group of workers are affected by the disease silicosis?*

No. 28 Answers

a1	Mikhail Gorbachev
b1	*Raisa (say: ry-ee-sa)*
a2	London
b2	*Ireland/Irish Republic/Eire*
a3	Baseball
b3	*Every four years*
a4	Lakes (in the English Lake District)
b4	*Windermere*
a5	David Bowie
b5	*New Zealand*
a6	Agatha Christie
b6	*Raymond Chandler*
a7	China
b7	*China*
a8	Nashville (Tennessee)
b8	*Tamla Motown Records*
a9	Asia (accept: Indian sub-continent)
b9	*Sri Lanka/Ceylon*
a10	12
b10	*1973*
a11	Afghanistan
b11	*Israel*
a12	Influenza
b12	*Miners (slate, coal, anthracite) (also stone-cutters)*

Tie-breaker

Q Who wrote the short novel *Breakfast at Tiffany's*?
A *Truman Capote (say: ca-po-tee)*

No. 29

a1   For whom would a *locum* normally deputize?

b1   *In what do underwriters deal?*

a2   In which city is Wenceslas Square?

b2   *In which city is the Prado?*

a3   Which film star's real name was Marion Morrison?

b3   *Which American child film star became the US representative to the United Nations in 1969?*

a4   Which pop group included Madame Cholet and Orinoco?

b4   *Which pianist played 'Sidesaddle' and later 'Roulette'?*

a5   On which river stands the English city of Cambridge?

b5   *On which river does Chester stand?*

a6   In which year did Hitler invade Austria?

b6   *Which war began in 1950?*

a7   Who was the highly successful scrum half and captain of the Welsh Rugby Union team until his retirement in 1978?

b7   *Which American baseball star was known as 'The Yankee Clipper' and was married (briefly) to Marilyn Monroe?*

a8   Who was prime minister of Great Britain from 1970 to 1974?

b8   *Who was prime minister of Great Britain from 1951 to 1955?*

a9   In which country was there a revolutionary group called the Mau Mau?

b9   *Which Russian leader was assassinated in Mexico in 1940?*

a10   Who wrote the novels *Brighton Rock* and *The Power and the Glory*?

b10   *Who wrote the novel* The Old Man and the Sea?

a11   In 1901, who sent a radio signal from Cornwall to Newfoundland?

b11   *What radio detection system was invented by Sir Robert Watson-Watt during the Second World War?*

a12   Which Russian musician composed *The Rite of Spring*?

b12   *Which famous Italian opera composer died in 1901?*

No. 29 Answers

a1   Doctor (accept: clergyman)
b1   *Insurance (accept: stocks)*
a2   Prague
b2   *Madrid*
a3   John Wayne
b3   *Shirley Temple (married name: Shirley Temple Black)*
a4   The Wombles
b4   *Russ Conway*
a5   Cam (accept: Granta)
b5   *Dee*
a6   1938
b6   *Korean War*
a7   Gareth Edwards
b7   *Joe DiMaggio*
a8   Edward Heath
b8   *Winston Churchill*
a9   Kenya
b9   *(Leon) Trotsky*
a10   Graham Greene
b10   *Ernest Hemingway*
a11   (Guglielmo) Marconi
b11   *Radar*
a12   (Igor) Stravinsky
b12   *(Giuseppe) Verdi*

Tie-breaker

Q Who was the American choreographer responsible for such films as *Forty-Second Street*, *Gold-Diggers of 1933* and *Dames*?
A *Busby Berkeley*

No. 30

a1   At the beginning of a game of snooker, how many red balls are on the table?

b1   *If, in darts, your score stands at 38, for what do you aim to win the game?*

a2   At what age can you legally buy cigarettes in Britain?

b2   *And what is the youngest age you can drink beer or wine when having a meal in a restaurant?*

a3   What was a Messerschmitt?

b3   *What is a 'STOL' aircraft?*

a4   In which country is Lake Como?

b4   *In which country is Lake Lucerne?*

a5   Which year was the Festival of Britain?

b5   *In 1932, where was a famous Harbour Bridge opened?*

a6   Of a psychiatrist and a psychoanalyst, which is certain to be medically qualified?

b6   *In what kind of illness does a paediatrician specialize?*

a7   According to the song, who used to wait underneath the lantern, by the barrack gate?

b7   *Who wrote and sang the protest ballad of the early sixties, 'The Times they are a-Changin'?*

a8   Which is the highest mountain in Africa?

b8   *Which is the highest – Ben Nevis, Mont Blanc, Snowdon?*

a9   Which president of Egypt nationalized the Suez Canal in 1956?

b9   *Who was emperor of Japan from 1926 to 1989?*

a10   In the cinema, who played a mafia leader in *The Godfather* and the hero's father in the 1978 version of *Superman*?

b10   *Which film star was married to Lauren Bacall and won an Oscar for his role in* The African Queen?

a11   In which country has a group calling itself ETA (say: ett-a) been fighting for freedom?

b11   *Which organization seeks to help prisoners of conscience?*

a12   Who became Poet Laureate in 1984?

b12   *Which poet wrote Old Possum's Book of Practical Cats?*

No. 30 Answers

a1   15
b1   *Double 19*
a2   16
b2   *16*
a3   German fighter plane (accept: bubble car)
b3   *Short take-off and landing*
a4   Italy
b4   *Switzerland*
a5   1951
b5   *Sydney*
a6   Psychiatrist
b6   *Children's diseases*
a7   Lilli Marlene
b7   *Bob Dylan*
a8   Kilimanjaro
b8   *Mont Blanc*
a9   President (Gamal Abdel) Nasser
b9   *Hirohito*
a10   Marlon Brando
b10   *Humphrey Bogart*
a11   Spain
b11   *Amnesty International*
a12   Ted Hughes
b12   *T. S. Eliot*

Tie-breaker

Q The subject of 'ethics' is concerned with what?
A *How people should behave; morality*

No. 31: Soap Sagas

Television soap operas became extremely popular forms of entertainment in the second half of this century. In which soap do or did the following locations feature?

a1 The Rover's Return
b1 *The Queen Vic*
a2 Ramsay Street
b2 *Southfork*
a3 Tarrant
b3 *Beckindale*
a4 'The Close'
b4 *Wentworth Detention Centre*

In which soap do or did the following characters appear?

a5 Billy Corkhill
b5 *Blake Carrington*
a6 Lou Beale
b6 *Ena Sharples*
a7 Benny Hawkins
b7 *Sue Ellen*
a8 Charlene Mitchell
b8 *Dr Gillespie*

Which character was or is played by these actors?

a9 Pat Phoenix
b9 *Larry Hagman*
a10 Ronald Allen
b10 *Charlton Heston*
a11 Joan Collins
b11 *Richard Chamberlain*
a12 Noele Gordon
b12 *Jason Donovan*

No. 31 Answers

a1   *Coronation Street*
b1   EastEnders
a2   *Neighbours*
b2   Dallas
a3   *Howards Way*
b3   Emmerdale Farm
a4   *Brookside*
b4   Prisoner: Cell Block H
a5   *Brookside*
b5   Dynasty
a6   *EastEnders*
b6   Coronation Street
a7   *Crossroads*
b7   Dallas
a8   *Neighbours*
b8   Dr Kildare
a9   Elsie Tanner (later Elsie Howard, Elsie Gregory) (in *Coronation Street*)
b9   *J. R. Ewing (in* Dallas*)*
a10 David Hunter (in *Crossroads*)
b10 *Jason Colby (in* The Colbys*)*
a11 Alexis Rowan (in *Dynasty*) (accept: Alexis Carrington, Colby, Dexter, etc.!)
b11 Dr Kildare
a12 Meg Richardson (in *Crossroads*)
b12 *Scott Robinson (in* Neighbours*)*

Tie-breaker

Q In the early days of *Coronation Street*, which character was caretaker at the Glad Tidings Mission Hall?
A Ena Sharples

No. 32

a1   In Britain, when does a person legally 'come of age'?

b1   *How old is an octogenarian?*

a2   Which county cricket team plays at home at the Oval?

b2   *Which county cricket team plays at home at Headingley?*

a3   On television, the crew of which spaceship had the mission 'to seek out new life and new civilizations, to boldly go where no man has gone before'?

b3   *On television, what is the name of the rabbit in the children's series,* The Magic Roundabout?

a4   Who was the first person to show it was possible to transmit pictures, and is known as 'the father of television'?

b4   *The aqualung was invented, in part, by which famous French under-sea explorer?*

a5   Which Royal prince is second in line to the throne?

b5   *Can you name the Duke of York's two daughters?*

a6   What was the name of the aircraft in which Charles Lindbergh first flew the Atlantic?

b6   *In 1930, who was the first woman to fly from Britain to Australia?*

a7   Anchorage and Fairbanks are cities in which American state?

b7   *In America, New York is at the mouth of which river?*

a8   Into which ocean does the River Congo (or River Zaire) flow?

b8   *Into which sea does the River Danube flow?*

a9   What is a futon?

b9   *For what would you use a kilner jar?*

a10   Which female singer had a hit with the song, 'Dominique'?

b10   *Which comedy pop group had a hit with the song 'Lily the Pink'?*

a11   For what is the Montessori Method used?

b11   *In medicine, of what is neurology the study?*

a12   If, in the Bible, you add together the number of Testaments, the number of Gospels and the number of Commandments, what is the total?

b12   *If you were driving at 50 mph, at how many kilometres per hour would you be going (approximately)?*

No. 32 Answers

a1	18
b1	*80 (or in their eighties)*
a2	Surrey
b2	*Yorkshire*
a3	Starship Enterprise (in *Star Trek*)
b3	*Dylan*
a4	John Logie Baird
b4	*Jacques Cousteau*
a5	Prince William (of Wales)
b5	*Beatrice and Eugenie*
a6	'Spirit of St Louis'
b6	*Amy Johnson*
a7	Alaska
b7	*Hudson (accept: East River)*
a8	(South) Atlantic
b8	*Black Sea*
a9	(Japanese) low-slung bed or mattress
b9	*To preserve fruit or vegetables (accept: preserving)*
a10	The Singing Nun (Soeur Sourire)
b10	*The Scaffold*
a11	Educating children
b11	*Nervous system (or the brain)*
a12	16
b12	*80 kph*

Tie-breaker

Q Which part of the body might suffer from stomatitis?
A *The mouth (inflammation of the mucous membrane)*

No. 33

a1   Who wrote the novel *Goldfinger?*

b1   *Who wrote the novel* The Guns of Navarone?

a2   Of which country was the Ayatollah Khomeini a ruler?

b2   *Which leader this century was known as 'il Duce' (say: doo-chay)?*

a3   For which city is Leonardo da Vinci an airport?

b3   *For which English city is Speke the airport?*

a4   In psychology, what is the opposite of an extrovert?

b4   *Which monkey has a blood factor otherwise found only in human blood?*

a5   In which city will you find the Trevi Fountain?

b5   *In which city is the cathedral of Notre Dame?*

a6   What have these in common: Scratchwood, Keele and Frankley?

b6   *What do Edinburgh, Chester and Chessington all have in common?*

a7   Which 'dance band' had a hit with 'Seven Tears'?

b7   *Which pop group won the Eurovision Song Contest with 'Making Your Mind Up'?*

a8   Of which American political party was President Lyndon Johnson a leading member?

b8   *Which general commanded the American forces in Europe at the time of D-Day?*

a9   Between the World Wars, Babe Ruth became a star in which sport?

b9   *Which Spaniard has been accepted as the leading European golfer since the early eighties?*

a10   Which is the RAF equivalent of the Army rank of captain?

b10   *What is the Army equivalent of the RAF rank of squadron leader?*

a11   Who was the first artistic director of Britain's National Theatre?

b11   *In 1935, she played Juliet. Fifty years later she starred in television's* Jewel in the Crown *series. Who was she?*

a12   Who was the chief star of the BBC radio programme, *Round the Horne?*

b12   *In which radio show did we hear about Ron and Eth Glum?*

No. 33 Answers

a1	Ian Fleming
b1	*Alistair Maclean*
a2	Iran
b2	*(Benito) Mussolini (of Italy)*
a3	Rome
b3	*Liverpool*
a4	Introvert
b4	*Rhesus monkey*
a5	Rome
b5	*Paris*
a6	All are motorway service stations
b6	*Zoos*
a7	Goombay Dance Band
b7	*Bucks Fizz*
a8	Democratic
b8	*Dwight D. Eisenhower*
a9	Baseball
b9	*Seve (Severiano) Ballesteros*
a10	Flight Lieutenant
b10	*Major*
a11	Laurence Olivier (later Lord Olivier)
b11	*Dame Peggy Ashcroft*
a12	Kenneth Horne
b12	Take It From Here

Tie-breaker

Q It's the lowest place on earth; it's so salty no fish can live in it –
and it's impossible to sink in it. What is it?

A *The Dead Sea*

No. 34

a1 What should you do with a pair of bongos?

b1 *Which musical instrument is associated with Liberace?*

a2 In Russia, what are the Urals?

b2 *In which country are the Cambrian Mountains?*

a3 Andrew Lloyd Webber composed the music for *Joseph and the Amazing Technicolor Dreamcoat*. Who wrote the lyrics?

b3 *Name the ukulele player who made popular the song 'I'm Leaning on a Lamppost'.*

a4 With which two comedians do we associate the phrase, 'You can't see the join'?

b4 *And in which television show did we regularly hear the phrase, 'And now for something completely different'?*

a5 For which month of the year is turquoise the birthstone?

b5 *For which month of the year is amethyst the birthstone?*

a6 Which Australian state lies to the north of New South Wales?

b6 *Which Australian state is a separate island?*

a7 Which play, first performed in 1904, features fairies and a villain called Captain Hook?

b7 *On which play by Bernard Shaw was the musical My Fair Lady based?*

a8 About which year is Stanley Kubrick's film that is sub-titled *A Space Odyssey*?

b8 *Who directed the films The Birds, North by Northwest and Psycho?*

a9 Which German scientist led the team which invented the V-2 rocket (the first true missile)?

b9 *Who designed the Morris Minor and later the Mini car?*

a10 What high office was held by Dr Robert Runcie?

b10 *In 1986, who became Archbishop of Cape Town?*

a11 Which two countries fought at the Battle of Tannenberg in 1914?

b11 *Which of these was a sea battle in the First World War: Arras, Jutland, Verdun?*

a12 In athletics, four field events involve jumping. Name three.

b12 *In athletics, there are four field events which involve throwing. Name three.*

No. 34 Answers

a1 Play them (they're small drums)
b1 *Piano*
a2 Mountains
b2 *Wales*
a3 Tim Rice
b3 *George Formby*
a4 Morecambe and Wise
b4 *Monty Python's Flying Circus*
a5 December
b5 *February*
a6 Queensland
b6 *Tasmania*
a7 *Peter Pan*
b7 *Pygmalion*
a8 2001
b8 *Alfred Hitchcock*
a9 Wernher von Braun
b9 *Alec Issigonis*
a10 Archbishop of Canterbury
b10 *Desmond Tutu*
a11 Germany and Russia
b11 *Jutland*
a12 Long jump, high jump, triple jump, pole vault
b12 *The hammer, the discus, the shot, the javelin*

Tie-breaker

Q 'I Get Around', 'Good Vibrations' and 'California Girls' were all popular hits for which group?
A *The Beach Boys*

No. 35

a1 In which European city would you be most likely to travel by gondola?

b1 *In which city is there a street called 'Unter den Linden'?*

a2 Which pop superstar released the albums, 'Off the Wall' and 'Thriller'?

b2 *Reginald Kenneth Dwight of Pinner in Middlesex is a pianist and supporter of Watford Football Club. By what name is he better known?*

a3 Who is the present Queen's eldest grandson?

b3 *What is the name of Princess Margaret's eldest child?*

a4 On which principal river does Dublin stand?

b4 *On which river stands the city of Nottingham?*

a5 Which very high office was held by Fisher of Lambeth?

b5 *What occupations have Russell, Losey and Fellini in common?*

a6 What is a psychosomatic illness?

b6 *What is the medical name for the collar-bone?*

a7 In which sport are Swinton and St Helens well-known teams?

b7 *Which Swedish tennis player was Wimbledon champion from 1976 to 1980?*

a8 Of which American political party was John F. Kennedy a leader?

b8 *What was the American president Richard Nixon's middle name?*

a9 Which American (Russian-born) science-fiction writer is famous for his *Foundation* trilogy?

b9 *What kind of novels are written by Jean Plaidy?*

a10 Who was the first man to fly the Channel by aeroplane?

b10 *Which airship made a round-the-world flight in 1929?*

a11 Which English county's industrial landscape was often painted by L. S. Lowry?

b11 *Guernica is a famous painting inspired by the Spanish Civil War. Who painted it?*

a12 Which Russian composed the musical narrative, *Peter and the Wolf*?

b12 *Which British composer founded the Aldeburgh Festival in Suffolk?*

No. 35 Answers

a1	Venice
b1	*Berlin*
a2	Michael Jackson
b2	*Elton John*
a3	Peter Phillips (son of the Princess Royal and Captain Mark Phillips)
b3	*(David) Viscount Linley*
a4	River Liffey
b4	*Trent*
a5	Archbishop of Canterbury
b5	*They are all film directors*
a6	One brought on by psychological causes
b6	*Clavicle*
a7	Rugby League
b7	*Bjorn Borg*
a8	Democratic
b8	*Milhous*
a9	(Isaac) Asimov
b9	*Historical novels (accept: historical romances, romantic novels)*
a10	(Louis) Bleriot (in 1909)
b10	*(Graf) Zeppelin*
a11	Lancashire
b11	*(Pablo) Picasso*
a12	(Sergei) Prokofiev
b12	*Benjamin Britten (Lord Britten)*

Tie-breaker

Q Who is this film star?: 'I was born in Massachusetts, USA; and studied acting in New York. I often, but not always, played cruel and selfish characters – as, for example, in the film *All about Eve*. In a much later film, I terrorized my screen sister and audiences – who worried about *Baby Jane*.'

A *Bette Davis (1908–1989)*

No. 36

a1   Who became prime minister of Britain in 1979?

b1   *Of which South American country has President Alfonsin been ruler?*

a2   In which sport or game was Cliff Thorburn a world champion?

b2   *Which snooker player gained the nickname 'Hurricane'?*

a3   What have these in common: Shannon, Lundy and South East Iceland?

b3   *What have these in common: Crosville, Ribble and Midland Red?*

a4   Who played the female lead in the film *The Sound of Music*?

b4   *Which film star was Liza Minelli's mother?*

a5   In which country is the city of Trieste?

b5   *In which Italian city would you find the Bridge of Sighs?*

a6   Who was head of state in Spain before Juan Carlos became king?

b6   *Over which country did the King of the Hellenes rule?*

a7   Which campaigning organization had a ship called the 'Rainbow Warrior'?

b7   *Which Townsend Thorensen car ferry capsized with tragic results off Zeebrugge in 1987?*

a8   If you drove south from the county Avon, which county would you enter next?

b8   *Which 'new' county was created in 1974 between Lincolnshire and North Yorkshire?*

a9   In a popular song, which musical instrument was called 'Tubby'?

b9   *For what would a musician use a 'plectrum'?*

a10   About which deaf and blind woman was the play (later filmed) called *The Miracle Worker*?

b10   *Which English nurse was shot by the Germans in 1915 for helping British soldiers?*

a11   Who was the first man to fly the Atlantic solo?

b11   *Who were the first two men to fly the Atlantic, non-stop?*

a12   In which year this century did hurricane-force winds devastate southern England?

b12   *In which year is Hong Kong due to become part of China?*

No. 36 Answers

a1	Margaret Thatcher
b1	*Argentina*
a2	Snooker
b2	*(Alex) Higgins*
a3	They're all sea areas (in the shipping forecasts)
b3	*All are bus companies*
a4	Julie Andrews
b4	*Judy Garland*
a5	Italy
b5	*Venice*
a6	General Franco
b6	*Greece*
a7	Greenpeace
b7	*Herald of Free Enterprise*
a8	Somerset
b8	*Humberside*
a9	Tuba
b9	*Plucking strings of an instrument (zither, guitar etc.)*
a10	Helen Keller
b10	*Edith Cavell*
a11	(Charles) Lindbergh (in 1917)
b11	*Alcock and Brown (in 1919)*
a12	1987
b12	*1997*

Tie-breaker

Q Which race starts at Cowes on the Isle of Wight and requires competitors to approach and return from the south-west coast of Ireland?

A *Fastnet Race (yachting)*

No. 37

a1 What was the name of Mickey Mouse's wife?

b1 *Name the cartoon cat who 'kept on walking'.*

a2 3½ pints of milk equals approximately how many litres?

b2 *If you buy a kilo package of sugar, what is the weight (approximately) in pounds?*

a3 Of which country has President Botha been ruler?

b3 *Of which country was David Ben Gurion Prime Minister?*

a4 Who composed the musicals *On the Town* and *West Side Story*?

b4 *Which American musician composed* An American in Paris *and the opera,* Porgy and Bess?

a5 Near which European city is Schiphol airport (say: ship-pol)?

b5 *For which English city is Squire's Gate the airport?*

a6 Who was the first Labour Member of Parliament?

b6 *Which former Labour minister was imprisoned as a fascist in 1940?*

a7 On stage, who was Chesney Allen's partner?

b7 *In the theatre, which writer and actor was known simply as 'Noël'?*

a8 Where in Liverpool were there race riots in 1981?

b8 *In 1987 Michael Ryan made the town of Hungerford into headline news. How?*

a9 Which Roman Catholic nun became famous for her work among the poor of Calcutta?

b9 *Who is generally said to be the greatest American architect of the century?*

a10 Who was Pope from 1958 to 1963?

b10 *This century, who was Pope for only 33 days?*

a11 The 1953 FA Cup Final is sometimes called 'The Matthews Final'. Which team won the final?

b11 *With which English league football club was George Best principally associated – and most successful?*

a12 Who wrote the novel *Kim*, first published in 1901?

b12 *Which writer created a hero called Aslan (who was a lion)?*

a1	Minnie
b1	*Felix*
a2	2
b2	*2.2 lb (accept: 2¼)*
a3	South Africa
b3	*Israel*
a4	(Leonard) Bernstein
b4	*(George) Gershwin*
a5	Amsterdam (in the Netherlands)
b5	*Blackpool*
a6	Keir Hardie
b6	*Sir Oswald Mosley*
a7	Bud Flanagan
b7	*Noël Coward*
a8	Toxteth (Liverpool 8)
b8	*He shot dead 14 people (and wounded 15) for no apparent reason*
a9	Mother Teresa
b9	*Frank Lloyd Wright*
a10	Pope John XXIII (born Angelo Roncalli)
b10	*John Paul I (in 1978)*
a11	Blackpool
b11	*Manchester United*
a12	Rudyard Kipling
b12	*C. S. Lewis (in The Lion, the Witch and the Wardrobe)*

Tie-breaker

Q What nationality was the surrealist painter René Magritte?
A *Belgian*

No. 38

a1 'Clunk click, every trip' was a slogan intended to encourage . . . what?

b1 *Which is the 'off-side' of a car?*

a2 Who was the star of the film *Crocodile Dundee?*

b2 *Who were the stars of the film* Duck Soup?

a3 In America which is the principal job of the FBI?

b3 *If you have committed regicide, what have you done?*

a4 What are: the Atheneum, the Carlton, the Reform?

b4 *And what are: Cheltenham, Benenden and Roedean?*

a5 In 1979, in which European country did workers win the right to join free trade unions?

b5 *And also in 1979, Abel Muzorewa became the first black prime minister of which country?*

a6 Who wrote the play *The Doctor's Dilemma?*

b6 *Who wrote the plays,* Blithe Spirit, Hay Fever *and* Private Lives?

a7 Which national leader had to flee his country in 1959 to escape from the Chinese?

b7 *Which country was ruled by Juan Peron (say: hwan pe-ron)?*

a8 Which Argentine cruiser was sunk by a British submarine during the Falklands War?

b8 *Henry VIII's flagship was rescued from the sea bed in 1982. What was she called?*

a9 Which university twice refused Mrs Thatcher an honorary degree?

b9 *In 1986, the 'Westland Affair' saw which Cabinet minister resign and stalk off along Downing Street?*

a10 Into which sea does the River Ribble flow?

b10 *Which is the principal river that flows into the Bristol Channel?*

a11 The busiest airport in the world is in America. Which is it?

b11 *Ronaldsway is an airport on which island?*

a12 Which famous black South African leader was released from prison in February 1990?

b12 *Emmeline, Christabel and Sylvia were all members of which family dedicated to women's rights?*

No. 38 Answers

a1	The wearing of car seat belts
b1	*The driver's side*
a2	Paul Hogan
b2	*The Marx Brothers*
a3	Crime detection, investigation
b3	*You have killed a king*
a4	London clubs; gentlemen's clubs
b4	*They are all girls' public schools*
a5	Poland
b5	*Rhodesia (later Zimbabwe)*
a6	G. B. Shaw
b6	*Noël Coward*
a7	Dalai Lama (of Tibet)
b7	*Argentina*
a8	General Belgrano
b8	*Mary Rose*
a9	Oxford
b9	*Michael Heseltine*
a10	Irish Sea
b10	*Severn*
a11	Chicago International
b11	*Isle of Man*
a12	Nelson Mandela
b12	*Pankhurst*

Tie-breaker

Q In which book will you read that: 'Whatever goes on two legs is an enemy. Whatever goes on four legs, or has wings, is a friend'?

A Animal Farm *by George Orwell*

No. 39

a1   What is Popeye's favourite vegetable?

b1   *What was the name of the Lone Ranger's horse?*

a2   With which means of transport is IATA concerned?

b2   *Of which country is KLM the national airline?*

a3   In 1981, who became president of Britain's National Union of Mineworkers?

b3   *'Solidarity' became a trades union movement in which country, principally?*

a4   Which famous female singing star was particularly associated with the songs 'Sing as We Go' and 'Sally in Our Alley'?

b4   *Who made famous the songs, 'Jake the Peg' and 'Tie Me Kangaroo Down, Sport'?*

a5   For what did Barbara Hepworth become famous?

b5   *As what did Artur Rubinstein achieve international fame?*

a6   Who wrote the novel *From Russia with Love*?

b6   *Which writer created Inspector Maigret?*

a7   Who became British prime minister after Harold Wilson in 1976?

b7   *Who was England's prime minister when India gained independence?*

a8   Why did Broadwater Farm become notorious in 1985?

b8   *November 1987 saw a tragic fire on London's Underground. At which station?*

a9   In which athletics event did Ed Moses become a champion?

b9   *'The Rockhampton Rocket', Rod Laver, was a champion in which sport?*

a10   Which city was once called Byzantium and Constantinople?

b10   *In which European country is the city of Turin?*

a11   Tumbledown Mountain is on which group of islands?

b11   *'Uluru' is an Aborigine name for which Australian landmark?*

a12   Arthur Miller's play, *The Crucible*, deals with witchcraft in which American town?

b12   *Who is the central character who is murdered in the play, Murder in the Cathedral?*

No. 39 Answers

a1   Spinach
b1   Silver
a2   Air travel (International Air Transport Association)
b2   Holland
a3   Arthur Scargill
b3   Poland
a4   Gracie Fields
b4   Rolf Harris
a5   (Abstract) Sculpture
b5   Pianist
a6   Ian Fleming
b6   (Georges) Simenon
a7   James Callaghan
b7   (Clement) Attlee (in 1947)
a8   For riots (in which a policeman was killed) (It's a housing estate in North London)
b8   King's Cross
a9   (High) hurdles; 400-metre hurdles
b9   Tennis
a10   Istanbul
b10   Italy
a11   Falklands (East Falkland)
b11   Ayers Rock
a12   Salem (Massachusetts)
b12   Thomas à Becket, Archbishop of Canterbury

Tie-breaker

Q Which island became the focus of a 'missile crisis' in 1962?
A *Cuba*

No. 40

a1   What is the capital of Greece?

b1   *Of which country is Lisbon the capital?*

a2   According to the First World War song, where was 'the sweetest girl I know'?

b2   *Which singer was called the 'Sweetheart of the Forces'?*

a3   From 1945, who was president of Yugoslavia?

b3   *Of which country was Jan (say: yan) Christiaan Smuts twice prime minister?*

a4   In which industry does BAFTA give awards?

b4   *A famous Hollywood film company uses the trademark of a mountain peak surrounded by a circle of stars. What is the name of the company?*

a5   For which English county did Geoffrey Boycott play cricket?

b5   *The ice-skaters Torvill and Dean became famous for skating to which composer's 'Bolero'?*

a6   Of which English county is the Isle of Sheppey a part?

b6   *Which island has a law-making council called the Tynwald?*

a7   Who wrote the play, *The Deep Blue Sea*?

b7   *Who wrote the long-running play,* The Mousetrap?

a8   On whom are Australians who live in the 'outback' of that country dependent for medical help?

b8   *What information does a pilot get from his altimeter?*

a9   Which two British political parties formed an alliance in 1981?

b9   *Which was regularly televised first, the House of Commons or the House of Lords?*

a10   Which major ship canal was completed in 1914?

b10   *Which major American seaway or canal was opened in 1959?*

a11   Where does the European Court of Justice meet?

b11   *By what abbreviation is the International Criminal Police Commission usually known?*

a12   'Sonny' Ramphal was secretary-general of which organization from 1975 to 1990?

b12   *In which country was Dr Sakharov banished for his beliefs?*

No. 40 Answers

a1   Athens
b1   *Portugal*
a2   Tipperary
b2   *Vera Lynn*
a3   Tito
b3   *South Africa*
a4   Film and television (British Academy of Film and Television Arts)
b4   *Paramount*
a5   Yorkshire
b5   *Ravel's*
a6   Kent
b6   *Isle of Man*
a7   Terence Rattigan
b7   *Agatha Christie*
a8   Flying doctors
b8   *His altitude or height, how high the plane is flying*
a9   Liberals, Social Democrats
b9   *House of Lords*
a10   Panama Canal
b10   *St Lawrence Seaway*
a11   The Hague (in the Netherlands) (accept: Den Haag)
b11   *Interpol*
a12   British Commonwealth
b12   *Soviet Union (Russia) (He was sent into 'internal exile')*

Tie-breaker

Q 'In a while, crocodile' was an answer to what remark in a classic film and pop hit of the fifties?
A 'See you later, alligator!'

No. 41: Hits from the Shows

In which musical does each of the following numbers occur?

a1 'On the Street Where You Live'
b1 'The Farmer and the Cowman'
a2 'We Said We Wouldn't Look Back'
b2 'Matchmaker, Matchmaker'
a3 'Some Enchanted Evening'
b3 'Good Morning, Starshine'
a4 'Day by Day'
b4 'Climb Every Mountain'
a5 'I Could Be Happy With You'
b5 'Shall We Dance?'
a6 'One'
b6 'Flash! Bang! Wallop!'
a7 'Luck be a Lady'
b7 'You've Got to Pick a Pocket or Two'
a8 'If You Could See Her Through My Eyes'
b8 'There's No Business Like Show Business'
a9 'Another Opening, Another Show'
b9 'Don't Cry for Me, Argentina'
a10 'Tonight'
b10 'Shakin' at the High School Hop'
a11 'I'll See You Again'
b11 'Let's Do a Deal'
a12 'The Lambeth Walk'
b12 'Easter Parade'

No. 41 Answers

a1	*My Fair Lady*
b1	Oklahoma!
a2	*Salad Days*
b2	Fiddler on the Roof
a3	*South Pacific*
b3	Hair
a4	*Godspell*
b4	The Sound of Music
a5	*The Boy Friend*
b5	The King and I
a6	*A Chorus Line*
b6	Half a Sixpence
a7	*Guys and Dolls*
b7	Oliver!
a8	*Cabaret*
b8	Annie Get Your Gun
a9	*Kiss Me Kate*
b9	Evita
a10	*West Side Story*
b10	Grease
a11	*Bitter Sweet*
b11	Charlie Girl
a12	*Me and My Girl*
b12	Holiday Inn

Tie-breaker

Q Who composed the musicals *Brigadoon, The Day Before Spring* and *Paint Your Wagon*?

A Frederick Loewe

No. 42

a1   In which game or sport is Gary Kasparov a champion?

b1   *In which sport did Evonne Cawley become famous?*

a2   In the 1942 film *A Yank at Oxford*, who played the Yank?

b2   *Norma Jean Baker became a film star and starred in* The Seven Year Itch, Bus Stop *and* Some Like it Hot. *What was her screen name?*

a3   In law, which kind of document has to be granted 'probate'?

b3   *How many people normally sit on a English jury?*

a4   What is, or was, the Luftwaffe?

b4   *Which is the world's oldest air force?*

a5   Which member of the Royal Family has a holiday home on the Caribbean island of Mustique?

b5   *Whom did Princess Margaret marry in 1960?*

a6   Which American base in Britain became famous in the eighties for the women protesters it attracted?

b6   *Orgreave in South Yorkshire became widely known during which industrial dispute?*

a7   In which English county are the Seven Sisters?

b7   *Which English county adjoins Cornwall?*

a8   What did Jack Teagarden, Benny Goodman and Tommy Dorsey all have in common?

b8   *Which Rodgers and Hammerstein musical is set in the American West?*

a9   What is the Army equivalent of the RAF rank of Marshal of the Royal Air Force?

b9   *What is the RAF equivalent of the Army rank of group captain?*

a10   What is the religion of most people in Afghanistan?

b10   *What is the principal religion of Albania?*

a11   Which writer is particularly associated with Ayot St Lawrence?

b11   *How did T. E. Lawrence (known as 'Lawrence of Arabia') die?*

a12   On stage which pop star has been Jesus in *Godspell*, Che Guevara and Lord Byron?

b12   *On stage, by what names are Dr Evadne and Dame Hilda better known?*

No. 42 Answers

a1	Chess
b1	*Tennis*
a2	Mickey Rooney
b2	*Marilyn Monroe*
a3	A will
b3	*12*
a4	German airforce
b4	*Britain's Royal Air Force (founded 1918)*
a5	Princess Margaret
b5	*Antony Armstrong-Jones (later he became the Earl of Snowdon)*
a6	Greenham Common
b6	*Miners' strike, 1984*
a7	(East) Sussex
b7	*Devon*
a8	Bandleaders (Big band, swing)
b8	*Oklahoma!*
a9	Field Marshal
b9	*Colonel*
a10	Muslim (Islam)
b10	*Muslim (Islam)*
a11	G. B. Shaw
b11	*He was killed in a motor-cycle accident*
a12	David Essex
b12	*Hinge and Bracket*

Tie-breaker

Q The Janata Party (or People's Front) is a political organization in which country?

A *India*

No. 43

a1   What is the capital of Finland?

b1   *Before re-unification what was the capital of West Germany?*

a2   In which country was there a secret police force called the KGB?

b2   *1981 saw the abolition of which means of execution in France?*

a3   'Just like that' was a catch phrase of which British comedian and conjuror?

b3   *Who originally became famous for his remark, 'You cannot be serious'?*

a4   In which English county is the town of Preston?

b4   *In which English county is the holiday resort, Hastings?*

a5   What had these in common: Michael Wilding, Mike Todd, Eddie Fisher, and Richard Burton?

b5   *Fantasia, Dumbo and Pinocchio are all famous cartoon films. Which studio made them?*

a6   With which kind of music do you associate Bill Haley?

b6   *What kind of dancing would you do at a Hoedown?*

a7   Eugene Terre Blanche has been an extreme right-wing leader in which country?

b7   *Of which country was Ferdinand Marcos president until 1986?*

a8   Steve Cram and Sebastian Coe have both held the world record in which athletic event?

b8   *Yachting: which country held the America's Cup from 1932 till 1983?*

a9   In 1958, the American submarine 'Nautilus' succeeded in crossing which ocean?

b9   *Which famous sailor is associated with the yacht, 'Gypsy Moth'?*

a10   Of which country has President Kaunda been the leader?

b10   *Of which country was Georges Pompidou Prime Minister?*

a11   Which diminutive and very young Russian gymnast was a star of the 1972 Olympics?

b11   *For which country did Diego Maradona play soccer?*

a12   As what did the American Martha Graham become famous?

b12   *As what has Judy Blume achieved fame?*

No. 43 Answers

a1 Helsinki
b1 *Bonn*
a2 Soviet Union (Russia)
b2 *Guillotine*
a3 Tommy Cooper
b3 *John McEnroe*
a4 Lancashire
b4 *Sussex (East)*
a5 All were husbands of Elizabeth Taylor
b5 *Walt Disney*
a6 Rock 'n' roll
b6 *Square dancing*
a7 South Africa
b7 *Philippines*
a8 The mile and/or 1500 metres
b8 *United States of America*
a9 Arctic Ocean
b9 *Sir Francis Chichester*
a10 Zambia
b10 *France*
a11 Olga Korbut
b11 *Argentina*
a12 Modern dancer and choreographer
b12 *Novelist; author of novels for teenagers*

Tie-breaker

Q Which comedy group used to sing, 'Ying-tong-iddle-i-po'?
A *The Goons (The Ying Tong Song)*

No. 44

a1 On which English racecourse is the Derby run?

b1 What ceremony takes place on Horse Guards Parade on the Sovereign's Official Birthday?

a2 What was the Black Bottom?

b2 In dance, what do you do when you pirouette?

a3 In the film, who played Dr Dolittle?

b3 In which film did Baloo sing about the 'bare necessities of life'?

a4 By what name are 'Las Malvinas' islands known in Britain?

b4 Las Palmas and Santa Cruz de Tenerife are the two main groups of which islands?

a5 In 1937, which airship burst into flames near New York?

b5 Which two countries jointly developed the aircraft Concorde?

a6 Which prime minister was assassinated by her own bodyguard in 1984?

b6 Yassir Arafat became a leader of which people?

a7 Hyde Park and Regent's Park both saw bomb explosions on the same day in 1982. Which organization was responsible?

b7 Where, in Britain, did a Trident airliner crash in June 1972, killing 118 people?

a8 Who was prime minister of Great Britain at the time of Edward VIII's abdication?

b8 Of which British political party was Arthur Balfour a leader?

a9 Former MI5 officer Peter Wright wrote a book which was headline news in 1987. What was its title?

b9 'Economical with the truth' became a diplomatic expression for . . . what?

a10 What tragedy at Bhopal in India killed at least 2,000 people in 1984?

b10 In which Indian city is the Sikh holy shrine, the Golden Temple?

a11 In which radio show did we used to hear the catch phrase, 'Give him the money, Barney!'?

b11 Who used the catchphrase, 'Here's to the next time'?

a12 In which art did Bertolt Brecht become famous?

b12 As what did Philip Larkin achieve fame?

No. 44 Answers

a1	Epsom
b1	*Trooping of the Colour*
a2	A dance (type of foxtrot)
b2	*Turn/spin round on one leg*
a3	Rex Harrison
b3	*Jungle Book*
a4	The Falkland Islands
b4	*Canary Islands*
a5	The Hindenburg
b5	*Britain and France*
a6	Mrs Indira Gandhi (India)
b6	*The Palestinians*
a7	IRA
b7	*Near Heathrow (accept: near Staines)*
a8	Stanley Baldwin
b8	*Conservative*
a9	Spycatcher
b9	*Lying, evading saying the truth*
a10	Leak from a chemical factory, a gas leak
b10	*Amritsar*
a11	*Have A Go*
b11	*Henry Hall*
a12	Theatre
b12	*Poet*

Tie-breaker

Q Which is the world's longest road tunnel?
A *St Gotthard Road Tunnel (southern Alps, in Switzerland)*

No. 45

a1 Which disc jockey uses the catch phrase, 'How's about that then, guys and gals'?

b1 *Whose catch phrase was 'You dirty rotten swine, you; you have deaded me!'?*

a2 Which is further north, Sardinia or Corsica?

b2 *To which country do the Azores islands in the Atlantic belong?*

a3 Which brothers starred in the film, *A Night at the Opera*?

b3 *Who was the star of the first successful talking feature film?*

a4 Until abolished in 1986, what was the GLC?

b4 *In which metropolitan area are Tameside, Trafford and Wigan?*

a5 In which country is the sea-port of Antwerp?

b5 *Which sea-port do sailors nickname 'Pompey'?*

a6 How did Chris Bonington become well-known in the sixties and seventies?

b6 *In which art has Peter O'Toole achieved fame?*

a7 Of which island is Honolulu the capital?

b7 *Which capital city is on Honshu island?*

a8 After the assassination of her husband, Cory Aquino became a political leader of which country?

b8 *Joshua Nkomo unsuccessfully aimed to become leader of which African nation when it became independent?*

a9 Which cricketer had a highest score of 452 not out – and made a duck in his last test innings as captain of Australia?

b9 *In swimming, who won seven gold medals at the Munich Olympics in 1972?*

a10 Of which country was Jack Lynch the prime minister?

b10 *Of which country was Sir Keith Holyoake prime minister?*

a11 In which year was the first motorway opened in Britain: 1951, 1959, or 1963?

b11 *In which year did commercial television begin in Britain: 1947, 1953, or 1955?*

a12 Who wrote the novel *The Hobbit*?

b12 *Under which pen-name did Eric Blair write?*

No. 45 Answers

a1   Jimmy Savile
b1   *Bluebottle (Peter Sellers in* The Goon Show*)*
a2   Corsica
b2   *Portugal*
a3   Marx Brothers
b3   *Al Jolson*
a4   Greater London Council
b4   *(Greater) Manchester*
a5   Belgium
b5   *Portsmouth*
a6   As a mountaineer
b6   *Acting*
a7   Hawaii
b7   *Tokyo*
a8   Philippines
b8   *Zimbabwe (formerly Rhodesia)*
a9   Donald Bradman
b9   *Mark Spitz*
a10   Eire; Ireland
b10   *New Zealand*
a11   1959
b11   *1955*
a12   J. R. R. Tolkien
b12   *George Orwell*

Tie-breaker

Q Who is this film director?: 'When I was a boy, I borrowed my
father's ciné camera to film toy trains. By the age of 21, I was
directing television series – including *Columbo*. I've made a
"purplish" story about racial conflict, and "lost" an ark.'
A *Steven Spielberg*

No. 46

a1 Which television presenter was famous for saying, 'Hello, good evening and welcome'?

b1 *Who led the team which created television's The Muppet Show?*

a2 Of which country is the island of Zealand a part?

b2 *To which country does the island of Corfu belong?*

a3 For which art did Maria Callas become famous?

b3 *Born Peggy Hookham, she became a famous ballerina, partnering Rudolf Nureyev. What was her stage name?*

a4 Which important bridge, east of London, was opened in 1991?

b4 *Roughly, in which direction from the Midlands does the M6 go?*

a5 Who was King of Great Britain from 1901 to 1910?

b5 *And who was King from 1910 to 1936?*

a6 Which continent has the longest coastline: Africa or Europe?

b6 *Which is the largest country in South America?*

a7 Which film star said (on screen), 'Why don't you come up sometime 'n' see me'?

b7 *Which star appeared in the film The Graduate and (in drag) in Tootsie?*

a8 Which great house in Derbyshire is sometimes called 'The Palace of the Peak'?

b8 *In which county is Wookey Hole?*

a9 Who composed the music for West Side Story?

b9 *Who composed the music for the musical, Starlight Express?*

a10 In which South American country did the final of the 1962 soccer World Cup take place?

b10 *In which country did the finals of the 1970 soccer World Cup take place?*

a11 Which American president became famous for his election slogan, 'Read my lips: no new taxes'?

b11 *Which president had a sign on his desk saying, 'The buck stops here'?*

a12 'Papa Doc' and 'Baby Doc' were both hated dictators in which country?

b12 *Enver Hoxha (say: hodja) was head of state of which country?*

No. 46 Answers

a1 David Frost
b1 Jim Henson
a2 Denmark
b2 Greece
a3 Opera (singing)
b3 Margot Fonteyn
a4 The Queen Elizabeth II Bridge (or Dartford Bridge)
b4 Northwards
a5 Edward VII
b5 George V
a6 Europe
b6 Brazil
a7 Mae West
b7 Dustin Hoffman
a8 Chatsworth House
b8 Somerset
a9 Leonard Bernstein
b9 Andrew Lloyd Webber
a10 Chile
b10 Mexico
a11 George Bush
b11 Harry S. Truman
a12 Haiti
b12 Albania

Tie-breaker

Q Robert Bolt's play *A Man for All Seasons* is about Sir Thomas
More and which English King?

A *King Henry VIII*

No. 47

a1   What is the capital of Norway?

b1   *Name the capital of Denmark.*

a2   Which of the Marx brothers had a cigar and moustache?

b2   *Which director of suspense movies always makes a brief appearance in each of his films?*

a3   Who led the winning side in the Spanish Civil War?

b3   *Who made Cuba a Communist state?*

a4   Which deputy chairman of the British Conservative party was also a very successful novelist?

b4   The Moon's a Balloon *was the autobiography of which actor?*

a5   One of President Theodore Roosevelt's distant cousins also became president of the United States. What was his name?

b5   *What was the first name of President Franklin D. Roosevelt's wife?*

a6   Soccer: Who won the World Cup in 1966?

b6   *And who was the English goalkeeper in that match?*

a7   Lech Walesa (say: wa-len-sa) led which campaign?

b7   *In the eighties, where were rebels known as 'Contras'?*

a8   Name one of the three Baltic states which were independent between 1920 and 1940 and again from 1991.

b8   *Can you name a European country which came into being at the end of the First World War?*

a9   Thelonius Monk became famous as what sort of musician?

b9   *Which English composer became famous for many film scores and for his suite, called 'Façade'?*

a10   Kenneth Clark became famous for a major cultural television series. What was it called?

b10   *On BBC television, who played Smiley in Smiley's People?*

a11   With which other country did Tanganyika merge to become Tanzania?

b11   *By what name (beginning with 'B') is the former African country of Bechuanaland now known?*

a12   Which dancer starred in such ballets as L'Après-midi d'un faun?

b12   *Which female dancer founded the Royal Ballet?*

No. 47 Answers

a1	Oslo
b1	*Copenhagen*
a2	Groucho
b2	*Alfred Hitchcock*
a3	General Franco
b3	*Fidel Castro*
a4	Jeffrey Archer
b4	*David Niven*
a5	Franklin D. Roosevelt
b5	*Eleanor*
a6	England
b6	*Gordon Banks*
a7	Solidarity (in Poland)
b7	*Nicaragua*
a8	Estonia, Latvia, Lithuania
b8	*Yugoslavia, Czechoslovakia*
a9	Jazz (pianist)
b9	*William Walton*
a10	*Civilisation*
b10	*Alec Guinness*
a11	Zanzibar
b11	*Botswana*
a12	Nijinsky
b12	*(Dame) Ninette de Valois*

Tie-breaker

Q Along which frontier were SWAPO forces active in the seventies?

A *Angola–Namibia*

No. 48

a1   In which country is the port of Bergen?

b1   *If you cross the Channel from Newhaven, in which French port do you expect to dock?*

a2   By what name has East Pakistan been known since 1971?

b2   *What was the former name of Sri Lanka?*

a3   With whom do we associate the phrase, 'Here's lookin' at you, kid'?

b3   *Which television detective is associated with the catch phrase, 'Who loves you, baby'?*

a4   In which mountain range is the Eiger?

b4   *What do we call the range of hills which forms the border between England and Scotland?*

a5   At which stadium in Belgium was there a football tragedy in 1985?

b5   *Soccer: who won the World Cup in 1974?*

a6   On television, on which sport was Kent Walton a famous commentator?

b6   *For his commentaries on which sport will Dan Maskell be remembered?*

a7   Which American leader is famous for a speech which included the words, 'I have a dream'?

b7   *Whose election campaign slogan was 'I like Ike'?*

a8   In the world of cinema, what is a 'spaghetti' western?

b8   *About what activity was the film, Pumping Iron?*

a9   Menachem Begin was prime minister of which country?

b9   *General Jaruzelski was formerly leader of which country?*

a10   Who composed many popular musicals and the song, 'Keep the Home Fires Burning'?

b10   *Who wrote the music which goes with the words, 'Land of Hope and Glory'?*

a11   In which English city is the Jorvik Viking Centre?

b11   *What was discovered at Sutton Hoo in Suffolk in 1939?*

a12   Beside being a Conservative, to which other political party did Winston Churchill belong during his life?

b12   *Which Labour minister inaugurated the National Health Service?*

No. 48 Answers

a1	Norway
b1	*Dieppe*
a2	Bangladesh
b2	*Ceylon*
a3	Humphrey Bogart
b3	*Kojak (Telly Savalas)*
a4	Alps
b4	*The Cheviots*
a5	Heysel Stadium, Brussels
b5	*West Germany*
a6	Wrestling
b6	*Tennis*
a7	Martin Luther King
b7	*Dwight D. Eisenhower (USA presidential election, 1952)*
a8	A western or cowboy film made outside America (possibly in Italy or Spain)
b8	*Body-building*
a9	Israel
b9	*Poland*
a10	Ivor Novello
b10	*Elgar (Sir Edward)*
a11	York
b11	*The remains of an Anglo-Saxon ship*
a12	Liberal
b12	*Aneurin Bevan*

Tie-breaker

Q Which British architect designed the new Stansted Airport?
A *Norman Foster*

No. 49

a1 Off the coast of which country is the island of Taiwan?
b1 *Of which country is Prince Edward Island a part?*
a2 In which ocean is the so-called Bermuda Triangle?
b2 *What kind of vessel is a U-Boat?*
a3 Who played Lawrence in the film, *Lawrence of Arabia?*
b3 *In which film did Orson Welles play Harry Lime?*
a4 In which country is the Nullarbor Plain?
b4 *In which country would you find the veldt?*
a5 Pipe, steel, wind and brass are all types of . . .what?
b5 *C60, C90 and C120 are all types of . . .what?*
a6 Yuri Andropov became president of which country in 1982?
b6 *Who became chancellor of West Germany in 1982?*
a7 Which English cathedral was set on fire by lightning in 1984?
b7 *Which English cathedral was rebuilt after the Second World War as a sign of reconciliation with Germany?*
a8 Which Democrat did Ronald Reagan defeat to become president in 1980?
b8 *Which American president resigned because of the Watergate scandal in 1974?*
a9 In yards, how long is a cricket pitch?
b9 *19 wickets were taken by one bowler in a 1956 cricket test match. Who was he?*
a10 'The Gang of Four' formed the new Social Democrat party in 1981. To which party did they formerly belong?
b10 *Which Welsh statesman started an old age pension scheme and became prime minister in 1916?*
a11 Which pop group sang about 'Baggy Trousers'?
b11 *Which pop group had hits with 'Painter Man', 'Rasputin' and 'Brown Girl in the Ring'?*
a12 Who led the Indian National Congress party for 20 years prior to Indian independence?
b12 *Who was the King's viceroy (or representative) in India at the time of independence?*

No. 49 Answers

a1	China
b1	*Canada*
a2	(North) Atlantic
b2	*Submarine (in German: Unter-See Boot, or under-sea boat)*
a3	Peter O'Toole
b3	*The Third Man*
a4	Australia
b4	*South Africa*
a5	Bands
b5	*Cassette tapes*
a6	Soviet Union
b6	*Helmut Kohl*
a7	York Minster
b7	*Coventry*
a8	Jimmy Carter
b8	*Richard Nixon*
a9	22
b9	*(Jim) Laker*
a10	Labour
b10	*Lloyd George*
a11	Madness
b11	*Boney M*
a12	Mahatma Gandhi
b12	*Louis Mountbatten (later: Earl Mountbatten of Burma)*

Tie-breaker

Q Which poet wrote about the Old Vicarage, Grantchester?
A *Rupert Brooke*

No. 50

a1 What is the capital of Brazil?

b1 *Of which country is Port of Spain the capital?*

a2 What is the official national anthem of the USA?

b2 *Which singer is associated with the song, 'Ol' Man River'?*

a3 Which two countries border the Bay of Biscay?

b3 *On which ocean does Peru have its seaboard?*

a4 Who was Richard Burton's co-star in the film *Cleopatra*?

b4 *Who is the male star in the film,* The French Lieutenant's Woman?

a5 Mysore, Hyderabad and Madras are all parts of which country?

b5 *The Polish port of Gdansk (say: gu-dansk) was formerly known by what name in Britain?*

a6 Where was Dr Garrett Fitzgerald prime minister?

b6 *Dr Kurt Waldheim was elected president of which country?*

a7 Daniel Kaminski played Walter Mitty and Hans Andersen on screen. What was his 'stage' name?

b7 *She was a musical comedy star, starred in* Wake Up and Dream *and later played Mrs Dale on BBC Radio. Who was she?*

a8 In 1985, there was a tragic fire at an English football ground. Which ground?

b8 *For which World Cup team did Eusebio play?*

a9 Who was the drummer in the group The Who?

b9 *Who developed a chain of shops specializing in traditional cotton fabrics and dresses which, by 1985, was known around the world?*

a10 Can you name a country (besides Britain) which joined the Common Market in 1973?

b10 *In which year was Winston Churchill first elected to Parliament?*

a11 Who wrote the novel *Catcher in the Rye*?

b11 *Who wrote the novel* To Kill a Mocking Bird?

a12 In which radio programme did we used to hear the catch phrase: 'And the next object is . . .'?

b12 *In which radio programme did we used to hear the catch phrase: 'After you Claude; No, after you, Cecil!'*

No. 50 Answers

a1	Brasilia
b1	*Trinidad (and Tobago)*
a2	'The Star Spangled Banner'
b2	*Paul Robeson*
a3	Spain and France
b3	*Pacific*
a4	Elizabeth Taylor
b4	*Jeremy Irons*
a5	India
b5	*Danzig*
a6	Ireland (Eire)
b6	*Austria*
a7	Danny Kaye
b7	*Jessie Matthews*
a8	Bradford
b8	*Portugal*
a9	Keith Moon
b9	*Laura Ashley*
a10	Denmark; Irish Republic
b10	*1900*
a11	J. D. Salinger
b11	*Harper Lee*
a12	Twenty Questions
b12	ITMA

Tie-breaker

Q In London, which Underground line was once known as the 'Tuppenny Tube'?

A *Central Line (Central Railway)*

No. 51: One Language, Two Nations

It has often been said that America and Britain are two nations separated by a common language – because, of course, words mean different things in the two countries.

What is the British equivalent of the following?

a1 Apartment
b1 Bill
a2 Cuffs
b2 Diaper
a3 Call collect
b3 Caravan
a4 Rubber
b4 A game of checkers
a5 Back-up lights (on a car)
b5 Odometer
a6 Barette
b6 Comforter

And what is the American equivalent of these British words?

a7 Wallet
b7 (Policeman's) truncheon
a8 Tap
b8 Spanner
a9 Post code
b9 Pelmet
a10 Lay-by
b10 Goose pimples
a11 Estate car
b11 Caretaker
a12 Courgettes
b12 Aubergine

a1	Flat
b1	*Banknote*
a2	Turn-ups
b2	*Nappy*
a3	Reverse charges
b3	*Convoy*
a4	Contraceptive, condom
b4	*A game of draughts*
a5	Reversing lights
b5	*Mileometer*
a6	Hair slide
b6	*Eiderdown*
a7	Billfold
b7	*Night stick*
a8	Faucet
b8	*Monkey wrench*
a9	Zip code
b9	*Valence*
a10	Pull-off
b10	*Goose bumps*
a11	Station wagon
b11	*Janitor*
a12	Zucchini
b12	*Egg plant*

Tie-breaker

Q What is the purpose of Callanetics?
A *To build up muscles, to develop muscle tone (through exercise)*

No. 52

a1 In which ocean are the Canary Islands?

b1 *In which continent is Nicaragua?*

a2 In which domestic product are you likely to find enzymes?

b2 *Besides tomatoes and meat, from what is tinned ravioli principally made?*

a3 Which south London exhibition centre burned down in 1936?

b3 *Whereabouts in London are the Crown Jewels now kept?*

a4 Which instrument did the jazz musicians Art Tatum and Earl Hines both play?

b4 *Which instrument did the jazz musician Dizzy Gillespie play?*

a5 Which radio sports commentator later became his country's leader?

b5 *And of which American state was Ronald Reagan formerly governor?*

a6 In which film did Bing Crosby first sing, 'White Christmas'?

b6 *Who was the Swedish star of the films* Queen Christina *and* Anna Karenina?

a7 Basrah is a port in which country?

b7 *In which country is the port of Aqaba?*

a8 Mrs Bandaranaike was prime minister of which island?

b8 *Before becoming involved in politics, what was Rajiv Gandhi's profession?*

a9 'Who shot JR?': to which television series did that question apply?

b9 *Which television private eye was played by Tom Selleck?*

a10 In gymnastics, what do we call the equipment which consists of two parallel bars at different heights?

b10 *And what do we call the vaulting horse which has two handles on top of it?*

a11 In which two cities or towns does the European parliament meet?

b11 *Which European 'Act' allows the free movement of money, goods and people within the EC?*

a12 Which female novelist wrote The Pursuit of Love and Love in a Cold Climate?

b12 *Which Russian author wrote* The Gulag Archipelago?

No. 52 Answers

a1 Atlantic
b1 (Central) America
a2 Detergent
b2 Semolina
a3 Crystal Palace
b3 Tower of London
a4 Piano
b4 Trumpet
a5 Ronald Reagan
b5 California
a6 Holiday Inn
b6 Greta Garbo
a7 Iraq
b7 Jordan
a8 Sri Lanka (formerly Ceylon)
b8 Airline pilot
a9 Dallas
b9 Magnum
a10 Asymmetric bars
b10 Pommel horse
a11 Strasbourg (France) and Luxembourg
b11 Single European Market Act
a12 Nancy Mitford
b12 Alexander Solzhenitsyn

Tie-breaker

Q The Seventh Seal, Wild Strawberries and Smiles of a Summer Night were all made by which Swedish film director?
A Ingmar Bergman

No. 53

a1   What sort of animals were Chi-Chi and An-An?

b1   *What are tigons and ligers?*

a2   Romanies and Diddikois are both names for which people?

b2   *From which country do 'Hispanic' people originate?*

a3   In Greece, what kind of food is moussaka?

b3   *And what kind of drink is Retsina?*

a4   Which couple became famous for their dancing in the film *Top Hat* and *Swing Time*?

b4   *In the film, The Wizard of Oz, who sang 'Over the Rainbow'?*

a5   Which part of a car's engine mixes petrol and air?

b5   *Which device in a car's engine drives the water pump and the alternator?*

a6   Which of the Queen's cousins was killed by the IRA in 1979?

b6   *Roddy Llewellyn was a close friend of which Royal Princess?*

a7   On board ship, what is the purpose of a gyroscope?

b7   *Which means of transport went into public use in 1965 (between the English mainland and the Isle of Wight)?*

a8   Bavaria and Saxony are both states within which country?

b8   *In which country is Legoland, a theme park made out of Lego?*

a9   Which famous production trio was the background team behind many popular music hits in the late eighties?

b9   *What was the first name and surname of Art Garfunkel's partner in a folk-rock duo in the sixties and seventies?*

a10   Who founded the Vietnamese communist party and became president of North Vietnam?

b10   *Who became president of Nationalist China on the island of Taiwan in 1949?*

a11   At which English football ground was there a major disaster in 1989, involving Liverpool fans?

b11   *In which country were the finals of the 1982 soccer World Cup?*

a12   In government, what is the job of the 'legislature'?

b12   *And what do we call the part of the government that puts the laws into effect?*

No. 53 Answers

a1 (Giant) pandas
b1 *Hybrid tigers/lions, cross-bred lions and tigers*
a2 Travelling people (gypsies)
b2 *Spain or Portugal*
a3 Baked aubergines and minced meat
b3 *Wine (flavoured with pine resin)*
a4 Fred Astaire and Ginger Rogers
b4 *Judy Garland*
a5 Carburettor
b5 *Fan belt*
a6 Earl Mountbatten (of Burma)
b6 *Princess Margaret*
a7 Either to improve the ship's stability (it counteracts the ship's movement) or to help the process of navigation (gyroscopic compass)
b7 *Hovercraft*
a8 Germany
b8 *Denmark*
a9 Stock, Aitken and Waterman
b9 *Paul Simon*
a10 Ho Chi Minh
b10 *Chiang Kai-Shek (Also known as: Jiang Jieshi)*
a11 Hillsborough (Sheffield Wednesday)
b11 *Spain*
a12 The passing of new laws
b12 *The executive (accept: the Cabinet or civil servants or Whitehall)*

Tie-breaker

Q Which indoor game involves penthouses, a net and a grille – and was popular with King Henry VIII?
A *Real tennis*

No. 54

a1   On television, who became famous for his Madhouse?

b1   *In which television hotel did a waiter come from 'Bar-th-elona'?*

a2   In which Italian cathedral is there a shroud thought by some to show the face of Christ?

b2   *What was the popular name of the special vehicle in which Pope John Paul II often toured the cities he visited?*

a3   Which sport was revolutionized by Kerry Packer?

b3   *Robin Cousins was a 1980 Olympic star in which sport?*

a4   As what did the Italian Tito Gobbi become famous?

b4   *In which profession did François Truffaut achieve fame?*

a5   The invasion of which country in 1990 brought about the Gulf War?

b5   *Which general commanded American forces in the Gulf War?*

a6   What form of transport was the Sinclair C5?

b6   *With which industry is the name Pilkington associated?*

a7   In which capital city was the 1916 Easter Rising?

b7   *Which European country conquered Ethiopia in 1936?*

a8   In France, to what do the initials TGV refer?

b8   *Before nationalization, which railway company ran the Cornish Riveria Express?*

a9   What was the Alexander Kielland?

b9   *Off what country's coast did the oil tanker Amoco Cadiz go aground and break up in 1978?*

a10   Which young star became a teen idol with his film *Rebel without a Cause*, released after his death in a car crash?

b10   *What film role has been played by Sean Connery, George Lazenby, Roger Moore and Timothy Dalton?*

a11   In 1960, who became president of Ghana?

b11   *Of which country was Julius Nyerere the first president?*

a12   Which system of medicine uses plants and minerals in very small quantities, and treats 'like with like'?

b12   *What name is given to the medical condition in which people suffer from a dangerous loss of body heat?*

No. 54 Answers

a1   Russ Abbot
b1   *Fawlty Towers*
a2   Turin
b2   *Pope-mobile*
a3   Cricket
b3   *Ice-skating*
a4   Singer, opera singer
b4   *Film direction*
a5   Kuwait
b5   *General (Norman) Schwarzkopf*
a6   Electric tricycle (very small)
b6   *Glass-making*
a7   Dublin
b7   *Italy*
a8   High-speed trains (Trains Grande Vitesse)
b8   *Great Western (GWR)*
a9   A (North Sea) oil platform (used as a 'hotel' for oil workers)
b9   *France's (Brittany)*
a10   James Dean
b10   *James Bond (007)*
a11   (Kwame) Nkrumah
b11   *Tanganyika and/or Tanzania (he was president of both)*
a12   Homoeopathic medicine
b12   *Hypothermia*

Tie-breaker

Q 'Highway 61 Revisited' and 'Blood on the Tracks' were both
albums released by which popular singer?
A Bob Dylan

No. 55

a1   What was the Holocaust?

b1   On which Japanese city was the second atomic bomb dropped?

a2   Ray Alan is a ventriloquist. What's the name of his dummy?

b2   Which ventriloquist do you associate with the dummy Archie Andrews?

a3   Who became Duke of Windsor in 1936?

b3   Who was the present Queen's father?

a4   In which London embassy was there a six-day siege in 1980?

b4   In which building did Prince Charles marry Lady Diana Spencer?

a5   Before invading the Falklands, which other British island was invaded by the Argentines in 1982?

b5   In 1963, a new island was volcanically created off Iceland. What is it called?

a6   Before marriage what was tennis star Evonne Cawley's surname?

b6   Boxers Alan Minter and Marvin Hagler fought at which weight?

a7   Until recent years, which metal was mined extensively in the county of Cornwall?

b7   Which country produces three quarters of the world's gold?

a8   In 1979, the Queen's art adviser was named as a Russian spy. What was his name?

b8   A Turkish gunman shot a religious leader in May 1981. Who was the victim?

a9   Who was the American president during the First World War?

b9   Which American president represented his country at the Yalta conference (at the end of the Second World War)?

a10   A father and daughter appeared together in the film On Golden Pond. What was their surname?

b10   The uncovering of which political scandal is described in the film, All the President's Men?

a11   In 1952, which was the first jet airliner to enter passenger service?

b11   Exactly what type of fuel do jet aircraft engines use?

a12   Shahpur Bakhtiar was appointed prime minister of Iran under which regime?

b12   In which country did the Khmer Rouge exercise power?

No. 55 Answers

a1   The systematic destruction of Jewish people by the Nazis in the Second World War
b1   *Nagasaki*
a2   Lord Charles
b2   *Peter Brough*
a3   Edward VIII
b3   *George VI*
a4   Iranian
b4   *St Paul's Cathedral*
a5   South Georgia
b5   *Surtsey*
a6   Goolagong
b6   *Middleweight*
a7   Tin (copper was also mined, but on a much smaller scale)
b7   *South Africa*
a8   Sir Anthony Blunt
b8   *Pope John Paul II*
a9   Woodrow Wilson
b9   *(Franklin D.) Roosevelt*
a10   Fonda (Henry and Jane)
b10   *Watergate*
a11   The Comet (the de Haviland Comet)
b11   *Kerosene (a type of paraffin)*
a12   Under the last Shah of Persia/Iran
b12   *Cambodia (Kampuchea)*

Tie-breaker

Q From which musical do the songs 'What's the Use of Wond'rin'?' and 'June Is Bustin' Out All Over' come?
A Carousel

No. 56

a1   Which comedian had the catch phrase, 'Shut that door'?

b1   *Whose catch phrase is or was 'I'm free'?*

a2   Which poisonous metal is used in sheets to make waterproof roofs?

b2   *Which rare, radioactive metal is used to provide energy in nuclear reactors?*

a3   For what was Sir Cecil Beaton principally famous?

b3   *For what was Sir Thomas Beecham famous?*

a4   According to the film title, which was the 'Longest Day'?

b4   *About which battle is the film, A Bridge Too Far?*

a5   In judo, what colour belt denotes a beginner?

b5   *Which Eastern martial art is called by a word which means, literally, 'open hands'?*

a6   Which television series was named after American mobile army surgical hospitals?

b6   *On television, who played Sergeant Bilko?*

a7   Which saint did Mrs Thatcher quote on first entering Downing Street as Prime Minister?

b7   *Which Tory MP was killed by a car bomb when driving out of the House of Commons car park?*

a8   Which city in the world has the largest population?

b8   *Which is the largest lake in the world?*

a9   Of which Caribbean island was Marcus Garvey a political leader?

b9   *Who became prime minister of Zimbabwe in 1980?*

a10   What sort of picture is a hologram?

b10   *What are polygraphs sometimes used to reveal?*

a11   Two Jumbo jets collided on the ground in 1977 to create the worst tragedy in aviation history. On which holiday islands did it occur?

b11   *Also in 1977, Archbishop Luwum was killed in mysterious circumstances. In which country?*

a12   Who wrote the novel Lolita?

b12   *Who wrote the novels Tropic of Cancer and Tropic of Capricorn?*

No. 56 Answers

a1 Larry Grayson
b1 John Inman
a2 Lead
b2 Uranium
a3 Photography (of glamorous people), also stage and film design
b3 Conducting; music
a4 D-Day (June 6th, 1944)
b4 Arnhem
a5 White
b5 Karate
a6 M*A*S*H
b6 Phil Silvers
a7 St Francis ('Where there is discord may we bring harmony . . .')
b7 Airey Neave
a8 Mexico City
b8 Caspian Sea
a9 Jamaica
b9 Robert Mugabe (say: mu-gah-bay)
a10 A three-dimensional one
b10 Whether someone is lying
a11 Canary Islands
b11 Uganda
a12 Vladimir Nabokov
b12 Henry Miller

Tie-breaker

Q Which is the largest library in the world?
A *The Library of Congress, Washington DC*

No. 57

a1   Tortillas are part of the staple diet of which country?

b1   *What would be sold in a pâtisserie department?*

a2   Of which family of animals are Koalas members?

b2   *What were Jespa, Gopa and Little Elsa?*

a3   Name the two men who star in the film *Butch Cassidy and the Sundance Kid*.

b3   *His real name was William Pratt, but by what name did he become famous for playing the Frankenstein monster?*

a4   In 1923, who married Lady Elizabeth Bowes-Lyon?

b4   *Which Royal Prince was born in April 1964?*

a5   Johan Cruyff (say: yo-han kroyff) played soccer for which country?

b5   *Ajax is the name of a famous football team – in which Dutch city?*

a6   Between which countries is the principality of Liechtenstein?

b6   *On the borders of which two countries are the Golan Heights?*

a7   Which actor played the television detective, Ironside?

b7   *Which actor played the television detective, Columbo?*

a8   Which republic's parliament consists of the Senate and the Dail (say: doyle)?

b8   *To what did the Ecology Party change its name in the mid-eighties?*

a9   Were the first old age pensions in Britain paid out in 1909, 1919, or 1945?

b9   *In which year did adoption become legal in Britain: 1827, 1926, or 1947?*

a10   Where does the International Court of Justice sit?

b10   *Where does the European Court of Justice sit?*

a11   Why did the artist Tom Keating become well known?

b11   *Who gave orders for Graham Sutherland's controversial portrait of Winston Churchill to be destroyed?*

a12   The black African leader Albert John Luthuli is famous for his autobiography. What is it called?

b12   *Which French existentialist thinker and author wrote a work called Being and Nothingness?*

No. 57 Answers

a1   Mexico
b1   *Cakes (accept: pastries)*
a2   Marsupials (accept: kangaroos) (they are not bears)
b2   *Lion cubs (in Born Free by Joy Adamson)*
a3   Paul Newman and Robert Redford
b3   *Boris Karloff*
a4   The Duke of York, later King George VI
b4   *Edward*
a5   Holland (the Netherlands)
b5   *Amsterdam*
a6   Switzerland and Austria
b6   *Israel and Syria*
a7   Raymond Burr
b7   *Peter Falk*
a8   Irish
b8   *The Green Party*
a9   1909
b9   *1926*
a10   The Hague (in the Netherlands)
b10   *Luxembourg*
a11   Forging or copying old masters
b11   *Lady Churchill*
a12   Let My People Go
b12   *Jean-Paul Sartre*

Tie-breaker

Q Which English artist is known for both a painting and a film
called *A Bigger Splash*?
A *David Hockney*

No. 58

a1   In the English legal system, what is another name for a JP (or justice of the peace)?

b1   *In law, what is a 'hung jury'?*

a2   In which sport did Zola Budd compete?

b2   *In which sport did Niki Lauda compete?*

a3   Which metal is a good conductor of heat and electricity and is used to make pipes for plumbing and wiring?

b3   *Which light, strong metal is used to make drink cans, kitchen foil and aircraft?*

a4   Which political party was led by President Jimmy Carter?

b4   *Of which American political party was Ronald Reagan a leading figure?*

a5   For which role was Jack Warner best known?

b5   *Which television comedian often wore a fez?*

a6   If you flew in a straight line from Tunisia to Egypt, which one intervening country would you cross?

b6   *Which country lies immediately south of Belgium?*

a7   Where did a nuclear disaster occur in April, 1986?

b7   *What tragedy occurred at Skopje in 1963?*

a8   In which film did Robert Shaw play Captain Quint?

b8   *Who was the star of the films* The Gold Rush, Modern Times *and* The Great Dictator?

a9   From 1978, who was the most important leader of China?

b9   *Who was the father of Indian Prime Minister Indira Gandhi?*

a10   In which year was Korea divided into North and South Korea: 1905, 1945, or 1951?

b10   *Until 1949, which European country governed Indonesia?*

a11   Who was the first musician to be made a life peer?

b11   *By what name was the jazz pianist William Basie more usually known?*

a12   In which Middle Eastern country did the Ba'ath Socialist party hold power?

b12   *In which Central American republic were Sandinista rebels active in the late seventies and eighties?*

No. 58 Answers

a1	Magistrate
b1	*One where the members cannot agree on a verdict*
a2	Athletics (track events)
b2	*Motor-racing*
a3	Copper
b3	*Aluminium*
a4	Democratic
b4	*Republican*
a5	Dixon of Dock Green (P. C. George Dixon)
b5	*Tommy Cooper*
a6	Libya
b6	*France*
a7	Chernobyl (in the Ukraine)
b7	*Earthquake*
a8	Jaws
b8	*Charlie Chaplin*
a9	Deng Xiaoping (also spelled in other ways: e.g. Teng Hsiao-p'ing)
b9	*Jawaharlal Nehru (India's first prime minister)*
a10	1945
b10	*The Netherlands (Holland)*
a11	Benjamin Britten
b11	*'Count' Basie*
a12	Iraq and/or Syria
b12	*Nicaragua*

Tie-breaker

Q Who first said, 'Because it was there' (when asked why he climbed a certain mountain)?

A *Sir Edmund Hillary, on having climbed Everest*

No. 59

a1 Which part of a hi-fi or home stereo system relies on lasers?

b1 *Which part of a car's engine sends sparks to the plugs?*

a2 In *Goldfinger*, what was the name of the villain with the dangerous hat?

b2 *Which was the Beatles' first film?*

a3 In Rugby Union internationals, what colour shirts does the England team wear?

b3 *What do we call the sport in which one person travels through the air in a harness under a triangular sail?*

a4 'Cosa nostra' is another name for which secret society?

b4 *Besides Italy, in which country has the Mafia been widely active this century?*

a5 Until 1941 which European power controlled the Lebanon?

b5 *Until independence in 1961, under which country's protection was Kuwait?*

a6 In which year did Britain have three kings?

b6 *Which king was married to Princess Mary of Teck?*

a7 Which radio programme was invented by Roy Plomley and was introduced by him until his death 44 years later?

b7 *Who was the star of the radio show, ITMA?*

a8 'Colonel' Tom Parker managed which pop star, who died in 1977?

b8 *Mark David Chapman shot dead which pop star in 1980?*

a9 Of which country was Bangladesh formerly a part?

b9 *Kowloon is part of which country or colony?*

a10 'The Earl of Avon' was the title taken by which former prime minister?

b10 *Former leader of the Liberal party Jeremy Thorpe was in court in 1979. On what charge?*

a11 In 1969, which colonel seized power in Libya?

b11 *Of which revolutionary group was Pol Pot the leader?*

a12 In which country did Steve Biko die in police custody in 1977?

b12 *Following an assassination, of which country did Mubarak become president?*

No. 59 Answers

a1   A CD player
b1   Distributor
a2   Oddjob
b2   A Hard Day's Night
a3   White
b3   Hang-gliding
a4   The Mafia
b4   United States of America
a5   France
b5   Britain
a6   1936 (George V, Edward VIII, George VI)
b6   George V
a7   *Desert Island Discs*
b7   Tommy Handley
a8   Elvis Presley
b8   John Lennon
a9   Pakistan (East Pakistan) and, before that, India
b9   Hong Kong
a10   Sir Anthony Eden
b10   (Plotting a) murder
a11   Colonel Qaddafi
b11   Khmer Rouge
a12   South Africa
b12   Egypt

Tie-breaker

Q Jimmy Porter, Alison and Cliff are characters in which British play, first performed in 1956?

A Look Back in Anger

No. 60

a1 In which Scottish region is Glasgow?

b1 *In which Scottish region is Ben Nevis?*

a2 In which sport is there a silly mid-off?

b2 *And in which sport is there a yellow jersey?*

a3 By what name is London's Central Criminal Court generally known?

b3 *If criminal law deals with people accused of committing a crime, what deals with cases where no crime has been committed?*

a4 Which war was ended by the American president Nixon giving the order to withdraw?

b4 *Who was shot by John Hinckley III in Washington in 1981?*

a5 Who played Hutch in *Starsky and Hutch*?

b5 *In the television series* The New Avengers, *who played Steed?*

a6 In 1933, who became Chancellor of Germany?

b6 *Josef Mengele was known as the 'Angel of Death'. With which concentration camp was this Nazi associated?*

a7 Which bank has regularly advertised itself with a black horse?

b7 *And which bank advertised itself as 'the listening bank'?*

a8 Which dull-coloured metal is used to coat or 'galvanize' steel to prevent rust?

b8 *Which strong, hard metal is used to make light-bulb filaments?*

a9 Athletes Harold Abrahams and Eric Liddell were commemorated in which film?

b9 *Which film star visited Hanoi to show her disapproval of America's role in the Vietnam War?*

a10 Which country or countries launched the Ariane rockets?

b10 *Which nation put Skylab into orbit?*

a11 Bishop Abel Muzorewa was a leader in which country?

b11 *Betty Williams and Mairead (say: mo'raid) Corrigan led a movement for peace – in which province?*

a12 Which famous poet of the First World War was shot dead just one week before the end of the war?

b12 *Which English poet was once married to the American poet, Sylvia Plath?*

No. 60 Answers

a1	Strathclyde
b1	*Highland*
a2	Cricket
b2	*Cycling*
a3	The Old Bailey
b3	*Civil law*
a4	Vietnam War
b4	*Ronald Reagan (also a policeman, a secret service agent and the president's press secretary)*
a5	David Soul
b5	*Patrick MacNee*
a6	Adolf Hitler
b6	*Auschwitz*
a7	Lloyds Bank
b7	*Midland Bank*
a8	Zinc
b8	*Tungsten*
a9	*Chariots of Fire*
b9	*Jane Fonda*
a10	European countries, jointly
b10	*United States of America*
a11	Rhodesia (later Zimbabwe)
b11	*Northern Ireland*
a12	Wilfred Owen
b12	*Ted Hughes*

Tie-breaker

Q Name four European countries in which communist governments lost power in 1989.

A *Poland, Hungary, East Germany, Czechoslovakia*

No. 61: Top of the Pops

Which pop star or group made it into the charts with these singles or albums?

a1 'Release Me', 'There Goes My Everything' and 'The Last Waltz'

b1 'Green, Green Grass of Home', 'I'll Never Fall in Love Again' and 'Delilah'

a2 'Super Trouper', 'Dancing Queen' and 'Waterloo'

b2 'Making Your Mind Up', 'Land of Make Believe' and 'My Camera Never Lies'

a3 'Every Picture Tells a Story', 'You Wear It Well' and 'Sailing'

b3 'Rocket Man', 'Crocodile Rock' and 'Daniel'

a4 'Only the Lonely', 'It's Over' and 'Oh, Pretty Woman'

b4 'Stand By Your Man', 'The Ways to Love a Man' and 'He Loves Me All the Way'

a5 'Tubular Bells'

b5 'Whiter Shade of Pale'

a6 'Alone Again (Naturally)', 'Clair' and 'Get Down'

b6 'Dark Side of the Moon' and 'Another Brick in the Wall'

a7 'Long Tall Sally', 'The Girl Can't Help It' and 'Lucille'

b7 'Cry', 'The Little White Cloud that Cried' and 'Here Am I – Brokenhearted'

a8 'Garden of Eden', 'Green Door' and 'Tower of Strength'

b8 'Never Do a Tango with an Eskimo', 'Dreamboat' and 'Stairway of Love'

a9 'Give Me Love', 'Try Some, Buy Some' and 'All Those Years Ago'

b9 'Another Day', 'Teddy Boy' and 'Wonderful Christmastime'

a10 'I Heard It through the Grapevine', and 'Neither One of Us'

b10 'I've Gotta Get a Message to You' and 'Don't Forget to Remember'

a11 'Happy to Be on an Island in the Sun' and 'When Forever Has Gone'

b11 'White Cliffs of Dover' and 'We'll Meet Again'

a12 'Fort Worth', 'Early Morning Rain' and 'Blue Train'

b12 'Wake Up Little Susie', 'All I Have to Do is Dream' and 'Bye Bye Love'

No. 61 Answers

a1   Engelbert Humperdinck
b1   *Tom Jones*
a2   Abba
b2   *Bucks Fizz*
a3   Rod Stewart
b3   *Elton John*
a4   Roy Orbison
b4   *Tammy Wynette*
a5   Mike Oldfield
b5   *Procol Harum*
a6   Gilbert O'Sullivan
b6   *Pink Floyd*
a7   Little Richard
b7   *Johnny Ray*
a8   Frankie Vaughan
b8   *Alma Cogan*
a9   George Harrison
b9   *Paul McCartney*
a10   Gladys Knight and the Pips
b10   *The Bee Gees*
a11   Demis Roussos
b11   *Vera Lynn*
a12   George Hamilton IV
b12   *The Everly Brothers*

Tie-breaker

Q Born Tommy Hicks, he had a hit with 'Little White Bull' and starred in *Half A Sixpence*. Who was he?

A *Tommy Steele*

No. 62

a1 Which comedian became famous for supposedly having short, fat, hairy legs?

b1 With which comedian do you associate Knotty Ash?

a2 What is kelp?

b2 What are krill?

a3 What is the square root of 361?

b3 What is a third minus a quarter?

a4 In which sport was Jan Kodes (say: yan ko-desh) a leading player?

b4 And in which sport did John Conteh compete?

a5 In the United States Congress, which is the name of the 'Upper House'?

b5 And what is the name of the 'Lower House'?

a6 On a London Underground diagram map, what colour is the Bakerloo line?

b6 On a London Underground map, what colour is the District line?

a7 Who starred in the film *The Deer Hunter*?

b7 In the 1978 re-make of Superman, who played Superman?

a8 The common unit for measuring electrical power equals 1,000 watts. What is it called?

b8 What name is commonly given to solid carbon dioxide used in refrigeration?

a9 In which year was the Battle of the Somme?

b9 In which year was the first Battle of Ypres (say: ee-preh)?

a10 Who wrote the novel *Catch-22*?

b10 Who wrote the 'Pop Larkin' novels?

a11 What do Europeans call the area Asians know as West Asia?

b11 Which island's name is derived from 'mel', the Latin word for honey?

a12 Sunnis (say: sunnies), Shiites (say: shee-ites) and Druze militia have all been fighting in recent years in which eastern Mediterranean city?

b12 Which terrorist group kidnapped and killed the former Italian prime minister, Aldo Moro?

No. 62 Answers

a1	Ernie Wise
b1	*Ken Dodd*
a2	(Dried and burned) seaweed
b2	*Small shrimp-like animals (they are an important item in the diet of other marine animals such as whales)*
a3	19
b3	*A twelfth*
a4	Tennis
b4	*Boxing*
a5	The Senate
b5	*The House of Representatives*
a6	Brown
b6	*Green*
a7	Robert de Niro
b7	*Christopher Reeve*
a8	Kilowatt
b8	*Dry ice*
a9	1916
b9	*1914*
a10	Joseph Heller
b10	*H. E. Bates*
a11	The Middle East
b11	*Malta*
a12	Beirut
b12	*Red Brigade*

Tie-breaker

Q The American city of New York consists of five boroughs. How many can you name?

A *Manhattan, the Bronx, Queens, Brooklyn and Staten Island*

No. 63

a1 Which famous actress stood out in the films, *One Million Years BC* and *The Biggest Bundle of Them All*?

b1 *Who was the young male star of the film* Saturday Night Fever?

a2 What is a dissident?

b2 *What is 'disinformation'?*

a3 Which member of the Cabinet presents the annual budget speech?

b3 *What title is given to the chairman or -woman of the House of Commons?*

a4 Why did the American millionaire Howard Hughes become notorious?

b4 *And also in the States, as what did Busby Berkeley achieve fame?*

a5 In which year was the Battle of Britain?

b5 *In which year did the Japanese bomb Pearl Harbor?*

a6 Who played Fletcher in *Porridge* and *Going Straight*?

b6 *In which series did Warren Mitchell first play Alf?*

a7 Between which cities did the Flying Scotsman train travel?

b7 *And between which cities did the Royal Scot travel?*

a8 Who became king of Spain in 1975?

b8 *In which year did Queen Elizabeth II celebrate her silver jubilee?*

a9 Which northern painter became famous for his 'matchstalk men'?

b9 *Which cartoonist created 'Li'l Abner'?*

a10 Which leader died in 1978 after only 33 days in office?

b10 *What nationality are the Papal Guards at the Vatican?*

a11 In 1976, three days of unrest and rioting resulted in 100 dead in which South African township?

b11 *UNITA was a nationalist movement in which African country?*

a12 Which influential book (the title of which became a slogan) was written by E. F. Schumacher?

b12 *Which doctor wrote* The Common Sense Book of Baby and Child Care?

No. 63 Answers

a1	Raquel Welch
b1	*John Travolta*
a2	Someone who disagrees with the policies of his or her own country
b2	*False information spread with the purpose of confusing others*
a3	Chancellor of the Exchequer
b3	*The Speaker, Mr (or Madame) Speaker*
a4	He was a recluse; always seeking total privacy
b4	*Choreographer; dance arranger*
a5	1940
b5	*1941*
a6	Ronnie Barker
b6	Till Death Us Do Part
a7	London and Edinburgh
b7	*London and Glasgow*
a8	King Juan Carlos
b8	*1977*
a9	L. S. Lowry
b9	*Al Capp*
a10	Pope John-Paul I
b10	*Swiss*
a11	Soweto
b11	*Angola*
a12	*Small is Beautiful*
b12	*(Benjamin) Spock*

Tie-breaker

Q Four English counties disappeared from the map in the 1974 local government reorganization. Can you name them?

A *Cumberland, Huntingdonshire, Rutland and Westmorland*

No. 64

a1 In which city is the Shankill Road?

b1 *In which English city did the IRA trigger the 1974 'Pub Bombings'?*

a2 For playing which musical instrument did Larry Adler become famous?

b2 *Musician Jacqueline du Pré had to give up her career owing to illness. What was her instrument?*

a3 What kind of missile is a SAM?

b3 *For what do the military initials SAS stand?*

a4 What substance has categories called Type A, Type AB and Type O?

b4 *Which organ of your body filters your blood fifty times a day?*

a5 Which motorway links South Wales and London?

b5 *Which motorway crosses the Pennines from Manchester to Leeds?*

a6 In the Korean War, which international force supported South Korea?

b6 *And, in the same war, which super-power supported North Korea?*

a7 By what nickname was the murderer Peter Sutcliffe generally known?

b7 *Which 'lucky' Earl was wanted for the murder of his child's nanny?*

a8 Until defecting to the West, which was tennis star Martina Navratilova's home country?

b8 *For which country did Rodney Marsh keep wicket?*

a9 Where in Britain is the National Railway Museum?

b9 *In which city is the Ashmolean Museum?*

a10 Which famous fictional barrister has been played on television by Leo McKern?

b10 *On television, who played 'Wonder Woman'?*

a11 Who wrote the novel *Saturday Night and Sunday Morning*?

b11 *Who wrote the novel Billy Liar?*

a12 Giscard d'Estaing (say: ji-skar dess-tan) became president of France in 1974. What was his first name?

b12 *Which was the last year in which Russia was ruled by a Tsar?*

No. 64 Answers

a1 Belfast
b1 *Birmingham*
a2 Harmonica (mouth organ)
b2 *Cello*
a3 Surface-to-air missile
b3 *Special Air Service*
a4 Blood
a4 Your kidneys
a5 M4
b5 *M62*
a6 United Nations
b6 *China*
a7 The Yorkshire Ripper
b7 *Earl of Lucan (Lord Lucan)*
a8 Czechoslovakia
b8 *Australia*
a9 York
b9 *Oxford*
a10 Rumpole (created by John Mortimer)
b10 *Lynda Carter*
a11 Alan Sillitoe
b11 *Keith Waterhouse*
a12 Valéry
b12 *1917*

Tie-breaker

Q In which Far Eastern country do the people live in traditional villages, pay no taxes, receive free services and mainly drive air-conditioned cars?

A *Brunei (offshore oil wells make it a very rich country)*

No. 65

a1   Which country is the home of the Datsun car company?

b1   *And which is the home country of the Fiat car company?*

a2   On television, which famous puppet was worked by Harry Corbett?

b2   *In which television programme was there a snail called Brian?*

a3   What do members of the House of Commons mean by 'another place'?

b3   *Who may not visit the House of Commons when it is in session?*

a4   By what name is the Windscale Nuclear plant now known?

b4   *Why did Flixborough on Humberside hit the headlines in 1974?*

a5   Which singer thanked heaven for little girls and had trouble remembering it well?

b5   *Which song (it became famous in the Second World War) was first sung by the German Lale Anderson?*

a6   What was the name of the Northern Ireland parliament building?

b6   *In which Northern Ireland city did the events known as 'Bloody Sunday' occur (in 1972)?*

a7   Why did Balcombe Street, London hit the headlines in December 1975?

b7   *A tragic London Underground train crash in 1975 killed 35. At which station?*

a8   As what did Ezra Pound achieve fame?

b8   *And as what did Sir John Barbirolli achieve fame?*

a9   From which country did the tennis star Ilie Nastase come?

b9   *Which was the home country of chess champion Bobby Fischer?*

a10   In which year was the African battle of El Alamein?

b10   *In which two years has Germany invaded Belgium?*

a11   In which year did the Vietnam War end?

b11   *In which year was the Russian October Revolution?*

a12   Which Irish poet wrote the poem 'The Lake Isle of Innisfree'?

b12   *Which poet wrote 'The Love Song of J. Alfred Prufrock'?*

No. 65 Answers

a1	Japan
b1	*Italy*
a2	Sooty (or Sweep)
b2	The Magic Roundabout
a3	House of Lords
b3	*The monarch*
a4	Sellafield
b4	*Chemical plant exploded, factory explosion (killing 28)*
a5	Maurice Chevalier
b5	*'Lili Marlene'*
a6	Stormont
b6	*Londonderry/Derry*
a7	Because of a siege (the IRA held two people hostage)
b7	*Moorgate*
a8	Poet
b8	*Conductor (accept: cellist)*
a9	Romania
b9	*United States of America*
a10	1942
b10	*1914, 1940*
a11	1975 (America withdrew in 1973)
b11	*1917*
a12	W. B. Yeats (say: yates)
b12	*T. S. Eliot*

Tie-breaker

Q Who is this famous actor?: 'I was born in Miami, USA. I took acting lessons at the American Negro Theatre in New York. I was in *The Blackboard Jungle*, but in my best-known film I was a New York cop, solving a murder in the heat of a small town in the south of the USA.'

A *Sidney Poitier (best-known film: In the Heat of the Night)*

No. 66

a1   What kind of food is pemmican?

b1   *And what kind of fruit or vegetable are capsicums?*

a2   Who played the Mafia chief in the film *The Godfather?*

b2   *Which comic actor starred in radio's* The Goon Show *and played Inspector Clouseau on screen?*

a3   Which illegal activity has been responsible for reducing the number of elephants in Africa?

b3   *Which virus was deliberately spread to control the number of rabbits?*

a4   What instrument was played by the musician Pablo Casals?

b4   *Which popular singer died on a Spanish golf course in 1977?*

a5   In the House of Lords, who are the Lords Spiritual?

b5   *Who presides over or 'chairs' the debates in the House of Lords?*

a6   Who was assassinated by a Bosnian student in 1914?

b6   *What world organization was founded at the end of the First World War?*

a7   On BBC radio, who sends a weekly *Letter from America?*

b7   *Who was the quizmaster of the television series* University Challenge?

a8   Name one of the countries which boycotted the 1980 Moscow Olympics.

b8   *Which country's headquarters were stormed in the Olympic Village at Munich in 1972?*

a9   After which American president were teddy bears named?

b9   *Dwight D. Eisenhower – what did the 'D' stand for?*

a10   On a London Underground diagram map, what colour is the Northern line?

b10   *On a London Underground diagram map, what colour is the Central line?*

a11   Who wrote the novel *The French Lieutenant's Woman?*

b11   *Who wrote the novel* A Clockwork Orange?

a12   Before being sent to prison for corruption, what was John Poulson's profession?

b12   *What took a man called Evel Knievel into the headlines?*

No. 66 Answers

a1	Concentrated food (usually dried beef)
b1	*Peppers*
a2	Marlon Brando
b2	*Peter Sellers*
a3	Poaching for ivory
b3	*Myxomatosis*
a4	Cello
b4	*Bing Crosby*
a5	The Bishops (and archbishops)
b5	*The Lord Chancellor*
a6	Archduke Ferdinand of Austria
b6	*League of Nations*
a7	Alistair Cooke
b7	*Bamber Gascoigne*
a8	United States of America, West Germany, Kenya
b8	*Israel's*
a9	Theodore ('Teddy') Roosevelt
b9	*David*
a10	Black
b10	*Red*
a11	John Fowles
b11	*Anthony Burgess*
a12	Architect
b12	*His stunts; driving a car over double-decker buses*

Tie-breaker

Q On whose BBC radio show did we used to hear the question, 'What's the recipe today?'?

A *Jimmy Young*

No. 67

a1   On which river does the town of Stockton stand?

b1   *And on which river does the city of Gloucester stand?*

a2   What is measured in ergs?

b2   *And what is meant by the Latin word 'ergo'?*

a3   Franz Beckenbauer captained which team in the 1974 soccer World Cup?

b3   *Which speedway team is nicknamed 'The Witches'?*

a4   A movement called 'Enosis' wanted the unification of which island with Greece?

b4   *Which war was ended by the Treaty of Panmunjon?*

a5   In the House of Commons, what is a Bill?

b5   *How many 'readings' are there to a Parliamentary Bill?*

a6   Which infamous leader committed suicide on April 30, 1945?

b6   *Manila, Rangoon and Singapore were all captured by which country in 1942?*

a7   On radio, where would you once have met Mr Growser, Dennis and Larry the Lamb?

b7   *On which sport was John Arlott a famous commentator?*

a8   Which is longer, the Suez or the Panama Canal?

b8   *Which sea lies between Iran and Saudi Arabia?*

a9   Which entrepreneur started cheap transatlantic flights on his so-called 'Skytrain'?

b9   *What kind of clothing was associated with the name 'Gannex'?*

a10   Who wrote the novels *The Odessa File* and *The Day of the Jackal*?

b10   *Who wrote the novels* Whisky Galore *and* Sinister Street*?*

a11   Which political system believes in a classless society with state-run means of production and trade?

b11   *What name is given to the socialist community farms found in Israel?*

a12   In which year did Britain have a three-day week (to conserve energy supplies)?

b12   *Which country celebrated its 'Bicentennial' in 1976?*

No. 67 Answers

a1	River Tees
b1	*Severn*
a2	Energy (accept: work)
b2	*Therefore*
a3	West Germany
b3	*Ipswich Town*
a4	Cyprus
b4	*Korean War*
a5	A proposed law, a proposed Act of Parliament
b5	*Three*
a6	Adolf Hitler
b6	*Japan*
a7	In 'Toytown'
b7	*Cricket*
a8	The Suez (it's twice as long)
b8	*Persian Gulf*
a9	Freddie Laker
b9	*Raincoats*
a10	Frederick Forsyth
b10	*Compton Mackenzie*
a11	Communism
b11	*Kibbutzim (kibbutzim is the plural of kibbutz)*
a12	1973–4
b12	*United States of America (1776–1976)*

Tie-breaker

Q Which British cruiser was reduced to a blazing hulk by Argentine Exocet missiles during the Falklands War?

A *HMS Sheffield*

No. 68

a1   In which section of the orchestra will you find a flautist?

b1   *Of which section of the orchestra is the tuba a part?*

a2   Who directed the films *ET* and *Close Encounters of the Third Kind*?

b2   *Who directed the cinema epic, The Ten Commandments?*

a3   In the Second World War, in which year did the Germans occupy Paris?

b3   *In which year during the Second World War was Germany defeated at the Battle of Stalingrad?*

a4   What medical term is given to the state of being very overweight?

b4   *Whereabouts in your body are your largest and strongest muscles?*

a5   What is the Army equivalent of the Naval rank of lieutenant?

b5   *What is the Naval equivalent of the Army rank of general?*

a6   The surname 'Singh' indicates membership of which religion?

b6   *To which city do Muslims hope to make a once-in-a-lifetime pilgrimage?*

a7   In which television series did we see Cowley, Doyle and Bodie?

b7   *Name the actor who played Kojak in the television series.*

a8   From which country did Israel capture the Gaza Strip in 1967?

b8   *And also in 1967, from which country did Israel take over the Golan Heights?*

a9   Of which country is the Indus the principal river?

b9   *In which country is the mouth (or delta) of the River Ganges?*

a10   Which former Labour MP faked his own disappearance on a Miami beach?

b10   *What post was held in the Soviet government for 28 years by Andrei Gromyko?*

a11   Of which country was William Taft president early this century?

b11   *Who was the first United States president to resign office?*

a12   Which metal is needed to provide the fuel for most nuclear power stations?

b12   *Which country produces the highest percentage of its electricity by nuclear power: France, Britain or the United States?*

No. 68 Answers

a1	Wind
b1	*Brass*
a2	Steven Spielberg
b2	*Cecil B. DeMille*
a3	1940
b3	*1942*
a4	Obese, obesity
b4	*The buttocks*
a5	Captain
b5	*Admiral*
a6	Sikhism
b6	*Mecca*
a7	The Professionals
b7	*Telly Savalas*
a8	Egypt
b8	*Syria*
a9	Pakistan
b9	*Bangladesh*
a10	John Stonehouse
b10	*Foreign Minister*
a11	United States of America (1909–1913)
b11	*President Nixon (1974)*
a12	Uranium
b12	*France*

Tie-breaker

Q What are the five major oceans of the world?
A *Arctic, Southern (accept: Antarctic), Atlantic, Pacific and Indian*

No. 69

a1   In which section of the orchestra does the viola play?

b1   *Of which section of the orchestra does the clarinet form a part?*

a2   Which religion celebrates its New Year during September or early October?

b2   *Which New Year festival occurs between 21st January and 19th February?*

a3   Into which movement were young people enrolled in Nazi Germany?

b3   *Who were on trial at the Nuremberg Trials in 1946?*

a4   For what do the initials PWR stand?

b4   *In Northern Ireland, for what do the initials UDA stand?*

a5   In the world of motoring, for what do the initials GT stand?

b5   *In the world of motor-cycle racing, for what do the initials TT stand?*

a6   Who played Rhett Butler in the classic film *Gone with the Wind*?

b6   *Who composed the music for the 1945 show* Carousel?

a7   Which country is ruled by King Hassan II?

b7   *On which island was Rauf Denktash a Turkish leader?*

a8   Who was the president of the USA just before Jimmy Carter?

b8   *On which American paper did the reporters work who uncovered the Watergate affair?*

a9   On television, who played Rigsby and Norman Tripper?

b9   *In which television serial is there a pub called the Woolpack?*

a10   This century, who composed an operatic version of *Midsummer Night's Dream*?

b10   *And who composed the opera* Madame Butterfly?

a11   In which continent is Papua New Guinea?

b11   *In which continent is Greenland?*

a12   Who wrote the novel *Cry, the Beloved Country*?

b12   *Who wrote the novels* Anglo-Saxon Attitudes, The Old Men at the Zoo *and* Hemlock and After?

No. 69 Answers

a1	String
b1	*Wind*
a2	Jewish
b2	*Chinese*
a3	The Hitler Youth Movement
b3	*Nazi leaders*
a4	Pressurized Water Reactor (type of nuclear reactor)
b4	*Ulster Defence Association*
a5	Grand Touring
b5	*Tourist Trophy*
a6	Clark Gable
b6	*Richard Rodgers*
a7	Morocco
b7	*Cyprus*
a8	Gerald Ford
b8	*The Washington Post*
a9	Leonard Rossiter
b9	*Emmerdale Farm*
a10	Benjamin Britten
b10	*Puccini*
a11	Oceania (accept: Australasia)
b11	*The Arctic*
a12	Alan Paton
b12	*Angus Wilson*

Tie-breaker

Q What are the 'Six Counties' of Northern Ireland?
A *Antrim, Armagh, Down, Fermanagh, Londonderry/Derry, Tyrone*

No. 70

a1 In Northern Ireland, who are or were known as the 'Provos'?

b1 *In Northern Ireland, what change happened to some courtroom procedures in 1973?*

a2 Which is the largest country by area in North America?

b2 *Which is the highest mountain in North America?*

a3 On television, who plays Arthur Daley?

b3 *In Coronation Street, which character was played by Doris Speed?*

a4 When is United Nations Day each year?

b4 *What famous event takes place at Munich in October?*

a5 Nine hands were shown clasped on a special British coin. Which coin?

b5 *What colour is the standard European Community passport?*

a6 What is the Naval equivalent of the Army rank of colonel?

b6 *What is the Army equivalent of the Naval rank of Admiral of the Fleet?*

a7 In which year did the Titanic sink?

b7 *In which year did the violence of the present troubles in Northern Ireland begin?*

a8 In Britain, which tax replaced purchase tax in 1973?

b8 *Which East European pact was formed to oppose NATO?*

a9 In which country would you find the Inuit people?

b9 *In which country was a 'terra cotta' army of 6,000 life-size models of soldiers uncovered in 1975?*

a10 In music, how many beats are there in a minim?

b10 *In music, how many beats are there in a semi-breve?*

a11 Which planet has two tiny moons called Phobos and Deimos?

b11 *And which planet has twenty moons, the biggest of which is called Titan?*

a12 Who wrote the 12-volume sequence of novels titled *A Dance to the Music of Time*?

b12 *Who wrote the novels* To the Lighthouse *and* The Waves?

No. 70 Answers

a1   Members of the 'Provisional' IRA (Irish Republican Army)
b1   *Trial without jury was introduced*
a2   Canada
b2   *Mount McKinley (in Alaska; 6194m)*
a3   George Cole
b3   *Annie Walker*
a4   October 24th
b4   *Beer festival (Oktoberfest)*
a5   50p piece (to celebrate membership of the Common Market)
b5   *Red*
a6   Captain
b6   *Field Marshal*
a7   1912
b7   *1969*
a8   VAT (Value Added Tax)
b8   *Warsaw Pact*
a9   Greenland; Arctic North America (Canada, Alaska)
b9   *China*
a10   2
b10   *4*
a11   Mars
b11   *Saturn*
a12   Anthony Powell
b12   *Virginia Woolf*

Tie-breaker

Q Which three countries make up the continent of North America?

A *Canada, United States, Mexico*

No. 71: Modern Abbreviations

The following abbreviations have all come into use in recent years. What do they each stand for or mean?

a1	K
b1	*PC*
a2	PIN
b2	*VCR*
a3	BMX
b3	*DBS*
a4	DTP
b4	*FTSE or Footsie*
a5	AIDS
b5	*CFC*
a6	CD-ROM
b6	*DAT*
a7	BSE
b7	*ECG*
a8	NIMBY
b8	*PEP*
a9	EPOS
b9	*ATM*
a10	EMS
b10	*TESSA*
a11	WYSIWYG
b11	*ERM*
a12	ME
b12	*RSI*

No. 71 Answers

a1 1,000

b1 *Personal computer*

a2 Personal identification number (used with cash machines, etc.)

b2 *Video cassette recorder*

a3 Bicycle moto-cross; cycle racing on dirt tracks

b3 *Direct broadcasting by satellite*

a4 Desk-top publishing; using a computer to produce books, etc.

b4 *Financial Times Stock Exchange 100 share index (shares of the 100 largest companies in Britain)*

a5 Acquired immune deficiency syndrome

b5 *Chlorofluorocarbon (gas used in aerosols, refrigerators, etc.)*

a6 Compact disc with 'read-only' memory

b6 *Digital audio tape*

a7 Bovine spongiform encephalopathy, 'mad cow disease'

b7 *Electrocardiogram (recording of the impulses in the heart)*

a8 'Not in my backyard'; person objecting to building scheme, etc. in his or her locality

b8 *Personal Equity Plan*

a9 Electronic point of sale; shop till system that reads bar-codes

b9 *Automated teller machine; 'hole-in-the-wall' cash machine*

a10 European Monetary System

b10 *Tax-exempt special savings account (UK tax-free savings account)*

a11 'What you see is what you get'; when computer screens show exactly what will be printed (and nothing else)

b11 *Exchange-rate mechanism (within the European Community)*

a12 A long-lasting illness; myalgic encephalomyelitis; sometimes cruelly called 'yuppy flu'

b12 *Repetitive strain injury; pains caused by extended keyboard use*

Tie-breaker

Q What is the OAU?
A *Organization for African Unity*

No. 72

a1 Which country is called the 'Land of the Midnight Sun'?

b1 *Two fifths of which European country was once covered by the sea, lakes or marsh?*

a2 In the 1919 pop music hit, what shouldn't you do 'on the way'?

b2 *And in another popular song in the same year, what were you 'forever blowing'?*

a3 What is the usual name for a motor cycle which has an engine capacity of less than 50cc?

b3 *And what does an octane rating indicate?*

a4 What is an architrave?

b4 *What is an inglenook?*

a5 Of which long-running television programme was Leonard Sachs the chairman?

b5 *On which quiz show do contestants have the choice of taking the money or opening the box?*

a6 In France, what is the Baccalaureate (say: back-a-lor-re-att)?

b6 *In England and Wales, which exams did the GCSE replace?*

a7 Where in the Netherlands is the seat of government?

b7 *Which is the capital city of the Netherlands?*

a8 In which film did Bogart say, 'Here's lookin' at you, kid'?

b8 *And which actress in the same film had the line, 'Play it, Sam. Play "As Time Goes By"'?*

a9 Which poet's verse autobiography is titled *Summoned by Bells*?

b9 *Which First World War poet wrote the poems 'Anthem for Doomed Youth' and 'Exposure'?*

a10 What were the Red Brigades?

b10 *In which country did the Frelimo movement fight for independence?*

a11 Which infamous Biblical character is also the title of an opera by Richard Strauss?

b11 *Who wrote the score for the musical, A Little Night Music?*

a12 In J. M. Barrie's play *The Admirable Crichton* (say: Cry-ton), what was Crichton's job?

b12 *Which London theatre was managed by Miss Lilian Baylis?*

No. 72 Answers

a1   Norway
b1   *The Netherlands*
a2   Dilly-dally ('Don't dilly-dally on the way')
b2   *Bubbles ('I'm forever blowing bubbles')*
a3   Moped
b3   *The power and/or quality of petrol*
a4   The frame round any doorway or window
b4   *Seat built into a wall (often beside a fireplace)*
a5   *The Good Old Days*
b5   Take Your Pick
a6   School examination taken at 17-plus
b6   *GCE 'O' (ordinary) level and CSE*
a7   The Hague
b7   *Amsterdam*
a8   Casablanca
b8   *Ingrid Bergman*
a9   John Betjeman
b9   *Wilfred Owen*
a10   *Marxist terrorist groups*
b10 *Mozambique*
a11   Salomé
b11 *Stephen Sondheim*
a12   Butler
b12 *The Old Vic*

Tie-breaker

Q Four film stars (Mary Pickford, Douglas Fairbanks, Charlie
Chaplin and D. W. Griffith) formed their own film company in
1919. What was it called?
A *United Artists*

No. 73

a1 What was the name of the first artificial satellite?

b1 *Which satellite carried the first television pictures across the Atlantic in 1962 (and was also the name of a pop record)?*

a2 Can you name a country (besides the United Kingdom) in which Rugby League is played?

b2 *How many players are there on a rounders team?*

a3 Which two countries generally have the 49th Parallel as their boundary?

b3 *In which province do the majority of French-speaking Canadians live?*

a4 Can you name a keyboard musical instrument besides the piano?

b4 *The saxophone will be found in which section of the orchestra?*

a5 Which United Nations organization agency is concerned with education, science and culture?

b5 *And which UN organization helps children in trouble?*

a6 In which Eastern country was there a revolution in 1949?

b6 *Which rebellion occurred in China at the start of the century?*

a7 Who sailed a yacht called 'Morning Cloud'?

b7 *Which politician, on stopping free milk supplies in schools, became known as 'the Milk Snatcher'?*

a8 Can you name a principal export of Finland?

b8 *And what is the main export of Iceland?*

a9 Who played Hudson in the television series *Upstairs, Downstairs?*

b9 *In a television soap opera, which famous character was played by Jean Alexander?*

a10 In 1900, which British wit and playwright died in poverty in Paris?

b10 *Who wrote a book called* Kim, *first published in 1901?*

a11 Which music hall artist sang the song 'I'm One of the Ruins Cromwell Knocked About a Bit'?

b11 *Which music hall star sang 'Roamin' in the Gloamin'?*

a12 A new form of public transport was seen in London's streets for the first time in 1903. What was it?

b12 *Which motoring organization was founded in 1905?*

No. 73 Answers

a1   Sputnik 1
b1   *Telstar*
a2   France, Australia, New Zealand
b2   *9*
a3   United States of America and Canada
b3   *Quebec*
a4   Organ, harmonium, accordion, harpsichord, clavichord, synthesizer, virginal, spinet
b4   *Woodwind*
a5   UNESCO (United Nations Education, Scientific and Cultural Organization)
b5   *UNICEF (United Nations International Children's Emergency Fund)*
a6   China
b6   *Boxer Rebellion*
a7   Edward Heath
b7   *Margaret Thatcher*
a8   Paper, paper products, wood
b8   *Fish*
a9   Gordon Jackson
b9   *Hilda Ogden (in Coronation Street)*
a10   Oscar Wilde
b10   *Rudyard Kipling*
a11   Marie Lloyd
b11   *Harry Lauder*
a12   Electric trams
b12   *AA (Automobile Association)*

Tie-breaker

Q Up to 1991, how long was the world's longest traffic jam: 7 miles, 21 miles, or 109 miles?

A *109 miles (towards Paris from Lyon, in 1980)*

No. 74

a1 Which TV star often said, 'He's done a whoopsie'?

b1 *Which radio and TV star used to start his shows by shouting 'Wakey, Wakey'?*

a2 In which town are the administrative headquarters of West Sussex?

b2 *And in which town or city are the administrative headquarters of West Yorkshire?*

a3 What were the 'Lusitania' and 'Mauretania'?

b3 *To which empire did the Battleship 'Potemkin' belong?*

a4 In which film did the two main characters describe their jobs by saying, 'We rob banks'?

b4 *In which film did Dustin Hoffman say, 'Mrs Robinson, you're trying to seduce me, aren't you?'?*

a5 In America, what is Mount St Helens?

b5 *In Holland, what is a 'polder'?*

a6 Which murderer was captured at sea in 1910, thanks to the use of radio?

b6 *Who were the Romanovs, who were put to death in a cellar in 1918?*

a7 The words of reggae music are often in which island's dialect?

b7 *What is distinctive about 'dub' reggae recordings?*

a8 Which is the richest country in the Middle East?

b8 *Is Saudi Arabia a republic, a kingdom or a dependency?*

a9 Who composed the music On Hearing the First Cuckoo in Spring?

b9 *Which Russian composed many ballet scores including* The Firebird *and* Petrushka?

a10 For what has Seamus Heaney become famous?

b10 *What was the profession of Mrs Lillie Langtry?*

a11 In opera, what name is given to a major solo song?

b11 *And also in opera, what name is given to a sung 'conversation' between two characters?*

a12 In which year did women (over 30) vote for the first time in Britain: 1911, 1918, or 1922?

b12 *Who was the first British woman MP to take her seat?*

No. 74 Answers

a1   Michael Crawford (Frank Spencer) in *Some Mothers Do 'Ave 'Em*
b1   *Billy Cotton*
a2   Chichester
b2   *Wakefield*
a3   Ocean liners (Cunard liners)
b3   *Russian*
a4   *Bonnie and Clyde*
b4   The Graduate
a5   A volcano (active in 1980)
b5   *Area of drained land, area reclaimed from the sea*
a6   Dr Crippen
b6   *The Russian Tsar and his family*
a7   Jamaican
b7   *No words, so DJs can 'rap' over them*
a8   Saudi Arabia
b8   *Kingdom*
a9   (Frederick) Delius
b9   *(Igor) Stravinsky*
a10   His poetry; as a poet
b10   *Actress*
a11   Aria
b11   *Recitative*
a12   1918
b12   *Nancy Astor (Lady Astor)*

Tie-breaker

Q Which Russian scientist became known for his studies of how dogs learned to expect food whenever a bell was rung?

A *(Ivan) Pavlov*

No. 75

a1   For which sport is Indianapolis especially famous?

b1   In which sport is the Curtis Cup awarded?

a2   Whose was the ragtime band in the popular hit of 1911?

b2   And in a 1908 hit, which moon was invited to 'shine on'?

a3   What is the official language of Brazil?

b3   What is the official language of Nicaragua?

a4   What type of food are vermicelli, macaroni and spaghetti?

b4   Which is the best source of protein: peanuts, eggs or rice?

a5   The comic actor Buster Keaton played an engine driver in which classic silent film?

b5   What was the name of the 'crazy cops' created by the film producer, Mack Sennett?

a6   In 1914, which country was likely to be split by the 'Home Rule' question?

b6   How did the suffragette Emily Davison die?

a7   Which author wrote the 'Forsyte Saga'?

b7   Who wrote the novel Anna of the Five Towns?

a8   Which country, principally, contains the homeland of the Kurdish people?

b8   Eritrea is a disputed part of which country?

a9   Which is the most crowded nation or state (that is, which is most densely populated)?

b9   And which is the most densely populated island in Europe?

a10   Which wealthy diamond-mine owner gave his name to a country in southern Africa?

b10   Which infamous Russian monk was murdered by supporters of the Tsar?

a11   Which part of England receives its programmes from the Winter Hill transmitter?

b11   Emley Moor television transmitter covers which part of England?

a12   What discovery was made by the archaeologist Howard Carter in 1922?

b12   Which Antarctic explorer said, 'I am just going outside and may be some time'?

No. 75 Answers

a1 Motor-racing
b1 *(Woman's) golf*
a2 Alexander ('Alexander's Ragtime Band')
b2 *Harvest moon ('Shine on Harvest Moon')*
a3 *Portuguese*
b3 *Spanish*
a4 *Pasta*
b4 *Peanuts*
a5 *The General (1927)*
b5 *Keystone Kops*
a6 *Ireland*
b6 *She threw herself under the King's horse in the Derby (1913)*
a7 *John Galsworthy*
b7 *Arnold Bennett*
a8 *Iraq*
b8 *Ethiopia*
a9 *Singapore*
b9 *Malta*
a10 Cecil Rhodes (Rhodesia)
b10 *Rasputin*
a11 Lancashire; northwest England
b11 *Yorkshire*
a12 Tomb of Egyptian boy-king, Tutankhamun
b12 *Captain Oates*

Tie-breaker

Q Who is this actor?: 'I made my first stage appearance in 1856 and often acted with Ellen Terry. I was one of the last great actor-managers and the first actor to be knighted, and I died in 1905.'

A Sir Henry Irving

No. 76

a1   A pop tune of 1902 asked someone: 'Won't you please come home'. Who was he?

b1   *In 1912 the singer Eugene Stratton had a hit song about a lily. It was called 'Lily of . . .' what or where?*

a2   By what name is the Spanish holiday coast north of Barcelona generally known?

b2   *And by what name is the southern coast of Spain (around Malaga) generally known?*

a3   Which is the principal city in the county of Tyne and Wear?

b3   *Which town or city is the administrative headquarters of Scotland's Tayside region?*

a4   In which film did Vivien Leigh say, 'Tomorrow is another day'?

b4   *To whom did Mae West say 'Why don't you come up sometime 'n' see me?' (in She Done Him Wrong)?*

a5   In which city are the administrative headquarters of Scotland's Lothian region?

b5   *And what is the 'capital' of Scotland's Highland region?*

a6   What is absolute alcohol?

b6   *What is ultrasonic sound?*

a7   1982 saw a new television channel start in Britain. What was it?

b7   *What is Sianel Pedwar Cymru?*

a8   What is the principal export of Kenya?

b8   *What is the principal export of Zambia?*

a9   Which church was formed in 1972 by the amalgamation of the Congregational and Presbyterian churches in England?

b9   *Members of which religious movement wear their hair in dreadlocks?*

a10   Where was a rebellion put down by Soviet troops in 1956?

b10   *Which country did Arab states fight in the 1973 Yom Kippur War?*

a11   Which novelist wrote The Portrait of a Lady?

b11   *Which author said (on reading his premature obituary) 'Reports of my death are greatly exaggerated'?*

a12   Whose last outpost, in 1917, was the Winter Palace?

b12   *At Christmas 1989, in which country was a Communist dictator overthrown?*

No. 76 Answers

a1   Bill Bailey
b1   *'Lily of Laguna'*
a2   Costa Brava
b2   *Costa del Sol*
a3   Newcastle upon Tyne
b3   *Dundee*
a4   Gone With the Wind
b4   *Cary Grant*
a5   Edinburgh
b5   *Inverness*
a6   Alcohol free of any water
b6   *Sound that is too high for the human ear to hear*
a7   Channel 4
b7   *The (fourth) Welsh television channel (literally: Channel 4 Wales)*
a8   Coffee and/or tea (Also animal hides)
b8   *Copper*
a9   United Reformed Church
b9   *Rastafarianism*
a10   Hungary
b10   *Israel*
a11   Henry James
b11   *Mark Twain*
a12   The Russian Tsar (Tsar Nicholas II)
b12   *Romania (President Ceausescu (say: chow-cheskew)*

Tie-breaker

Q In 1935 the British Government asked the scientist Robert Watson-Watt to invent an anti-aircraft 'death ray'. He said it was impossible. What did he invent instead?

A *Radar (first radar system for detecting enemy planes)*

a1 With which political party do you associate William Whitelaw?

b1 *And with which party do you associate Jo Grimond?*

a2 Which early rock musician was known as 'Chuck'?

b2 *With which group did the pop musician Sting perform for a period?*

a3 Which town is the administrative headquarters of the Isle of Wight?

b3 *In which city are the administrative headquarters of Hampshire?*

a4 What was the name of the bear on *The Muppet Show*?

b4 *On television's* Muppet Show, *which animals were famous for space travel?*

a5 Who wrote the play, *French Without Tears*?

b5 *In 1901 a play called* Three Sisters *was first performed in Moscow. Who is it by?*

a6 Which French scientist was the first woman to win a Nobel prize (for discoveries about radioactivity)?

b6 *Which scientist first split the atom by artificial means?*

a7 As what did Henri de Toulouse-Lautrec (who died in 1901) achieve fame?

b7 *Which American artist became famous for his paintings of Campbell's soup cans and Marilyn Monroe?*

a8 What is the official language in Nigeria?

b8 *What is the official language in the African country, Congo?*

a9 Who wrote the novel *The Moon and Sixpence*?

b9 *Which author (who died in 1905) wrote* Around the World in 80 Days?

a10 Before independence, which European country ruled Libya?

b10 *And which European country ruled Tunisia?*

a11 Which modern poet was also a librarian in Hull?

b11 *Which Merseyside poet was also a member of the pop group, The Scaffold?*

a12 What is a pulsar?

b12 *And what is a quasar? (The first was discovered in 1963)*

a1 Conservative
b1 *Liberal*
a2 (Charles) 'Chuck' Berry
b2 *The Police*
a3 Newport
b3 *Winchester*
a4 Fozzie
b4 *Pigs*
a5 Terence Rattigan
b5 *(Anton) Chekhov*
a6 Madame (Marie) Curie
b6 *(Professor Ernest) Rutherford*
a7 Artist, painter of scenes at the Moulin Rouge
b7 *Andy Warhol*
a8 English
b8 *French*
a9 (William) Somerset Maugham
b9 *Jules Verne*
a10 Italy
b10 *France*
a11 Philip Larkin
b11 *Roger McGough*
a12 A star which sends out a series of bleeps; very dense stars; a type of neutron star (discovered in 1967)
b12 *A 'quasi-stellar radio source'; a very distant source of radio waves (they may be 'black holes' at the centres of distant galaxies)*

Tie-breaker

Q What four colours are generally used in colour printing?
A *Yellow, magenta, cyan (blue) and black*

No. 78

a1 Of what common device or implement was there a type called a Brownie?

b1 What device was first marketed in 1901 by a man called King Camp Gillette?

a2 On television, who travelled by Tardis?

b2 What was the name of the short, fat, dumpy robot in the film Star Wars?

a3 How many watts make a kilowatt?

b3 How many watts make a megawatt?

What are the capitals of the following Canadian provinces?

a4 Ontario

b4 Manitoba

a5 Newfoundland

b5 Alberta

a6 Nova Scotia

b6 Quebec

a7 Name two of the Goons

b7 Who was the smallest of the comedy team, the Goodies?

a8 Beatrix became queen of which country in 1980?

b8 Which monarch died in January, 1901?

a9 Long, medium and short waves are used in . . . what?

b9 For what purpose are ultra-high frequency (or UHF) radio waves used?

a10 Who wrote the children's 'Peter Rabbit' books?

b10 Which author wrote The Call of the Wild and White Fang?

a11 As what did Auguste Rodin achieve fame?

b11 As what did Sarah Bernhardt achieve fame?

a12 In 1917, which party did Lenin lead to power in Russia?

b12 Which political party was founded by the Italian Benito Mussolini in 1919?

No. 78 Answers

a1   Camera
b1   *Safety razor*
a2   Dr Who
b2   *R2D2*
a3   1,000
b3   *1,000,000 (one million)*
a4   Toronto
b4   *Winnipeg*
a5   St John's
b5   *Edmonton*
a6   Halifax
b6   *Quebec*
a7   Spike Milligan, Harry Secombe, Peter Sellers (Michael Bentine, briefly)
b7   *Bill Oddie*
a8   The Netherlands
b8   *Queen Victoria*
a9   Radio transmission
b9   *Television transmission*
a10   Beatrix Potter
b10   *Jack London*
a11   As a sculptor
b11   *Actress*
a12   Bolshevik
b12   *Fascist*

Tie-breaker

Q   What was made illegal in Britain in October 1915, in the hope of cutting down the consumption of alcohol?

A   *'Treating', or the buying of 'rounds' in public houses (punishment for those caught was £100 fine or six months in jail)*

No. 79

a1 What have the following in common: Etna, Vesuvius and Stromboli?

b1 *What have the following in common: Maggiore, Garda and Como?*

a2 Which fictional detective had to be brought back to 'life' in 1903?

b2 *Which county is visited by tourists interested in the novels of Thomas Hardy?*

a3 What is an ocarina?

b3 *And what is an oculist?*

a4 Which war ended in 1902?

b4 *In which year was the so-called 'Winter of Discontent'?*

a5 Which organization links the police forces of 146 countries?

b5 *What is OPEC?*

a6 Which besieged South African town, commanded by Colonel Baden Powell, was relieved in 1900?

b6 *Which South African town was relieved after a 118-day siege earlier in 1900?*

a7 Until 1905, which country ruled Norway?

b7 *Which Scandinavian country became independent of Russian rule in 1917?*

a8 In the film *I'm No Angel*, which actress said, 'Beulah, peel me a grape'?

b8 *In which film did Greta Garbo say 'I want to be alone' (to John Barrymore)?*

a9 Which is the principal city on New Zealand's southern island?

b9 *Which is the largest city in New Zealand?*

a10 As what did the American Ogden Nash achieve fame?

b10 *As what did the Italian Enrico Caruso achieve fame?*

a11 Which Irish nationalist (famous for his diaries) was hanged for treason in 1916?

b11 *In Irish history, which party was supported by Sir Edward Carson?*

a12 Which Welsh poet wrote: 'The Hunchback in the Park', 'After the Funeral' and 'Poem in October'?

b12 *Who wrote the poems 'Bagpipe Music' and 'Prayer Before Birth'?*

No. 79 Answers

a1   All are (Italian) volcanoes
b1   *All are (Italian/Alpine) lakes*
a2   Sherlock Holmes
b2   *Dorset*
a3   Musical instrument (played by blowing)
b3   *Specialist in eye diseases*
a4   Boer War
b4   *1978–9*
a5   Interpol (International Criminal Police Organization)
b5   *Organization of Petroleum Exporting Countries*
a6   Mafeking
b6   *Ladysmith*
a7   Sweden
b7   *Finland*
a8   Mae West
b8   *Grand Hotel*
a9   Christchurch
b9   *Auckland*
a10   Poet
b10   *As a singer (tenor)*
a11   (Sir Roger) Casement
b11   *Ulster Unionists*
a12   Dylan Thomas
b12   *Louis MacNeice*

Tie-breaker

Q In 1903, the king and queen of which middle-European country were shot in a bedroom cupboard?

A *Serbia (King Alexander and Queen Draga)*

No. 80

a1 On television, which comic character regularly asked, 'Permission to speak, sir?'?

b1 *In Dallas, who played J. R. Ewing?*

a2 Cagliari is the capital of which Mediterranean island?

b2 *And Palermo is the capital of which other Mediterranean island?*

a3 In the thirties and forties, as what did Ambrose achieve fame?

b3 *Which chain of shops was run by Joseph Sieff?*

a4 Which three Scandinavian countries have ruling royal families?

b4 *How did Princess Grace of Monaco die (in 1982)?*

a5 Which English Major led Arabs into Damascus to free it from the Turks?

b5 *In which country did Mahatma Gandhi first campaign?*

a6 Why is Knock (say: nok) in Ireland visited by many people each year?

b6 *Which police force is based at New Scotland Yard?*

a7 Which theory was proposed by Albert Einstein in 1905?

b7 *For what medical research and practice did Patrick Steptoe become famous?*

a8 Can you name one of the two independent countries situated within Italy?

b8 *Between which two countries is the tiny state of Andorra?*

a9 The sign of the treble clef in music means that the notes following it will be played on the piano by which hand?

b9 *In music, what is the smallest interval?*

a10 'Me Tarzan . . . You Jane' was spoken to Maureen O'Sullivan by which actor in the film *Tarzan the Ape Man?*

b10 *In which film did Anthony Parkins have the line, 'Mother – what's the phrase – isn't quite herself today'?*

a11 Of which church organization is Terry Waite a member?

b11 *Which emperor had the title 'Lion of Judah'?*

a12 Who was re-elected prime minister of Britain in 1900?

b12 *Sir Henry Campbell-Bannerman became prime minister in 1906. Which party did he lead?*

No. 80 Answers

a1	Lance-Corporal Jones (Clive Dunn), in *Dad's Army*
b1	*Larry Hagman*
a2	Sardinia
b2	*Sicily*
a3	Bandleader
b3	*Marks and Spencer*
a4	Norway, Sweden, Denmark
b4	*In a car crash*
a5	T. E. Lawrence, Lawrence of Arabia
b5	*South Africa*
a6	It's a religious shrine; a Catholic place of pilgrimage
b6	*Metropolitan Police*
a7	Theory of (special) relativity
b7	*Test-tube babies; fertilization of the egg in a test tube*
a8	Vatican City, San Marino
b8	*France and Spain*
a9	Right hand
b9	*A semi-tone (half a tone)*
a10	Johnny Weissmuller (in fact he said 'Tarzan . . .Jane', pointing first to himself and then to her)
b10	Psycho
a11	Church Army
b11	*Haile Selassie of Ethiopia/Abyssinia*
a12	Lord Salisbury
b12	*Liberal*

Tie-breaker

Q The film *The Old California* was famous for being the first film to be made in which town?

A *Hollywood (in 1910)*

No. 81: Do You Speak the Language?

In Cockney rhyming slang, what is meant by each of the following?

a1   Would you Adam-and-Eve it?
b1   *Get up them apples!*
a2   I must get me barnet cut
b2   *That's a smart pair of daisies*
a3   Wot smashin' bacons!
b3   *'E pinched me bottle!*

And what does a Liverpudlian (or 'Scouser') mean by the following?

a4   A proddy-dog
b4   *A pur of kecks*
a5   It's crackin de flags
b5   *Cack-'anded*
a6   The bone orchard
b6   *To sag off*

'Geordie' is the dialect or 'language' spoken on Tyneside. What do the following mean?

a7   Whey aye!
b7   *Whist!*
a8   Hadaway!
b8   *Hinny*
a9   Clarty
b9   *Galluses*

And what does an Australian mean by the following?

a10   Jumbuck
b10   *Joey*
a11   Don't come the raw prawn!
b11   *Rattle your dags*
a12   Chunder
b12   *Tube*

No. 81 Answers

a1   Would you believe it?
b1   *Stairs (apples and pears)*
a2   I need a haircut (Barnet Fair)
b2   *That's a fine pair shoes/boots (daisy roots)*
a3   What fine legs (bacon and eggs)
b3   *He pinched my bottom (bottle and glass)*
a4   A protestant
b4   *A pair of trousers*
a5   The weather is very hot
b5   *Left-handed (accept: awkward, clumsy)*
a6   The cemetery
b6   *To play truant*
a7   Of course!
b7   *Be quiet!*
a8   Begone!
b8   *Dear or darling (a term of endearment)*
a9   Muddy
b9   *(Men's) braces*
a10   Sheep
b10   *Baby kangaroo*
a11   Don't try to fool me!
b11   *Get a move on*
a12   Vomit
b12   *Can (of beer)*

Tie-breaker

Q Cornwall has its own language. Which days of the week do you
think are: De Merth, De Mergher and De Yow?
A *Tuesday, Wednesday and Thursday*

No. 82

a1 In the films, who played Rocky?

b1 *Whose catch phrase is or was 'Rock on, Tommy'?*

a2 If something is porous, what can pass through it?

b2 *And if something is translucent, what can pass through it?*

a3 In which sport did Bill Beaumont captain England?

b3 *In which sport did David Gower captain England?*

a4 What is the cost of eight items, each costing £2.10?

b4 *And what is the cost of 32 items each costing 30p?*

a5 What is 51 divided by 7, to two decimal places?

b5 *And what is 85 divided by 6, also to two decimal places?*

a6 What is the tangent of a circle?

b6 *How many faces has a squared-based pyramid?*

a7 Which mountain range separates Argentina and Chile?

b7 *Which river separates the two historic towns of Buda and Pest?*

a8 In which famous house did Queen Victoria die?

b8 *At Windsor, in which chapel are members of the Royal Family buried?*

a9 Milan is the capital of which Italian region?

b9 *And Florence is the capital of which Italian region?*

a10 In which town are the administrative headquarters of North Yorkshire?

b10 *In which town are the administrative headquarters of Northumberland?*

a11 Which crime writer created a detective called Commander Adam Dalgleish?

b11 *And which writer created Chief Inspector Reg Wexford?*

a12 In physics, what do we call the external agency which can change the state of rest or motion of a body?

b12 *Which of the following substances will not combine with Oxygen: Gold, Mercury, Carbon, Sulphur, Hydrogen?*

No. 82 Answers

a1	Sylvester Stallone
b1	*(Bobby) Ball (to Tommy Cannon)*
a2	Liquids or gas
b2	*Light*
a3	Rugby Union
b3	*Cricket*
a4	£16.80
b4	*£9.60*
a5	7.28
b5	*14.16*
a6	A line which touches it once and only once
b6	*5*
a7	Andes
b7	*Danube*
a8	Osborne House, Isle of Wight
b8	*St George's*
a9	Lombardy
b9	*Tuscany*
a10	Northallerton
b10	*Morpeth*
a11	P. D. James
b11	*Ruth Rendell*
a12	Force
b12	*Gold*

Tie-breaker

Q Until 1954, which three countries made up French Indo-China?
A *Vietnam, Laos, Cambodia (Kampuchea)*

a1 If you describe something as a rip-off, what would you mean?

b1 *If you buy a hatchback, can you say precisely what you would be acquiring?*

a2 If we say someone 'rabbits on' about something, what do we mean?

b2 *What do we mean if we say that a building is listed?*

a3 If you buy something that is zero-rated, which tax does not apply to it?

b3 *Can you explain what a Catch-22 situation is?*

a4 In the area of house purchasing, what does 'gazumping' mean?

b4 *In the area of foreign policy, what is 'the domino theory'?*

a5 On which river is the former West German capital of Bonn?

b5 *On which river is the historic French town of Rouen?*

a6 Which is the smallest country in the Common Market?

b6 *Which was the largest republic within the USSR?*

a7 Which European country's stamps and coins bear its old Latin name, Helvetia?

b7 *On which country's coins can be found the slogan, 'Liberty, Equality, Brotherhood' (or 'Fraternity')*

a8 In which television series were Doris, Bruno and Miss Sherwood regular characters?

b8 *In which television series did we meet Donna, Ray and Cliff?*

a9 What name do we give to the resistance encountered when one solid body moves while in contact with another?

b9 *What do we call the force with which a celestial body, such as the Earth or Moon, attracts an object?*

a10 What colour are copper sulphate crystals?

b10 *What colour is Potassium Permanganate when dissolved in water?*

a11 Whose diary was actually written by Sue Townsend?

b11 *Who, supposedly, wrote the 'Dear Bill' letters which appeared in the magazine Private Eye?*

a12 In soccer, when does a drop ball occur?

b12 *On a motor-racing track, what does a white flag indicate?*

No. 83 Answers

a1 It was a swindle; not worth the money paid for it; cheat

b1 *A car with a sloping rear door opening upward (semi-estate car)*

a2 He/she talks at great length (irrelevantly or repetitively)

b2 *It has special architectural interest (no demolition without special authority)*

a3 VAT

b3 *One in which you can't win*

a4 Raising the price after agreeing to sell (before contract signed) when a second, more 'generous' buyer comes along

b4 *One event sparks off a chain of similar ones*

a5 Rhein

b5 *Seine*

a6 Luxembourg

b6 *Russian Federation*

a7 Switzerland

b7 *France*

a8 *Fame*

b8 Dallas

a9 Friction

b9 *Gravity*

a10 Blue

b10 *Purple/deep red*

a11 Adrian Mole

b11 *Denis Thatcher*

a12 After a suspension of play which began with the ball in play

b12 *There's a service car on the circuit*

Tie-breaker

Q What are the ten events of the Olympic Decathlon?

A *100m, 110m hurdles, 400m, 1500m races, long jump, high jump, pole vault, shot put, javelin, discus*

No. 84

a1 What's another name for a meteorological area of low pressure?
b1 *Which country's parliament is called the Knesset?*
a2 In *EastEnders*, who was played by Leslie Grantham?
b2 *What is an incisor?*
a3 Where is the Sea of Tranquility?
b3 *'Ferrous' refers to which metal?*

What are the capital cities of the following Australian states and territories?

a4 New South Wales
b4 *Victoria*
a5 Queensland
b5 *Western Australia*
a6 Northern Territory
b6 *South Australia*
a7 Which university opened near Brighton in 1961?
b7 *Which university opened near Colchester in 1964?*
a8 Where might you find cueing and anti-skating devices?
b8 *What familiar product is graded in ASA and/or DIN?*
a9 Which pop star had hits with 'Gamblin' Man', 'Cumberland Gap' and 'Does Your Chewing Gum Lose Its Flavour'?
b9 *'Sunshine Superman' and 'Mellow Yellow' were hits for which pop star?*
a10 Which body of men elects the Pope?
b10 *Which French girl was canonized in 1920?*
a11 Which novel features Ralph, Jack and Piggy?
b11 *Which novelist created the character Gandalf the Wizard?*
a12 What particular discovery was made by the physician anatomist William Harvey?
b12 *Sir Ronald Ross won a Nobel prize for his discoveries connected with – which illness?*

No. 84 Answers

a1   Depression/cyclone
b1   *Israel*
a2   Den Watts, Dirty Den
b2   *Tooth (used for cutting)*
a3   On the Moon
b3   *Iron*
a4   Sydney
b4   *Melbourne*
a5   Brisbane
b5   *Perth*
a6   Darwin
b6   *Adelaide*
a7   University of Sussex
b7   *University of Essex*
a8   On a record player/turntable deck
b8   *Photographic film*
a9   Lonnie Donegan
b9   *Donovan*
a10   The Sacred College of Cardinals; cardinals of the Roman Catholic Church
b10   *Joan of Arc*
a11   *Lord of the Flies* (by William Golding)
b11   *J. R. R. Tolkien*
a12   Circulation of the blood
b12   *Malaria*

Tie-breaker

Q How many of the seven Welsh counties created in 1974 can you name?

A *Clwyd, Dyfed, Gwent, Gwynedd, Powys, Mid-Glamorgan, South Glamorgan and West Glamorgan*

No. 85

a1 On television, what was the name of the waiter in *Fawlty Towers*?

b1 *Which American TV series had as its stars Sharon Gless and Tyne Daly?*

a2 In Moscow, what was the Lubyanka?

b2 *What is 'Izvestia'?*

a3 What do the figures '007' mean in the James Bond books?

b3 *And what is the name of M's secretary in many of the Bond films and books?*

a4 What is the normal temperature of your body in degrees Celsius?

b4 *In physics, what do we call a quantity which has both magnitude and direction?*

a5 Which of the following metals does not react with water: Calcium, Copper, Iron, Potassium, Sodium?

b5 *Can you name the three bones in the middle ear?*

a6 Which comedian had success in the pop charts with 'Tears', 'Happiness' and 'Love is Like a Violin'?

b6 *Which vocalist often used to sing while sitting in a rocking chair?*

a7 Besides the board and the pieces, what do you need to play Backgammon?

b7 *In which game might you land on Mayfair or a railway station?*

a8 Prior to 1974, what were the three Ridings of Yorkshire?

b8 *After the Second World War, which three countries occupied West Germany?*

a9 In 1921, what chemical gave hope to diabetics?

b9 *If you suffer from xenophobia, what do you dislike?*

a10 Which Adriatic country came into being at the end of the First World War?

b10 *To which country did the Ottoman Empire belong (till it was broken up in 1920)?*

a11 Which university opened in Staffordshire in 1962?

b11 *Which university opened in Birmingham in 1966?*

a12 On which river does the German city of Frankfurt stand?

b12 *On which river is the French city of Lyon?*

No. 85 Answers

a1	Manuel
b1	*Cagney and Lacey*
a2	A notorious prison
b2	*Russian newspaper*
a3	He is licensed to kill
b3	*Miss Moneypenny*
a4	36.9 (allow 36 or 37)
b4	*A vector*
a5	Copper
b5	*Malleus, incus, stapes (also known as hammer, anvil, stirrup)*
a6	Ken Dodd
b6	*Val Doonican*
a7	Dice
b7	*Monopoly*
a8	North, West, East
b8	*United Kingdom, United States of America and France*
a9	Insulin
b9	*Foreigners, strangers, other countries*
a10	Yugoslavia
b10	*Turkey*
a11	Keele
b11	*University of Aston (in Birmingham)*
a12	Main (say: mine)
b12	*Rhône*

Tie-breaker

Q Who is this actress?: 'For several seasons, I was the leading lady in Miss Horniman's repertory company in Manchester. To celebrate our golden wedding, my husband and I appeared in *Eighty in the Shade*. Down in Leatherhead, they graciously named a theatre after me'.

A *Dame Sybil Thorndike (1882–1976)*

No. 86

a1 In snooker, how many points are scored when you pot the pink?

b1 *And how many when you pot the blue?*

a2 Galerie Lafayette is a department store in which capital city?

b2 *Which is the most famous department store in London's Knightsbridge?*

a3 In which types of food do we find Vitamin C?

b3 *Can you name the type of food in which we find Vitamin D?*

a4 In which battle was Germany defeated in August and September 1940?

b4 *In which battle was Germany defeated in October and November 1942?*

a5 In which musical is everything 'up-to-date in Kansas City'?

b5 *In which musical is the song 'If I Were a Rich Man'?*

a6 What kind of ship is sometimes described as a 'ro-ro'?

b6 *The world's largest ship was destroyed by rocket attack in 1976. What type of ship was it?*

a7 In which year was the first flight of the supersonic plane, Concorde: 1969, 1972, or 1976?

b7 *And in which year did Concorde enter scheduled service?*

a8 In which county is Welwyn Garden City?

b8 *Which major new town or city has been developed in Buckinghamshire since 1967?*

a9 Who wrote *The Spy Who Came in from the Cold*?

b9 *Who wrote* Where Eagles Dare *and* The Guns of Navarone?

a10 On which planet did the spaceships Viking 1 and 2 land in 1975?

b10 *Which planet did Mariner 2 fly by in 1962?*

a11 Male members of which religion wear a turban to cover their uncut hair?

b11 *Shinto is the folk religion of which country?*

a12 What is the UPU?

b12 *What is GATT?*

No. 86 Answers

a1 6
b1 *5*
a2 Paris
b2 *Harrods*
a3 Fruit, green vegetables
b3 *Liver, dairy products, eggs, fish*
a4 Battle of Britain
b4 *El Alamein*
a5 *Oklahoma!*
b5 Fiddler on the Roof
a6 Roll-on, roll-off car ferry
b6 *Oil tanker (the 'Seawise Giant')*
a7 1969
b7 *1976*
a8 Hertfordshire
b8 *Milton Keynes*
a9 John Le Carré
b9 *Alistair Maclean*
a10 Mars
b10 *Venus*
a11 Sikhism
b11 *Japan*
a12 Universal Postal Union (Co-ordinates international post)
b12 *General Agreement on Tariffs and Trade*

Tie-breaker

Q Which are the four open tennis competitions a player must win
to achieve the 'Grand Slam'?
A *French, Australian, US and Wimbledon Opens*

No. 87

a1 What do we call a car built before 1918?

b1 *And what name is given to a car built between 1918 and 1930?*

a2 Where in London are most of the Henry Wood Promenade Concerts held?

b2 *What is the STD code for inner London?*

a3 On which part of the body does a cardiac surgeon specialize?

b3 *On which parts of the body do orthopaedic surgeons work?*

a4 About a million people died in which siege during the Second World War?

b4 *And in which country's civil war did another 1½ million die between 1967 and 1969?*

a5 As what did Ralph Vaughan Williams achieve fame?

b5 *As what did Bertrand Russell achieve fame?*

a6 At which university did St Catherine's, St Peter's and St Antony's colleges open during this century?

b6 *Which university opened at Guildford in 1966?*

a7 Chief Detective Superintendent Lockhart was the central character of which television series?

b7 *On television, Barry Foster plays a Dutch detective called . . .?*

a8 Which author created the fictional village of Thrush Green?

b8 *What was the title of Muriel Spark's novel about a distinctive Edinburgh teacher?*

a9 What is the name of the neck of water which separates European and Asian Turkey?

b9 *The Gulf of Bothnia separates which two northern countries?*

a10 On which London Underground line is the longest tunnel?

b10 *Which northern city re-introduced a street tramway system in 1992?*

a11 About what would you consult *Grove's Dictionary*?

b11 *Which magazine, originally reprinting condensations of articles from other magazines, first appeared in 1922?*

a12 Which playwright wrote the line, 'Very flat, Norfolk'?

b12 *Which French playwright wrote the farces A Flea in Her Ear and Look After Lulu?*

No. 87 Answers

a1	A veteran
b1	*Vintage*
a2	Royal Albert Hall
b2	*071*
a3	The heart
b3	*Bones (and joints)*
a4	Siege of Leningrad (St Petersburg)
b4	*Nigeria (accept: Biafra)*
a5	Composer
b5	*Philosopher (contributor to many radio programmes)*
a6	Oxford
b6	*University of Surrey*
a7	*No Hiding Place*
b7	*Van der Valk*
a8	Miss Read
b8	The Prime of Miss Jean Brodie
a9	The Bosporus
b9	*Sweden and Finland*
a10	Northern (Morden–East Finchley via Bank) (17.3 miles)
b10	*Manchester*
a11	Music
b11	*Reader's Digest*
a12	Noël Coward
b12	*Georges Feydeau*

Tie-breaker

Q How many points is the maximum break in snooker?
A 147

No. 88

a1   In which city is the department store called Macy's?

b1   *And in which city is the department store called GUM?*

a2   In Germany, what is the Bundesbahn (say: bun-des-barn)?

b2   *What are or were: Delta, Eastern and Braniff?*

a3   Which is the largest civil engineering project this century?

b3   *In the world of transport, what were Counties, Kings and Castles?*

a4   On television's *New Avengers*, who played Purdey?

b4   *Grace Metalious wrote a novel which inspired a film and a television series. It was called . . .?*

a5   Which country suffered most casualties in the Second World War?

b5   *Where was the television series* Enemy at the Door *set?*

a6   In London, which title role in an Andrew Lloyd Webber musical did Michael Crawford create?

b6   *Who wrote (and performed) the songs 'Mad Dogs and Englishmen' and 'Mrs Worthington'?*

a7   In which year was the Wall Street Crash in America?

b7   *Since its foundation in 1929, which has been the world's smallest independent country?*

a8   In which Welsh county is the new town of Cwmbran (say: koom-bran)?

b8   *Which major new town has been developed in Shropshire since 1963?*

a9   Which glamorous male film star appeared in *The Four Horsemen of the Apocalypse* and *The Sheik*?

b9   *What was the nickname of the Hollywood star, Roscoe Arbuckle?*

a10   The inventor of which rapid-fire machine gun died in 1903?

b10   *Which material was invented by Leo Baekeland in 1907?*

a11   Which is the more flexible plastic – polystyrene, polypropylene or polyester?

b11   *Which purified element is used to make the chips in microprocessors?*

a12   Did aspirin go on sale for the first time in 1905, 1923, or 1931?

b12   *In which year was the first radio broadcast of speech and music?: 1906, 1920, or 1923?*

No. 88 Answers

a1	New York
b1	*Moscow*
a2	Railway system
b2	*(American) airline companies*
a3	The Channel Tunnel
b3	*(Express) steam locomotives (on the Great Western Railway)*
a4	Joanna Lumley
b4	*Peyton Place*
a5	Soviet Union
b5	*Channel Islands*
a6	*Phantom of the Opera*
b6	*Noël Coward*
a7	1929
b7	*Vatican City State*
a8	Gwent
b8	*Telford*
a9	Rudolf Valentino
b9	*Fatty (Arbuckle)*
a10	(Richard) Gatling
b10	*Bakelite*
a11	Polyester
b11	*Silicon*
a12	1905
b12	*1906*

Tie-breaker

Q 1934 saw the introduction of high street shops offering a useful domestic service. What were they?

A *Launderettes*

No. 89

a1   Which television series features Del and Rodney?

b1   *In which series did Penelope Keith play Mrs Forbes-Hamilton?*

a2   In which sport were Maureen Connolly and Margaret Court champions?

b2   *For which sport did Lucinda Green become famous?*

a3   Which country is the world's largest producer of wool?

b3   *What is the principal business or industry in Monaco?*

a4   In which musical did we see the Ascot Gavotte?

b4   *In which musical was there a lonely goatherd?*

a5   Before transistors were used in radios, what did their job?

b5   *Was the first electric washing machine made in 1906, 1931, or 1948?*

a6   The 'Third World' includes the developing countries. Which is the 'First World'?

b6   *And which is (or was) the 'Second World'?*

a7   Which item of clothing was first put on the market in 1937 by a New York and London company?

b7   *On a clothing label, what symbol indicates a garment may be dry-cleaned?*

a8   Where, in 1918, did the German naval fleet sink itself?

b8   *In which building near Paris was the First World War peace treaty signed?*

a9   In area, which is the largest: Isle of Man, Isle of Wight, Anglesey?

b9   *Which Welsh county does not have a coastline?*

a10   About which fictional character's complaint did Philip Roth write a novel?

b10   *American author Anita Loos became popular with a novel about a blonde flapper – called . . . what?*

a11   Who would receive training at RADA?

b11   *As a preparation for which job might you obtain the CQSW?*

a12   Which university opened in Greater Manchester in 1967?

b12   *Which university opened at Coleraine in Northern Ireland in 1965?*

No. 89 Answers

a1	*Only Fools and Horses*
b1	To The Manor Born
a2	Tennis
b2	*(3-day) Eventing; horse-riding*
a3	Australia
b3	*Tourism and/or gambling*
a4	My Fair Lady
b4	The Sound of Music
a5	Valves
b5	*1906*
a6	Western Europe, North America and Australasia
b6	*The Soviet Union and what was formerly communist Eastern Europe (it is disputed whether China is in the 'Second' or 'Third' world)*
a7	Nylons (NY – Lon)
b7	*A circle*
a8	Scapa Flow, Scotland
b8	*Palace of Versailles*
a9	Anglesey
b9	*Powys*
a10	Portnoy (*Portnoy's Complaint*)
b10	Gentlemen Prefer Blondes
a11	Actors/Actresses (Royal Academy of Dramatic Art)
b11	*Social worker (Certificate of Qualification in Social Work)*
a12	University of Salford
b12	*New University of Ulster*

Tie-breaker

Q Which was the first European country to give women the vote?
A Finland (1906)

No. 90

a1   Which horse was the first to win the Grand National three times?

b1   *In darts, what is the highest score you can achieve with one dart?*

a2   Who were 'White' Russians?

b2   *In 1906, what was a 'Silver Ghost'?*

a3   The invasion by Germany of which country brought Britain into the Second World War?

b3   *Which country was occupied by Germany in the 1938 'Anschluss'?*

a4   Of what is laurel an emblem?

b4   *Of which country is the peacock an emblem?*

a5   On television, in which series did we meet Inspector Jack Regan and Detective Sergeant Carter?

b5   *And what is meant by the underworld expression, 'the Sweeney'?*

a6   In which county is the new town of Crawley?

b6   *In which English county is the new town of Washington?*

a7   By what nickname was Wild West show owner William Cody generally known?

b7   *Which early film star became known as 'The World's Sweetheart'?*

a8   In the Spanish Civil War, was the Falange Party fascist or communist?

b8   *On which island has tension between Tamil Indians and native inhabitants led to violence?*

a9   Which fictional detective lives in a village called St Mary Mead?

b9   *Which novelist invented the Drones Club?*

a10   Which Irishman wrote the mammoth novel *Ulysses*?

b10   *Which Czech-Jewish author wrote The Trial?*

a11   Alongside which West German river is a major coal-mining, steel and industrial region?

b11   *Which important dam was completed on the River Nile in 1970?*

a12   What fraction of the human body is water?

b12   *In medicine, for what are gamma rays used?*

No. 90 Answers

a1	Red Rum
b1	60
a2	Non-Communists
b2	*A Rolls-Royce motor-car*
a3	Poland
b3	*Austria*
a4	Victory
b4	*India*
a5	The Sweeney
b5	*The Flying Squad*
a6	(West) Sussex
b6	*Tyne and Wear*
a7	Buffalo Bill
b7	*Mary Pickford*
a8	Fascist
b8	*Sri Lanka*
a9	Miss Marple
b9	*P. G. Wodehouse*
a10	James Joyce
b10	*Franz Kafka*
a11	Ruhr
b11	*Aswan Dam*
a12	Two thirds
b12	*To kill cancer cells*

Tie-breaker

Q In which sport do you 'take the drop'?
A *Surfing*

No. 91: The First World War

a1 By when was the War meant to be all over?

b1 *What shocked the generals at Christmas 1914?*

a2 Which side won the Battle of Mons?

b2 *Which army was defeated at Tannenberg?*

a3 Where, according to Sir Edward Grey, were the lamps going out?

b3 *According to a famous recruiting poster, what did the women of Britain say to their menfolk?*

a4 Until his death in 1916 who was Britain's Secretary of State for War?

b4 *What was the name of the infamous sea-battle off Denmark in 1916?*

a5 Where was 'no man's land'?

b5 *Which new so-called 'Motor Monsters' were first used in 1916?*

a6 In which year did the Somme campaign begin?

b6 *Which Field Marshal directed the British at the start of this campaign?*

a7 In 1915, how were Norfolk towns hit by German fire?

b7 *On which peninsula in the Dardanelles did the Allies seek to establish a base?*

a8 Which English poet died en route to the Dardanelles?

b8 *What was the nickname of German airman Baron Manfred von Richthofen?*

a9 Who became British prime minister halfway through the War?

b9 *Who had been prime minister at the start of the War?*

a10 What were 'doughboys'?

b10 *What was 'Big Bertha'?*

a11 On what charge was the dancer Mata Hari put to death?

b11 *Into what were the Royal Flying Corps and Royal Naval Air Service merged in 1918?*

a12 For what are Siegfried Sassoon and Isaac Rosenberg remembered?

b12 *And for what are Sir John Sergeant and John Nash remembered?*

No. 91 Answers

a1 Christmas
b1 *Brief peace in the trenches, fraternization between armies*
a2 Germany
b2 *The Russian*
a3 All over Europe
b3 *'Go'*
a4 Lord Kitchener
b4 *Jutland*
a5 Between the opposing front lines
b5 *Tanks*
a6 1916
b6 *Sir Douglas Haig*
a7 By Zeppelin raids
b7 *Gallipoli*
a8 Rupert Brooke
b8 *The Red Baron*
a9 (David) Lloyd George
b9 *(Herbert) Asquith*
a10 American soldiers
b10 *A huge German gun*
a11 Spying (espionage)
b11 *RAF (Royal Air Force)*
a12 Their war poetry
b12 *Their war paintings*

Tie-breaker

Q Who wrote the words, 'They shall not grow old as we that are left grow old'?

A *Laurence Binyon*

No. 92

a1 What is Princess Margaret's second Christian name?
b1 Which royal duke was killed in a flying accident in 1942?
a2 Of which American state is Sacramento the capital?
b2 Which dance, popular in the twenties, was named after a city in South Carolina?
a3 What is the usual word for a motorway in the United States of America?
b3 And what is a motorway called in Germany?
a4 What is sumo?
b4 And where or what is Sumatra?
a5 On television, who plays Ken Boon?
b5 On television, who plays Hadleigh?
a6 In which year did we see the first pocket calculators: 1969, 1971, or 1974?
b6 In which year did we see the first digital watches: 1963, 1968, or 1971?
a7 A gruelling 19-day cycle race was run for the first time in 1903. What was it called?
b7 To see which sport would you travel to Ripon in Yorkshire?
a8 What is a TriStar (say: try-star)?
b8 What are the Triads?
a9 Which airport is sometimes known by the initials LHR?
b9 Entebbe Airport is in which African country?
a10 In 1900, which empire stretched from Constantinople and Baghdad westwards through Egypt to Tripoli?
b10 In which war early in the century did Britain imprison women and children in concentration camps?
a11 Which American humourist wrote *Guys and Dolls*?
b11 Which American novelist wrote the 'sex-change' novel Myra Breckinridge?
a12 Which South American country was still a département of France in 1991?
b12 In which country is there an area called the Mato Grosso?

No. 92 Answers

a1 Rose
b1 *(George) Duke of Kent*
a2 California
b2 *Charleston*
a3 Freeway or highway
b3 *Autobahn*
a4 Japanese wrestling
b4 *Largest island of Indonesia (south of Singapore)*
a5 Michael Elphick
b5 *Gerald Harper*
a6 1971
b6 *1971*
a7 Tour de France
b7 *Horse-racing*
a8 (American) airliner
b8 *Members of a Chinese secret society (said to be involved in drugs and gambling)*
a9 London Heathrow
b9 *Uganda (near Kampala)*
a10 Turkish or Ottoman
b10 *Boer War (in southern Africa)*
a11 Damon Runyon
b11 *Gore Vidal*
a12 French Guiana
b12 *Brazil*

Tie-breaker

Q On which radio show did the presenter regular ask, 'Are you courting?' or 'Tell us, have you had any embarrassing moments?'?

A Have A Go *(with Wilfred Pickles)*

No. 93

a1 In which sport was Jack Hobbs a star?

b1 *Which sportsman, known as 'W. G.', died in October 1915?*

a2 Where were a group of part-time policemen known as B-Specials?

b2 *And to which religion or order did they belong?*

a3 Which American secret society used violence to defend white supremacy over blacks and Jews?

b3 *Who said, 'There will be no whitewash at the White House'?*

a4 Who was the star of the early film comedy *Cops*?

b4 *Who starred in the film The Man Who Fell to Earth?*

a5 The composer of the 'Savoy Operas' died in 1900. Who was he?

b5 *Who composed 'Rhapsody in Blue'?*

a6 Who wrote the thriller *The Eagle Has Landed*?

b6 *About which Roman Emperor did Robert Graves write two novels?*

a7 As what did Alexander Skriabin (say: scree-a-bin) become famous?

b7 *As what did Professor A. J. 'Freddie' Ayer achieve fame?*

a8 Who was Geraldo?

b8 *And for playing which instrument did Semprini become famous?*

a9 Which political party held its first rally in 1923, led by an Austrian corporal and decorator?

b9 *And which world leader resigned in 1923, after a serious stroke?*

a10 Who was Tsar of Russia in the early years of the century?

b10 *Of which country was David Lange (say: longi) prime minister?*

a11 Which churchman became the first leader of independent Cyprus in 1960?

b11 *Who became the first president of the Turkish Republic in 1923?*

a12 In which year did Britain first have a Labour prime minister?

b12 *In which year were Australian Aborigines given the vote: 1947, 1973, or 1981?*

No. 93 Answers

a1   Cricket
b1   W. G. Grace, the cricketer
a2   Northern Ireland
b2   Protestant, the Protestant Orange Order
a3   Ku Klux Klan
b3   President Nixon (during the Watergate affair)
a4   Buster Keaton
b4   David Bowie
a5   Sir Arthur Sullivan
b5   George Gershwin
a6   Jack Higgins
b6   Claudius (I, Claudius; Claudius the God)
a7   Composer
b7   Philosopher (member of television's Brains Trust)
a8   Bandleader (became famous in London in the thirties)
b8   Piano
a9   National Socialist (Nazi)
b9   (Vladimir) Lenin
a10   Nicholas II
b10   New Zealand
a11   Archbishop Makarios
b11   (Mustafa) Kemal Atatürk
a12   1924
b12   1973

Tie-breaker

Q Which European city was the last to be liberated in the Second World War?

A Prague

No. 94

a1   In the Second World War, what was the BEF?

b1   *And for what did the initials ARP stand?*

a2   What was Babe Ruth's sport?

b2   *And what was Wally Hammond's sport?*

a3   Which singer recorded the album 'Born in the USA'?

b3   *Which female vocalist became famous as lead singer of the group, The Supremes?*

a4   As what did Lord Northcliffe achieve fame?

b4   *Who was the philanthropist who died in 1922, having founded a village for his workers called Bournville?*

a5   Where do the Masai people live?

b5   *And in which country do Sherpas live?*

a6   Which cat and mouse were invented in 1939 by Fred Quimby, William Hanna and Joseph Barbera?

b6   *Which cartoon character derived his strength from spinach?*

a7   In which country is the city of Isfahan?

b7   *In which capital city is there a royal enclave known as the 'Forbidden City'?*

a8   Antonio Salazar was dictator of which European country?

b8   *Which statesman was buried in the village of Colombey-les-Deux-Eglises in November 1970?*

a9   In which year did Britain introduce decimal currency?

b9   *And when that happened, what was the new value of the old 'florin' coin?*

a10   What was the name (or nickname) of the American woman who became a successful painter at the age of 78?

b10   *Which artist can be said to have invented Cubism?*

a11   Who wrote the novels *Howards End* and *A Room With a View*?

b11   *Who wrote the novel* The Great Gatsby?

a12   Which radio family lived in Parkwood Hill?

b12   *In which long-running comedy radio programme did Richard Murdoch star with Kenneth Horne?*

No. 94 Answers

a1	British Expeditionary Force
b1	*Air-raid precautions*
a2	Baseball
b2	*Cricket*
a3	Bruce Springsteen
b3	*Diana Ross*
a4	Newspaper owner (died 1922, founded the *Daily Mail* in 1896)
b4	*(George) Cadbury*
a5	East Africa (highlands of Kenya and Tanzania)
b5	*Nepal*
a6	Tom and Jerry
b6	*Popeye*
a7	Iran
b7	*Beijing (Peking), in China*
a8	Portugal
b8	*(Charles) de Gaulle*
a9	1971
b9	*10p*
a10	Grandma Moses (Anna Mary Robertson Moses)
b10	*Picasso (also Braque)*
a11	E. M. Forster
b11	*F. Scott Fitzgerald*
a12	The Dales (*Mrs Dale's Diary*)
b12	*Much-Binding-in-the-Marsh*

Tie-breaker

Q What were 'The Four Freedoms', the democratic ideals proposed jointly by Franklin D. Roosevelt and Winston Churchill in 1941?

A *Freedom of Expression, Freedom of Worship, Freedom from Fear, Freedom from Want*

No. 95

a1   Which boy's comic, launched in 1950, featured Dan Dare?

b1   And, pre-war, which comic featured Corky the Cat?

a2   In which sport was Donald Budge a champion?

b2   Which was Sam Snead's sport?

a3   For which instrument was Harry James renowned?

b3   And Fats Waller?

a4   Julius, Arthur and Leonard were the real names of which film star brothers?

b4   What was the screen name of the actress V. M. Leigh Holman?

a5   Who attempted (in 1923) to start a revolution in a beer hall or cellar?

b5   Which capital city did the Russians capture on 13th April, 1945?

a6   Which famous bomber of the Second World War was made by Boeing?

b6   Besides the Fortress, what was America's other main bomber in the same war?

a7   Which American president was assassinated in 1901?

b7   Which American politician was assassinated in 1968?

a8   Before the Second World War, as what did the Swiss known as 'Grock' become famous?

b8   Which world-famous clown first appeared in Britain in Bertram Mills Circus in 1930?

a9   In which country is the city of Timbuktu?

b9   Which is the highest capital city in the world?

a10   Which comedian had the nickname 'The Prime Minister of Mirth'?

b10   What was the nickname of the American comedian, Jimmy Durante?

a11   What was the pen-name of the creator of the fictional hero, Bulldog Drummond?

b11   Pelham Grenville were the first names of which novelist?

a12   What name was given to German air raids on historic or beautiful towns in the Second World War?

b12   In the Second World War, on which island did the British intern foreign nationals and those whose loyalty was suspect?

No. 95 Answers

a1	*The Eagle*
b1	*The Dandy*
a2	Lawn tennis
b2	*Golf*
a3	Trumpet
b3	*Piano*
a4	(Groucho, Harpo and Chico) Marx
b4	*Vivien Leigh*
a5	Adolf Hitler (and Erich van Ludendorff)
b5	*Vienna*
a6	Flying Fortress
b6	*Liberator*
a7	William McKinley
b7	*Bobby (Robert) Kennedy*
a8	Circus clown
b8	*Coco*
a9	Mali
b9	*La Paz (Bolivia)*
a10	George Robey
b10	*Schnozzle*
a11	Sapper
b11	*P. G. Wodehouse*
a12	Baedeker Raids
b12	*Isle of Man*

Tie-breaker

Q Who is this actress?: 'I first acted in 1888 and was once described as "a glorious, impossible woman". It was I who said, "It doesn't matter what you do in the bedroom as long as you don't do it in the streets and frighten the horses." My great friend was Bernard Shaw.'

A *Mrs Patrick Campbell (1865–1940)*

No. 96

a1   In which sport did Bobby Moore captain England?

b1   *What was the nickname of the heavyweight boxer, Joe Louis?*

a2   Which comedian had as his catch phrase, 'Can you hear me, mother?'?

b2   *Which diminutive comedian had as his catch phrases 'I thank you' (pronounced 'Ay theng yow') and 'Before your very eyes'?*

a3   What was the name of Superman's girlfriend?

b3   *In the Walt Disney cartoons, who was Pluto?*

a4   'Tiger Ray' was the signature tune of which popular bandleader?

b4   *And whose signature tune was 'Say it with Music'?*

a5   In which country is the 'lost city' of the Incas, rediscovered in 1911?

b5   *In which country is the royal burial ground, the Valley of the Kings?*

a6   As what did the American Charles Manson become notorious?

b6   *Ethel Le Nève was mistress and accomplice to which famous murderer?*

a7   As what did Sir Frederick Ashton achieve fame?

b7   *Which scout became famous for organizing the scouting 'Gang Shows'?*

a8   Next to which city is Pearl Harbor naval base?

b8   *In the Second World War, which European capital did American troops liberate two days before D-Day?*

a9   Which organization once had its headquarters at London's Savoy Hill?

b9   *From where in London did the BBC transmit its first regular television programmes?*

a10   In the thirties, what was the 'China Clipper'?

b10   *And what was the 'Tiger Moth'?*

a11   Which American radio play caused panic in the streets in 1938?

b11   *Which cult television series invented a ministry for silly walks and featured a dead parrot?*

a12   Who wrote the science-fiction anti-war novel Slaughterhouse Five?

b12   *Who wrote the book The Female Eunuch?*

No. 96 Answers

a1	Soccer
b1	*The Brown Bomber*
a2	Sandy Powell
b2	*Arthur Askey*
a3	Lois Lane
b3	*The dog*
a4	Harry Roy
b4	*Jack Payne*
a5	Peru
b5	*Egypt*
a6	Murderer (of Sharon Tate and others)
b6	*Dr Crippen*
a7	Choreographer (accept: ballet dancer)
b7	*Ralph Reader*
a8	Honolulu
b8	*Rome*
a9	BBC
b9	*Alexandra Palace*
a10	A giant flying-boat
b10	*Bi-plane; training aircraft*
a11	*War of the Worlds* (produced by Orson Welles)
b11	Monty Python's Flying Circus
a12	Kurt Vonnegut
b12	*Germaine Greer*

Tie-breaker

Q In 1925, what was painted on British roads for the first time, in an attempt to reduce accidents?

A *White lines*

No. 97

a1   Which politician was born on 13th October 1925 in Grantham?

b1   *Which politician has been credited with advising the unemployed: 'On yer bike'?*

a2   What name was given to the hosts and entertainers at Butlins' Holiday Camps?

b2   *Which English seaside resort has the longest pier?*

a3   Which city is the Big Apple?

b3   *Which city is a holy city for three world religions?*

a4   In which daily paper did the picture strip 'Jane' appear?

b4   *In which comic did Lord Snooty first appear?*

a5   Which comedian reminisced about 'the day war broke out'?

b5   *By what name were Nervo and Knox, Naughton and Gold, and Flanagan and Allen known when they appeared together on stage?*

a6   In the post-Second World War years, what was Godfrey Evans' great contribution to England's cricket?

b6   *The cricketer Denis Compton became famous for appearing in advertisements – for what?*

a7   Who wrote the hit of the thirties, 'Stardust'?

b7   *Which American musician was known as the 'King of Swing'?*

a8   Michael Collins was a politician and leader of which country?

b8   *Why did Bernadette Devlin become well known in 1969?*

a9   Which French minister of war became famous for his 'line' of fortifications along the French-German frontier?

b9   *What name was given to the large balloons flown over towns and harbours in war-time to discourage enemy aircraft?*

a10   During the Second World War, why were Alvar Lidell, Frank Phillips and John Snagge household names?

b10   *In which radio series did we hear the catch phrases 'Don't forget the diver' and 'I don't mind if I do'?*

a11   As what did Josephine Baker win fame in the twenties?

b11   *Which famous paperback book publishing company was started by Sir Allen Lane?*

a12   In 1925, Eisenstein directed a film about which battleship?

b12   *In the world of films, for what do the initials MGM stand?*

No. 97 Answers

a1	Margaret Thatcher
b1	*Norman Tebbit*
a2	Redcoats
b2	*Southend-on-Sea*
a3	New York
b3	*Jerusalem (Judaism, Christianity, Islam)*
a4	*Daily Mirror*
b4	The Beano
a5	Robb Wilton
b5	*The Crazy Gang*
a6	As wicket-keeper
b6	*Brylcream*
a7	Hoagy Carmichael
b7	*Benny Goodman*
a8	Ireland (Irish Free State)
b8	*Ulster MP, sentenced for incitement to riot*
a9	Maginot (say: maj-in-oh)
b9	*Barrage balloons*
a10	They were radio newsreaders
b10	ITMA *(Tommy Handley's* It's That Man Again*)*
a11	As a dancer (in French nightclubs)
b11	*Penguin Books*
a12	Potemkin (*The Battleship Potemkin*)
b12	*Metro-Goldwyn-Mayer*

Tie-breaker

Q Who first said, 'We are all the president's men'?
A *Dr Henry Kissinger (justifying the US invasion of Cambodia)*

No. 98

a1　On television, whose catch phrase became 'Didn't he do well?'?

b1　Which entertainer said, 'I've arrived and to prove it, I'm here'?

a2　If you were on the 'Bluebell', how would you be travelling?

b2　What is the name of the transcontinental railway across Russia?

a3　Which series of children's cartoon characters was created by Roger Hargreaves?

b3　Who wrote about a bear called Winnie-the-Pooh?

a4　What was the name of the first British aircraft carrier?

b4　Which British liner made her maiden transatlantic voyage in 1936?

a5　By which river do the Abu Simbel temples stand?

b5　In which country is the Kruger National Park?

a6　What was the surname of the entertainer 'Two-Ton Tessie'?

b6　Which radio and television comedian was known for his schoolmasterly catch phrase, 'Wake up at the back, there!'?

a7　Which international prizes were first awarded in Norway and Sweden in 1901?

b7　The flag or sign of the International Red Cross is basically a reversal of which country's flag?

a8　What was Oh! Calcutta!?

b8　Which 'opera' includes the song 'Mack the Knife'?

a9　In the Second World War, what was 'pool'?

b9　What nickname was generally given to flying bombs in the Second World War?

a10　Which poet was rude enough to write, 'Come friendly bombs and fall on Slough'?

b10　Which modern British prime minister's wife published a volume of her poems?

a11　What was the name of the Communist family which savagely ruled Romania until 1989?

b11　In which country was Adolf Eichmann executed in 1962?

a12　Which Russian soccer team made a famous tour of Britain immediately after the Second World War?

b12　At which Scottish football ground did 66 people die when a barrier collapsed in 1971?

No. 98 Answers

a1 Bruce Forsyth
b1 *Max Bygraves*
a2 By (steam) train; it's a preserved railway line
b2 *Trans-Siberian Railway*
a3 Mr Men
b3 *A. A. Milne*
a4 'Ark Royal'
b4 *'The Queen Mary'*
a5 Nile (Moved to avoid being flooded during the building of the Aswan Dam)
b5 *South Africa*
a6 O'Shea
b6 *Jimmy Edwards*
a7 Nobel Prizes
b7 *Switzerland's*
a8 Theatrical sex revue (1970)
b8 *The Threepenny Opera*
a9 Unbranded petrol
b9 *Doodle bugs (or buzz bombs)*
a10 (Sir John) Betjeman
b10 *Mary Wilson*
a11 Ceauşescu (say: chow-cheskew)
b11 *Israel*
a12 Moscow Dynamo
b12 *Ibrox Park (Glasgow Rangers)*

Tie-breaker

Q Which play by Peter Shaffer reconstructs the last ten years of the life of Mozart?

A Amadeus

No. 99

a1 What was the 'Tirpitz'?

b1 *Who or what was 'Arkle'?*

a2 In 1970, which golfer became the first Briton for 50 years to win the US Open?

b2 *In 1986, Mike Tyson won which sporting title?*

a3 Which 'layer' around the Earth prevents dangerous ultraviolet radiation from harming us?

b3 *In space exploration, what is linked with the name 'Hubble'?*

a4 Which ruler's real surname was Schickelgruber?

b4 *Where in Germany was the annual rally of the Nazi party held?*

a5 The 1923 Cup Final was the first major event staged in which sporting stadium?

b5 *Of which football club did Matt Busby become manager in 1945?*

a6 Which major West European power left NATO in 1966?

b6 *Where are the headquarters of the Council of Europe?*

a7 'Buddy, Can You Spare a Dime?' was a popular song during the American depression. Which singer made it a hit?

b7 *T. H. White's story of King Arthur, The Once and Future King, became a musical – under what title?*

a8 In British education, what is 'LMS'?

b8 *And in the world of transport, what was 'LMS'?*

a9 In which country is the city, Da Nang?

b9 *What is the capital city of Slovakia?*

a10 Which Nazi minister for propaganda was known as 'the Mouth'?

b10 *Who was head of the Gestapo and the SS, (he committed suicide in 1945)?*

a11 Just three aircraft were available to defend Malta in 1940. What were their names?

b11 *Which British pilot (who lost both legs before the war) became an ace pilot during the Second World War?*

a12 Who wrote A la Recherche du Temps Perdu?

b12 *Which Polish-born author, who wrote in English, told many stories about the sea and the Far East?*

No. 99 Answers

a1 German battleship
b1 *Race-horse*
a2 Tony Jacklin
b2 *(WBC) World heavyweight champion*
a3 Ozone layer
b3 *The Hubble Space Telescope (launched 1990)*
a4 Adolf Hitler
b4 *Nuremberg*
a5 Wembley
b5 *Manchester United*
a6 France
b6 *Strasbourg (in France)*
a7 Bing Crosby
b7 *Camelot*
a8 Local management of schools
b8 *London, Midland and Scottish Railway*
a9 South Vietnam
b9 *Bratislava*
a10 Goebbels
b10 *(Heinrich) Himmler*
a11 'Faith', 'Hope' and 'Charity'
b11 *Douglas Bader*
a12 (Marcel) Proust
b12 *Joseph Conrad*

Tie-breaker

Q Which country had an internal security force known as STASI?
A *East Germany (German Democratic Republic)*

No. 100

a1   Where, in the United States, is Disney World?

b1   *And in which state in the USA is Disneyland?*

a2   Which part of the body is affected by dermatitis?

b2   *Which type of flu killed almost 3,000 people in Britain in one week in 1970?*

a3   What, in the Second World War, were Weights and Capstan?

b3   *What were Grants, Shermans and Cromwells?*

a4   Of which country is Orange Free State a part?

b4   *Of what origin were the large group of people expelled from Uganda in 1972?*

a5   Who or what are gauchos?

b5   *And what is a gaudy?*

a6   Which Australian batsman made a sensational debut in England in 1930?

b6   *Who was Britain's champion racing jockey in the thirties (and after the Second World War)?*

a7   'Coco' was the nickname of which famous French fashion queen?

b7   *Besides being a dancer, who or what was Nijinsky?*

a8   What giant carving has been cut into the Black Hills of Dakota?

b8   *The merchant ship called 'The Savannah of America' was famous for its means of propulsion. Why?*

a9   From the twenties onwards, which country embarked on a series of Five-Year Plans?

b9   *In 1948 and 1949, which city was saved by an 'airlift'?*

a10   'Are You Experienced?' and 'Electric Ladyland' were albums issued by which pop guitarist and singer?

b10   *Which rock guitarist played with the Yardbirds and Cream, and had his own Rainbow Concert?*

a11   Which country was formed in 1963 by the merging of Malaya, Singapore, Sabah and Sarawak?

b11   *For what was Monte Bello island used in October 1952?*

a12   Which two countries fought at the Battle of Tsushima in 1905?

b12   *In 1935, where on the continent were British troops sent to keep the peace?*

No. 100 Answers

a1 Florida
b1 *California*
a2 The skin
b2 *Hong Kong flu (Hong Kong A2 virus)*
a3 Brands of cigarettes
b3 *Tanks*
a4 South Africa
b4 *Asian ('Ugandan Asians')*
a5 South American cowboys
b5 *College or university reunion, entertainment*
a6 Don Bradman
b6 *Gordon Richards*
a7 (Gabrielle) Chanel (say: sha-nell)
b7 *A champion racing horse*
a8 Statues of four American presidents (Washington, Jefferson, (Theodore) Roosevelt and Lincoln)
b8 *First nuclear-powered merchant ship*
a9 Soviet Union (USSR)
b9 *Berlin*
a10 Jimi Hendrix
b10 *Eric Clapton*
a11 Malaysia
b11 *The testing of Britain's first atomic bomb*
a12 Japan and Russia
b12 *The Saar*

Tie-breaker

Q *Towards a New Architecture* was written by which Swiss-French architect in 1923?

A *Le Corbusier (Charles-Edouard Jeanneret)*

No. 101: More Modern Lingo

What is meant by the following words and phrases, which have all entered the language in recent years?

a1 Advertorial
b1 *Affinity card*
a2 Callanetics (say: cal-a-ne-ticks)
b2 *The chattering classes*
a3 Def
b3 *A Denver boot*
a4 'E' or Ecstasy
b4 *A graphic novel*
a5 'Fatwa' or 'Fatwah'
b5 *Intifada*
a6 A ligger
b6 *Mondo*
a7 A Sloane Ranger
b7 *Quorn (as you might find it in a supermarket)*
a8 'Slo-mo' (as used in the media and the world of films)
b8 *A sound bite*
a9 A spin doctor (as used in the world of politics)
b9 *Sampling (as practised in the world of music)*
a10 A white knight (as used in the financial world)
b10 *Black Monday (again, as in the financial world)*
a11 Paintball
b11 *A rah-rah skirt*
a12 The Gaia theory
b12 *Jojoba (say: ho-ho-ba)*

No. 101 Answers

a1 A newspaper advertisement written to look like an article
b1 *A credit card issued to a particular group (e.g. supporters of a charity)*
a2 A physical exercise programme
b2 *Members of the educated middle classes who read the 'quality' newspapers and who hold opinions about topical matters*
a3 'Cool', excellent, great (slang)
b3 *A wheel clamp*
a4 A (hallucinogenic) drug
b4 *A book-length story in comic strip format*
a5 A ruling given by an Islamic leader; a decree
b5 *An Arab uprising*
a6 A 'sponger' or freeloader; a party-crasher
b6 *'Utterly', extremely (slang)*
a7 An upper-class, very conventional young person (especially one who lives in a fashionable area of London – e.g. Chelsea)
b7 *Vegetable protein, vegetarian meat substitute*
a8 Slow motion
b8 *A short extract from a recorded speech or interview*
a9 A political spokesman employed to make news sound favourable
b9 *Re-using short pieces of music in a new composition*
a10 A company that rescues one facing a hostile takeover bid
b10 *The day of the stock market crash (19th October, 1987)*
a11 A type of 'war-game' in which bright paint is fired at the 'enemy'
b11 *Type of skirt worn by American cheerleaders*
a12 Theory that the Earth adapts itself in order to survive
b12 *A desert shrub; oil (from that shrub) used in cosmetics*

Tie-breaker

Q On which Far Eastern island are there amusement parks called the Great World, the Gay World and the New World?
A Singapore

No. 102

a1 What kind of food are Brie (say: bree) and cottage?

b1 *Gorgonzola is a town in which country?*

a2 Who crashed a car at Chappaquiddick in 1969?

b2 *And what was the name of his passenger, who drowned?*

a3 In which sport is the Calcutta Cup a trophy?

b3 *And which two countries compete for the Calcutta Cup?*

a4 Which building, near Agra, is said to look its best in moonlight?

b4 *In 1939, which country changed its name to Thailand?*

a5 Which disease is sometimes called 'MS'?

b5 *What is caries?*

a6 Which spaceship carried the first men to walk on the Moon?

b6 *In space, what is thought to cause a 'black hole'?*

a7 In the Second World War, what did 'ack-ack' mean?

b7 *During the Second World War, what was 'Bully Beef'?*

a8 Of which country was Alexander Dubcek (say: dub-check) a ruler?

b8 *Of which country was John G. Diefenbaker prime minister from 1957 to 1963?*

a9 What was the native country of Samuel Beckett (author of *Waiting for Godot*)?

b9 *Who wrote the farces* Rookery Nook, The Cuckoo in the Nest *and* Thark?

a10 On radio what is 'BFBS'?

b10 *Which radio station broadcast for many years on 208 metres?*

a11 What nationality was the composer Béla Bartók?

b11 *What nationality was the composer Arnold Bax?*

a12 In which year was the British electricity supply system privatised?

b12 *In which year did the nationalized British Railways come into being?*

No. 102 Answers

a1   Cheese
b1   *Italy (near Milan)*
a2   Senator Edward Kennedy
b2   *Mary Jo Kopechne*
a3   Rugby Union
b3   *England and Scotland*
a4   Taj Mahal
b4   *Siam*
a5   Multiple sclerosis (say: skluh-roh-sis)
b5   *Tooth decay*
a6   Apollo 11
b6   *The explosion of a large star*
a7   Anti-aircraft
b7   *Corned beef*
a8   Czechoslovakia
b8   *Canada*
a9   Ireland
b9   *Ben Travers*
a10   British Forces Broadcasting Service
b10   *Radio Luxembourg*
a11   Hungarian
b11   *British*
a12   1990
b12   *1948*

Tie-breaker

Q *The Big Sleep, Farewell My Lovely and The High Window are novels by which American crime writer?*
A *Raymond Chandler*

No. 103

a1 In the film *Kind Hearts and Coronets*, who played eight different roles?

b1 *Who were the two stars of the 1946 film* Brief Encounter?

a2 On which sport does Peter Bromley commentate?

b2 *With which sport has the commentator Brian Johnston especially been associated?*

a3 What is the purpose of a hospice?

b3 *What is a hologram?*

a4 What was the surname of Ronald and Reginald, gangland twins in east London, jailed in 1969?

b4 *Which civil rights leader did James Earl Ray shoot dead in 1968?*

a5 What is a herbivore?

b5 *Which kind of tree was ravaged by disease in the seventies?*

a6 Which sport (in Britain) do the Barbarians play?

b6 *In which sport might you compete for the Admiral's Cup?*

a7 In the Second World War, what was the WAAF?

b7 *Also in the Second World War, what was ENSA?*

a8 Who wrote the book *My Family and Other Animals*?

b8 *Who wrote books called* The Human Zoo *and* The Naked Ape?

a9 What is measured in ampères?

b9 *What is measured in watts?*

a10 Which South African doctor pioneered human heart transplant surgery?

b10 *Research by Enrico Fermi led to the building of the first nuclear . . . what?*

a11 Who became chancellor of West Germany in 1969?

b11 *Sir Joshua Hassan was chief minister of which British colony?*

a12 As what did Arnold Schoenberg become famous?

b12 *Walter Sickert died in 1942. What was his trade or profession?*

No. 103 Answers

a1	Alec Guinness
b1	*Celia Johnson, Trevor Howard*
a2	Racing
b2	*Cricket*
a3	To care for the dying, the terminally ill
b3	*A picture which appears to have depth; a 3-D picture*
a4	Kray
b4	*Martin Luther King*
a5	An animal that feeds only on plants
b5	*Elm (Dutch elm tree disease)*
a6	Rugby Union
b6	*Yachting*
a7	Women's Auxiliary Air Force
b7	*Entertainments National Service Association (entertainment for the troops)*
a8	Gerald Durrell
b8	*Dr Desmond Morris*
a9	Electric current
b9	*Electrical power*
a10	Dr Christiaan Barnard
b10	*Reactor*
a11	Willi Brandt
b11	*Gibraltar*
a12	Composer (of 'modern' music)
b12	*Artist*

Tie-breaker

Q The films *Brighton Rock*, *Fame is the Spur* and *Lucky Jim* were made by which pair of brothers?

A (John and Roy) Boulting

No. 104

a1 On television, who originally presented *Take Your Pick*?

b1 *And who presented* Double Your Money?

a2 Which is the most westerly point on the English mainland?

b2 *Which is the most important city in Scotland's Grampian region?*

a3 Which theatrical satire, devised by Joan Littlewood, attacked aspects of the First World War?

b3 *In which musical did the cast first face the audience nude (in 1968)?*

a4 In Second World War slang, what were 'angels'?

b4 *In Second World War RAF slang, what were 'cookies'?*

a5 For which soccer club did Jimmy Armfield play?

b5 *For which country did Danny Blanchflower play soccer?*

a6 What is particular about a 'geostationary' satellite?

b6 *What is the source of 'geothermal' energy?*

a7 Which British politician made a controversial speech in 1968 about 'rivers of blood'?

b7 *Which British prime minister tried to be reassuring about 'the pound in your pocket'?*

a8 What is the purpose of antibodies, medically speaking?

b8 *In the human body, what is a capillary?*

a9 Who composed a piece of music called 'On Hearing the First Cuckoo in Spring'?

b9 *Who composed a suite of music called 'The Planets'?*

a10 Which author created the character Horatio Hornblower?

b10 *Which novelist created the private eye Philip Marlowe?*

a11 Who directed the films *A Clockwork Orange* and *2001: A Space Odyssey*?

b11 *Which stage actor directed himself in the films* Henry V, Hamlet *and* Richard III?

a12 Which British painter created a huge tapestry for Coventry Cathedral and became famous for controversial portraits?

b12 *Which English test cricketer became a bishop in the Church of England?*

No. 104 Answers

a1 Michael Miles (Des O'Connor hosts the revised version of the show)

b1 *Hughie Green*

a2 Land's End

b2 *Aberdeen*

a3 *Oh, What a Lovely War!*

b3 Hair

a4 Friendly aircraft

b4 *Bombs*

a5 Blackpool

b5 *Northern Ireland*

a6 It stays in the same place above the Earth

b6 *The heat inside the Earth, found in rocks, geysers, etc.*

a7 Enoch Powell

b7 *Harold Wilson*

a8 To protect us from disease; to fight disease

b8 *A tiny blood vessel*

a9 Frederick Delius

b9 *(Gustav) Holst*

a10 C. S. Forester

b10 *Raymond Chandler*

a11 Stanley Kubrick

b11 *Laurence Olivier*

a12 Graham Sutherland

b12 *David Sheppard*

Tie-breaker

Q For which sport do you need a loft, a basket or transporter crate and a special type of clock?

A *Pigeon-racing*

No. 105

a1 American, Australian and Canadian are all codes of which sport?

b1 *Which sport can be indoor, lawn or crown?*

a2 In England, which two counties surround the Wash?

b2 *Which English city has road tunnels called Kingsway and Queensway?*

a3 By what name was the comedian Arthur Stanley Jefferson (who was born at Ulverston in England) internationally known?

b3 *Which newspaper tycoon drowned in 1991?*

a4 What is measured in ohms?

b4 *Of what is a hertz a measure?*

a5 Who was Che Guevara (say: chay gw-var-a)

b5 *Who became leader of the Palestine Liberation Organization in 1969?*

a6 Which county cricket team plays at home at Lords?

b6 *Which county cricket team plays at home at the Oval?*

a7 Which writer created William (of the 'Just William' stories)?

b7 *Which writer's stories were televised as Tales of the Unexpected?*

a8 In which film about two hustlers trying to live in New York did Dustin Hoffman star with Jon Voight?

b8 *In which film about a motor-bike ride across America did Dennis Hopper star with Peter Fonda?*

a9 What nationality was the composer Dmitri Shostakovich?

b9 *What nationality was the composer Jean (say: jan) Sibelius?*

a10 In which year was the treaty signed bringing into existence the Irish Free State (or Irish Republic)?

b10 *In which year did the Spanish Civil War begin?*

a11 Which long-running radio programme was regularly introduced by 'Uncle Mac'?

b11 *With which radio programme was Jack de Manio associated?*

a12 In the Second World War, what was the ATS?

b12 *During the Second World War, where did 'Bevin Boys' work?*

No. 105 Answers

a1 Football
b1 *Bowls*
a2 Lincolnshire, Norfolk
b2 *Liverpool (Merseyside)*
a3 Stan Laurel
b3 *Robert Maxwell*
a4 Electrical resistance
b4 *Wave frequency*
a5 Latin (or Central) American guerrilla leader or revolutionary
b5 *Yassir Arafat*
a6 Middlesex
b6 *Surrey*
a7 Richmal Crompton
b7 *Roald Dahl*
a8 *Midnight Cowboy*
b8 *Easy Rider*
a9 Russian
b9 *Finnish*
a10 1921
b10 *1936*
a11 *Children's Hour* (Derek McCulloch)
b11 *Today*
a12 Auxiliary Territorial Service
b12 *Down mines (instead of in the forces)*

Tie-breaker

Q Who is this composer?: 'One of my earliest hits was the First World War song, 'Keep the Home Fires Burning'. Since then, I became better known as the writer of romantic musicals. My career took off one glamorous night, and my final word was gay.'

A Ivor Novello

No. 106

a1   Can you name an African country which took part in the 1992 cricket World Cup?

b1   *Where is the 'All-England' Club?*

a2   Counting all its forms, which language is spoken by the most people?

b2   *Which two Chinese words symbolize male and female, day and night, sky and earth?*

a3   About which part of the world does the novelist Catherine Cookson write?

b3   *Daphne du Maurier wrote a novel about which Cornish inn?*

a4   In politics, what is (or was) the CP?

b4   *In a computer, what is the CPU?*

a5   Pasolini, Polanski and Visconti were or are all . . .what?

b5   *For which kind of film did the American director John Ford become especially famous?*

a6   Which event brought the United States into the Second World War?

b6   *Did bread rationing begin in Britain in 1940, 1942, or 1946?*

a7   What was the name of the toy animal with whom Annette Mills appeared on early children's television programmes?

b7   *Who were the three regular characters on television's The Flowerpot Men?*

a8   From what do we get ambergris?

b8   *Who or what was Alban Berg?*

a9   Is the element radon a metal, a gas or an alkali?

b9   *Is the element cadmium a gas, a metal or an alkali?*

a10   Why was Bikini Atoll in the news in 1946?

b10   *In the late sixties, what was Biba?*

a11   In which capital did Russian tanks crush a movement for freedom in 1968?

b11   *Which country seized control of Albania in 1939?*

a12   In which year this century was the most serious flooding of Britain's east coast?

b12   *In which year was the British coal industry nationalized?*

No. 106 Answers

a1   South Africa or Zimbabwe
b1   *Wimbledon, south-west London (tennis)*
a2   Chinese
b2   *Yin and yang*
a3   Tyneside; northeast England
b3   *Jamaica Inn*
a4   Communist Party
b4   *Central processing unit (the part that controls the circuits and holds the memory)*
a5   Film directors
b5   *Westerns (Stagecoach, The Man Who Shot Liberty Valance, etc)*
a6   Bombing of Pearl Harbor
b6   *1946*
a7   Muffin the Mule
b7   *Bill and Ben and Little Weed*
a8   The sperm-whale (it's used in perfumery)
b8   *(Austrian) composer*
a9   A gas
b9   *A metal*
a10   It was used for atom bomb tests
b10   *Department store or boutique for young women*
a11   Prague
b11   *Italy*
a12   1953
b12   *1947*

Tie-breaker

Q In which group did pop guitarist Eric Clapton play 'Five Long Years' and 'Louise'?
A *The Yardbirds*

No. 107

a1 When was 'Put out that light' a slogan?

b1 *What is a 'Black Box'?*

a2 In which political party has Barbara Castle been a key figure?

b2 *By what first name was the Labour politician Cripps always known?*

a3 For what does PAYE stand?

b3 *As a human group, what are WASPs?*

a4 In the television comedy series *Open All Hours*, who played Arkwright?

b4 *Who was the star of television's I Love Lucy?*

a5 What is measured by an ammeter?

b5 *What does a hygrometer measure?*

a6 In which sport has Jonah Barrington been a British champion?

b6 *What was Leslie Ames' sport?*

a7 Who wrote *The Murder of Roger Ackroyd*?

b7 *Which novelist wrote* Tender is the Night?

a8 In which year did Britain invade Suez?

b8 *In which year did British troops first go into action in Belfast in the present troubles?*

a9 In which country has Salvador Allende (say: ay-yen-deh) been a radical leader?

b9 *What did Edwin 'Buzz' Aldrin achieve on July 21, 1969?*

a10 Who directed the films *The Music Lovers, The Devils* and *Tommy*?

b10 Blazing Saddles, Young Frankenstein *and* Silent Movie *were all comedies directed by . . . whom?*

a11 Which basketball team or troupe has toured the world and has the signature tune 'Sweet Georgia Brown'?

b11 *In archery, what colour is the centre of the target?*

a12 What post has been held by John Masefield and Cecil Day Lewis?

b12 *What genetic structure was discovered by Francis Crick and James Watson?*

No. 107 Answers

a1   During a Black Out, in the Second World War
b1   Flight recorder in an aircraft, designed to survive any accident
a2   Labour
b2   Stafford (Sir Stafford Cripps)
a3   Pay As You Earn
b3   White Anglo-Saxon Protestants
a4   Ronnie Barker
b4   Lucille Ball
a5   The strength of an electrical current
b5   The amount of moisture in the air
a6   Squash
b6   Cricket (England wicket-keeper)
a7   Agatha Christie
b7   F. Scott Fitzgerald
a8   1956
b8   1969
a9   Chile
b9   He was the second man to walk on the Moon
a10   Ken Russell
b10   Mel Brooks
a11   Harlem Globetrotters
b11   Gold (accept: yellow)
a12   Poet Laureate
b12   DNA (the molecule that contains genetic information)

Tie-breaker

Q Which British sculptor became famous (or infamous) for his smooth stone figures, sometimes of human torsos, sometimes of shapes which included holes in them?

A *Henry Moore*

No. 108

a1 Who used Scuds?

b1 *In the Second World War, what was a Dornier?*

a2 Which county cricket team plays at home at Old Trafford?

b2 *Which county cricket team plays at home at Edgbaston?*

a3 What is the BMA?

b3 *What is the BSI?*

a4 Which singer had hits with 'Mary's Boy Child' and 'Island in the Sun'?

b4 *And which British singer had hits with 'Someone Else's Baby' and 'What Do You Want If You Don't Want Money'?*

a5 As what did Alexander Korda become famous?

b5 *As what did the American Aaron Copland become famous?*

a6 About which profession did Richard Gordon write a series of comic novels?

b6 *About which profession did Henry Cecil write comic novels?*

a7 In our cities, what is the major source of the poison, carbon monoxide?

b7 *In a car's exhaust system, what is the purpose of the baffle?*

a8 In which year did Sir Winston Churchill die: 1958, 1964, or 1965?

b8 *Was the death penalty finally abolished in Britain in 1947, 1963, or 1969?*

a9 On television, for what was Eileen Fowler once famous?

b9 *Who was the first presenter in Britain of the television series* This Is Your Life?

a10 What is the biomass (say: bi-o-mass)?

b10 *What eventually happens to biodegradable matter?*

a11 Who wrote the novel *A Kind of Loving*?

b11 *Who wrote the science-fiction novel* Fahrenheit 451?

a12 What is the currency of South Africa?

b12 *What is the currency of Mexico?*

No. 108 Answers

a1 Iraq (missiles in the Gulf War)
b1 German aircraft
a2 Lancashire (at Manchester)
b2 Warwickshire (Birmingham)
a3 British Medical Association
b3 British Standards Institution
a4 Harry Belafonte
b4 Adam Faith
a5 Film producer and director
b5 Composer
a6 Doctors; medical (*Doctor in the House*, etc.)
b6 The law; barristers (Brother-in-Law, etc.)
a7 Car exhausts
b7 To reduce noise
a8 1965
b8 1969
a9 Keep-fit programmes
b9 Eamonn Andrews
a10 The total amount of plant and animal life on Earth
b10 It rots; is broken down by bacteria
a11 Stan Barstow
b11 Ray Bradbury
a12 Rand
b12 Peso

Tie-breaker

Q In which sport do blue and black play against red and yellow?
A Croquet (*blue and black balls always play against the red and yellow balls*)

No. 109

a1 What is the currency of Japan?

b1 What is the currency of Italy?

a2 Which country built the ill-fated airship, the R101?

b2 What kind of aircraft is a Tornado?

a3 Which popular pianist always had as his 'trademark' a candelabra on his piano?

b3 And which clean-cut American singer of the fifties had as his trademark his white 'bucks' (or shoes)?

a4 Which country was the home of 'Tito-ism'?

b4 Which country has been divided by the 38th Parallel?

a5 What is or was a Poseidon C-3?

b5 Of what is 'hydragas' a type?

a6 What is aerodynamics?

b6 What is an aileron?

a7 What is cartography?

b7 In business, what is a cartel?

a8 Which Russian composed a 'Sabre Dance' and a ballet called Spartacus?

b8 Who composed the 'Liberty Bell' and 'Washington Post' marches?

a9 In which European mainland country is cricket regularly played?

b9 In or near which capital city does the soccer team Anderlecht play?

a10 What is your profession if you have the letters ARIBA after your name?

b10 And which musical instrument do you play if you can use the letters ARCO after your name?

a11 Which woman crime writer created the character Mr Ripley?

b11 Which author created the lawyer Perry Mason?

a12 Athol Fugard is a famous South African. What is his profession?

b12 What has been the profession of the Italian, Federico Fellini?

No. 109 Answers

a1 Yen
b1 *Lira*
a2 Britain
b2 *(Jet) fighter*
a3 Liberace
b3 *Pat Boone*
a4 Yugoslavia
b4 *Korea*
a5 Submarine-launched missile
b5 *Car suspension system*
a6 The study of the effect of moving gases; the forces that act on objects moving in the air
b6 *Movable flap on an aircraft wing (which controls the movements of the aircraft)*
a7 The making of maps or charts
b7 *Union of manufacturers (etc.) to control production, prices, etc.*
a8 (Aram) Khachaturian
b8 *(John Philip) Sousa*
a9 Netherlands (accept also Denmark)
b9 *Brussels*
a10 Architect (Associate of the Royal Institute of British Architects)
b10 *Organ (Associate of the Royal College of Organists)*
a11 Patricia Highsmith
b11 *Erle Stanley Gardner*
a12 Playwright
b12 *Film director*

Tie-breaker

Q How did the first man in space, Yuri Gagarin, die?
A *He was killed in a plane crash in 1968 (a Mig fighter he was piloting crashed into the ground)*

No. 110

a1   What is a derrick?

b1   What is Prestel?

a2   For what is fibreglass wool used?

b2   What is fibrositis?

a3   Which company developed the Xerox (say: zir-rox) copier?

b3   Which company developed the Walkman?

a4   What kind of books were written by Zane Grey?

b4   Which character is the most famous creation of the novelist Edgar Rice Burroughs?

a5   What nickname did 617 Squadron acquire after causing widespread flooding in the Ruhr Valley?

b5   What was the nickname of the 7th Armoured Division, which saw action in North Africa?

a6   Which county cricket team plays at home at Trent Bridge?

b6   Which county cricket team plays at home on the St Lawrence ground?

a7   Which disease was first noted when 34 people died at a convention of the American Legion in 1976?

b7   For what has Papworth in Cambridgeshire become famous?

a8   Who originally sang about Mr Wu cleaning windows?

b8   Who was famous for singing 'Wish Me Luck', 'I Took My Harp to a Party' and 'Walter, Walter'?

a9   What is an AGR?

b9   What is the concern of the organization ASH?

a10   As what did Fred Hoyle achieve fame?

b10   What was the trade or profession of the German, Rainer Werner Fassbinder?

a11   In which country is the currency the zloty (say: zhwo-tee)?

b11   And in which country is the currency the rupee?

a12   On what day of the week are Mardi Gras (say: mar-dee grah) carnivals properly held?

b12   What day of the week is Ascension Day?

No. 110 Answers

a1 Framework of girders over an oilwell that supports the drilling machinery; a crane

b1 Information system accessed by phone and a television set

a2 Insulation of buildings; to conserve heat

b2 Inflammation of the muscles; rheumatic disorder

a3 Rank

b3 Sony

a4 Westerns

b4 Tarzan

a5 Dam-busters

b5 Desert Rats

a6 Nottinghamshire

b6 Kent (at Canterbury)

a7 Legionnaires' disease

b7 It's a hospital (heart transplant surgery)

a8 George Formby

b8 Gracie Fields

a9 Advanced Gas-cooled Reactor

b9 It is against the ill-effects of smoking (Action on Smoking and Health)

a10 Astronomer and/or science fiction writer

b10 Film director (and actor)

a11 Poland

b11 India (and Pakistan, Sri Lanka)

a12 Tuesday (Shrove Tuesday; in French Mardi = Tuesday)

b12 Thursday

Tie-breaker

Q Which two American universities row a boat race on the Thames River in Connecticut?

A Harvard and Yale

No. 111: A la Carte

Recent years have brought foreign restaurants to Britain, and many more people 'eat out' than used to. But how much do you really know about the terms you see on the menu and in cookery books? What is the meaning of the following?

a1	Aspic
b1	*Au Gratin*
a2	Bisque
b2	*Blanch*
a3	Borsch
b3	*Bouillabaisse*
a4	Bouquet Garni
b4	*Canapé*
a5	Caviare
b5	*Chowder*
a6	Compote
b6	*Crêpe Suzette*
a7	Croûtons
b7	*Cutlets*
a8	Devilled
b8	*En Brochette*
a9	Filet Mignon
b9	*Fondue*
a10	Fricassée
b10	*Hollandaise*
a11	Lyonnaise
b11	*Marinade*
a12	Mignon
b12	*Petits Fours*

No. 111 Answers

a1 Jelly made with either meat, fish or vegetable stock

b1 *Food cooked and covered with breadcrumbs*

a2 A cream soup prepared from game, fish or vegetables

b2 *Plunging into boiling water for a brief time only*

a3 A soup from Russia which includes beetroot, vegetables and beef

b3 *A fish soup*

a4 Mixed herbs tied in muslin and used to season foods

b4 *A piece of toast which is topped with any savoury*

a5 The roe (eggs) of the sturgeon

b5 *A thick soup made from vegetables or fish cooked in milk*

a6 Fruit cooked slowly in a syrup, often served in a stemmed glass dish

b6 *A thin pancake, often cooked in wine or spirits*

a7 Small squares of toast

b7 *Meat cut from the ribs or legs of beef, lamb, veal or pork*

a8 Cooked with sauce or hot seasoning

b8 *Food which is cooked on a skewer*

a9 A small strip of meat – usually beef

b9 *A dish made from breadcrumbs, cheese, eggs and milk*

a10 Braised or sometimes stewed, as with chicken, etc.

b10 *A sauce, served hot, made from the yolks of eggs and butter*

a11 Food seasoned with parsley, onions, etc.

b11 *A mixture of vinegar, wine, spices, in which meat or fish is left to soak to gain extra flavour*

a12 A tender cut of beef, without any bone

b12 *Small iced cakes cut into fancy shapes*

Tie-breaker

Q In 1951 which novelist and historian edited the first edition of *The Good Food Guide?*

A Raymond Postgate

No. 112

a1   Between which two cities did the Golden Arrow train run?

b1   *Which luxury train did Agatha Christie use as a setting for a crime?*

a2   What was an 'Instamatic'?

b2   *What are 'Craven A'?*

a3   In which British city is Sauchiehall (say: sock-i-hall) Street?

b3   *And in which city has streets called Dale Street, Paradise Street and Scotland Road?*

a4   Which American pop singer starred in the television series *The Partridge Family*?

b4   *Who had pop hits with 'Puppy Love' and 'Too Young'?*

a5   In which country would you be if you holidayed in the Dordogne (say: door-doyne)?

b5   *And in which country is the Algarve?*

a6   What product or technique was invented by Clarence Birdseye in 1930?

b6   *What gadget was first known as the 'Drunkometer'?*

a7   What composer is honoured at the Bayreuth (say: by-royt) Festival each summer?

b7   *Which saint is honoured in Lourdes in France each February?*

a8   Which novelist wrote the blockbusters *Hotel* and *Airport*?

b8   *What was the name of the novel about a public school master, written by James Hilton?*

a9   What was the trade or profession of John Huston?

b9   *Which French film actor and director created the character Monsieur Hulot (say: huw-lo)?*

a10   Which western was based on the Japanese film *Seven Samurai*?

b10   *In which film did John Wayne play a one-eyed Marshal?*

a11   By what abbreviation is trinitrotoluene known?

b11   *And by what name are the Allied Powers in Europe's supreme headquarters known?*

a12   In which country do cricket teams compete for the Sheffield Shield?

b12   *Which country was re-admitted to international cricket in 1991?*

No. 112 Answers

a1 London and Paris
b1 *The Orient Express*
a2 A small camera (which used small flash bulbs)
b2 *A type of cigarette*
a3 Glasgow
b3 *Liverpool*
a4 David Cassidy
b4 *Donny Osmond*
a5 France
b5 *Portugal*
a6 Frozen food
b6 *Breathalyser*
a7 (Richard) Wagner
b7 *St Bernadette*
a8 Arthur Hailey
b8 *Goodbye, Mr Chips*
a9 Film director (and writer) (*The African Queen*, etc.)
b9 *Jacques Tati*
a10 *The Magnificent Seven*
b10 True Grit
a11 TNT
b11 *SHAPE (Supreme Headquarters Allied Powers in Europe)*
a12 Australia
b12 *South Africa*

· Tie-breaker

Q Can you give three examples of 'alternative energy'?
A *Solar power, wind power, hydroelectricity, power derived from tides*

No. 113

a1 Who sang 'Congratulations' in the Eurovision Song Contest?

b1 *When the Beatles started their own record label, what did they call it?*

a2 Which car was nicknamed the 'Beetle'?

b2 *Of what make of car is or was the Robin a type?*

a3 Who led the miner's union in a strike in the eighties?

b3 *In Britain, in which year was the General Strike?*

a4 What is REME?

b4 *What is a QC?*

a5 Opened in 1937, the Golden Gate bridge crosses which bay?

b5 *Which bridge across a harbour opened in 1932?*

a6 In which country is the Camargue?

b6 *And in which country are the Catskill Mountains?*

a7 What is the name of Tarzan's chimpanzee friend?

b7 *What was the name of the bear who sang 'The Bare Necessities' in the film of Jungle Book?*

a8 Which company invented paper handkerchiefs in 1924?

b8 *What useful domestic or office product was first marketed by the 3M Company in 1928?*

a9 Which American comedian became famous for his 'driving instructor' and 'introducing tobacco' sketches?

b9 *On television, which couple were 'Happy Ever After'?*

a10 Which city is served by Orly Airport?

b10 *Which city is served by Ben Gurion International Airport?*

a11 Who wrote the novel Lucky Jim?

b11 *Who wrote the novels First Among Equals and Kane and Abel?*

a12 What has been Stephen Roche's sport?

b12 *And what has been Katarina Witt's (say: Vitt's) sport?*

No. 113 Answers

a1	Cliff Richard
b1	*Apple*
a2	Volkswagen
b2	*Reliant*
a3	Arthur Scargill
b3	*1926*
a4	Royal Electrical and Mechanical Engineers
b4	*Queen's Counsel*
a5	San Francisco
b5	*Sydney Harbour Bridge*
a6	France
b6	*United States of America*
a7	Cheta
b7	*Balloo*
a8	Kleenex
b8	*Scotch tape (cellulose adhesive tape) (NB 'Cellotape' is the trade name of a later, rival product)*
a9	Bob Newhart
b9	*Terry and June (Terry Scott and June Whitfield played Terry and June Fletcher)*
a10	Paris
b10	*Tel Aviv*
a11	Kingsley Amis
b11	*Jeffrey Archer*
a12	Cycling
b12	*Ice-skating*

Tie-breaker

Q 913 people committed suicide together in Guyana in 1978. What did they have in common?

A *All were members of a religious cult, the People's Temple (leader: Reverend Jim Jones)*

No. 114

a1 On television, which cartoon or puppet characters were associated with Wimbledon?

b1 *And in which cartoon or puppet television series did we meet Dougal, Florence and Zebedee?*

a2 In which English city is the Bull Ring?

b2 *In which university city is there a street called the High?*

a3 At which sport did Rachel Heyhoe-Flint captain England?

b3 *For which county did Geoffrey Boycott play cricket?*

a4 In the term 'street cred', what is 'cred' short for?

b4 *Who, cruelly, became known as 'Crumblies'?*

a5 What is TM?

b5 *What is or was a UDC?*

a6 Standard 8 and Super 8 are (or were) both types of . . . what?

b6 *V-8 was a type of . . . what?*

a7 Which 1939 film featured the Cowardly Lion?

b7 *Which 1966 film was about Elsa the Lioness?*

a8 Which event takes place in Oberammergau in Germany every ten years?

b8 *Which event takes place at Llangollen (say: thllan-goth-len) in Wales each July?*

a9 In 1963, who sang 'Take these Chains from My Heart'?

b9 *Which pop group had their first hit in 1964 with 'The House of the Rising Sun'?*

a10 Who was Will Fyffe?

b10 *How did Clare Francis become famous?*

a11 What type of transport flew successfully for the first time in 1936?

b11 *What useful device was first installed at a crossroads in Cleveland, Ohio in 1914?*

a12 What was special about the steam locomotive 'Evening Star'?

b12 *And what was special about the steam locomotive 'Mallard'?*

No. 114 Answers

a1 The Wombles
b1 The Magic Roundabout
a2 Birmingham
b2 Oxford
a3 Women's cricket
b3 Yorkshire
a4 Credibility
b4 Elderly people (in young people's slang)
a5 Transcendental Meditation
b5 Urban District Council
a6 Home-movie film
b6 Car engine
a7 The Wizard of Oz
b7 Born Free
a8 The Passion Play (presenting the life of Jesus)
b8 International Eisteddfod (a festival of music and other arts)
a9 Ray Charles
b9 The Animals
a10 Scottish comedian
b10 (Solo) yachtswoman
a11 Helicopter (Focke Fa-61, in Germany)
b11 Traffic lights
a12 It was the last one built for British Railways
b12 For many years, it held the speed record for steam locomotives

---

Tie-breaker

Q Edvard Munch painted a famous picture of a person running towards us, hands clasped round the face and mouth wide open. What is it called?

A The Scream (*also known as* The Cry)

No. 115

a1 Which sport is somewhat like bowls but is played on ice?
b1 *And also in Scotland, which sport is played at Carnoustie?*
a2 In which country are the Dolomites?
b2 *And in which country are the Ardennes?*
a3 Of what make of car were Sprites and Dolomites both types?
b3 *Of what make of car were Consuls and Zephyrs both types?*
a4 In London, what is 'the V and A'?
b4 *And what is UCL?*
a5 Which disc jockey is nicknamed 'Fluff'?
b5 *Which pop group had hits with 'Shang-a-lang' and 'Summerlove Sensation'?*
a6 In Britain, which tax replaced the rates?
b6 *Who sends you a 'notice of coding'?*
a7 Who wrote the novel Casino Royale?
b7 *Who wrote the novel The Thirty-Nine Steps?*
a8 Which city is served by Tempelhof Airport?
b8 *Which city is served by a railway station called St Lazare (say: san la-zar)?*
a9 Which comedian was known as 'the Cheekie Chappie'?
b9 *Which female comedian was famous for her nursery school sketches?*
a10 What twin disasters hit San Francisco in 1906?
b10 *Which 'fault' makes San Francisco vulnerable to earthquakes?*
a11 On film, what was the name of Gene Autry's horse?
b11 *And Tom Mix's horse?*
a12 In which country was the French fortress Dien Bien Phu?
b12 *In which country, principally, was the Ho Chi Minh trail?*

No. 115 Answers

a1	Curling (played especially in Scotland)
b1	*Golf*
a2	Italy
b2	*Belgium (and France and Luxembourg)*
a3	Triumph
b3	*Ford*
a4	Victoria and Albert Museum
b4	*University College London*
a5	Alan Freeman
b5	*Bay City Rollers*
a6	Community Charge (poll tax)
b6	*The Inland Revenue*
a7	Ian Fleming
b7	*John Buchan*
a8	Berlin
b8	*Paris*
a9	Max Miller
b9	*Joyce Grenfell*
a10	Earthquake and subsequent fire
b10	*San Andreas*
a11	Champion
b11	*Tony*
a12	Indo-China (accept: Vietnam)
b12	*Laos*

Tie-breaker

Q Who is this star of musical comedy?: 'My last great role was in *Charley Girl* in 1969, but I'd also been in *The Belle of New York*. My greatest role was, however, in *The Merry Widow*'.

A Evelyn Laye

No. 116

a1 What is a roadster?

b1 *In which country did Saab and Volvo cars originate?*

a2 What is Godzilla?

b2 *And what is gazpacho?*

a3 'Bye Bye Love', 'Cathy's Clown' and 'Wake Up Little Susie' were all hits for whom?

b3 *And for whom were 'Summertime Blues', 'Nervous Breakdown' and 'Something Else' all hit records?*

a4 Which very tall building was opened in London in 1965?

b4 *Which tall skyscraper was opened by President Hoover in 1931?*

a5 In which sport or entertainment did Henry Higgins become the first successful Englishman?

b5 *By what married name did the British tennis player Ann Haydon become well known?*

a6 On television, what was *Crackerjack*?

b6 *On television, what was The Six-Five Special?*

a7 To which country does Ascension Island belong?

b7 *In which ocean is the island of Tristan da Cunha?*

a8 What was ILEA?

b8 *For what is BNFL an abbreviation?*

a9 Which woman was convicted of the so-called 'Moors Murders'?

b9 *And who was her male partner-in-crime?*

a10 Which screen detective has been played by both Margaret Rutherford and Joan Hickson?

b10 *And which one by Peter Ustinov and David Suchet?*

a11 Which general won power in China in 1927?

b11 *Who expelled Trotsky from the Soviet Communist Party?*

a12 Which is the most north-easterly state in the USA?

b12 *Which Australian state forms the north-eastern part of that country?*

No. 116 Answers

a1 An open car; often a two-seater
b1 *Sweden*
a2 Film monster (Japanese)
b2 *(Spanish) soup, served hot or cold*
a3 The Everly Brothers
b3 *Eddie Cochran*
a4 Post Office Tower
b4 *Empire State Building*
a5 Bull-fighting
b5 *Ann Jones (Ann Haydon-Jones)*
a6 Children's variety show
b6 *Pop music show*
a7 United Kingdom (Britain)
b7 *South Atlantic*
a8 Inner London Education Authority
b8 *British Nuclear Fuels*
a9 Myra Hindley
b9 *Ian Brady*
a10 Miss Marple (Agatha Christie)
b10 *Hercule Poirot*
a11 Chiang Kai-shek
b11 *Joseph Stalin*
a12 Maine
b12 *Queensland*

Tie-breaker

Q By what name did the 'pre-selective multiphone' invented by John C. Danton in 1905 come to be known?

A Juke box

No. 117

a1 What was the Cakewalk?
b1 *And what is a catwalk?*
a2 According to Vera Lynn, where did a nightingale sing?
b2 *In popular music, who was 'the Old Groaner'?*
a3 What was Ted Dexter's sport?
b3 *In which sport has Geoff Dyson been a coach?*
a4 For what has Dounreay in Scotland become famous?
b4 *And for what sort of building has Brent Cross in north London become famous?*
a5 In law, what is a legatee?
b5 *What is the legal term for giving false testimony?*
a6 On film, what was the name of the Lone Ranger's horse?
b6 *And of Roy Rogers' horse?*
a7 What type of craft was the SRN-1?
b7 *Of what make of car is the 2CV a type?*
a8 What is crêpe de chine?
b8 *And what is crème de menthe?*
a9 In Rhodesia, what was UDI?
b9 *And which Rhodesian prime minister declared UDI?*
a10 On whose side was Italy at the end of the First World War?
b10 *In the First World War, on whose side was Holland?*
a11 Which American state lies south of Alabama and Georgia?
b11 *Which American state lies south of Oklahoma?*
a12 Who wrote *The Grapes of Wrath*?
b12 *Who wrote The Maltese Falcon?*

a1 A dance (popular in 1900)

b1 *Narrow passageway or platform on which fashion shows are held (or platform surrounding a large machine)*

a2 In Berkeley (say: barclay) Square

b2 *Bing Crosby*

a3 Cricket

b3 *Athletics*

a4 Fast breeder reactor; nuclear power station

b4 *Shopping centre*

a5 One to whom a legacy is bequeathed

b5 *Perjury*

a6 Silver

b6 *Trigger*

a7 Hovercraft

b7 *Citroën*

a8 A silk fabric

b8 *A (green) peppermint liqueur (drink) (accept: peppermint)*

a9 Unilateral Declaration of Independence

b9 *Ian Smith*

a10 The Allies; Britain and France

b10 *It was neutral*

a11 Florida

b11 *Texas*

a12 John Steinbeck

b12 *Dashiell Hammett*

Tie-breaker

Q What was the name of the first type of wide-screen film?

A *Cinemascope*

No. 118

a1 For what did Mary Whitehouse start a campaign?

b1 *Who is said to be 'infallible'?*

a2 In which sport did Gentlemen play Players?

b2 *Which sport is played by the Harlequins?*

a3 What is meant by 'to go', when speaking of food?

b3 *What is or was a 'closed shop'?*

a4 For whom were 'Great Balls of Fire' and 'Whole Lotta Shakin'' hit records?

b4 *Which pianists were known as 'Fats'?*

a5 Which film studio created the cartoon rabbit, Bugs Bunny?

b5 *And who provided the voice for Bugs Bunny?*

a6 What is meant by Kamikaze?

b6 *What were cami-knickers?*

a7 In which film did Julie Walters play an Open University student who fell in love with her English tutor (played by Michael Caine)?

b7 *On television, which British King has been famously played by Edward Fox?*

a8 What is a megaton?

b8 *What is 0.125 expressed as a fraction?*

a9 In 1914, in which country was Sarajevo (where the Archduke Ferdinand was assassinated)?

b9 *In which country is Mons, the site of a First World War battle?*

a10 What is the everyday name for nitrous oxide?

b10 *What is the chemical name for common salt?*

a11 Which author, who died in 1928, wrote of an area he called Wessex?

b11 *Who wrote a novel about an otter called Tarka?*

a12 Of which country was Sukarno president?

b12 *Of which country (until his assassination) was Dr Verwoerd prime minister?*

No. 118 Answers

a1 'Cleaner' television

b1 *The Pope*

a2 Cricket

b2 *Rugby Union*

a3 Take-away, 'eat out'

b3 *An arrangement which requires workers to be members of a trade union*

a4 Jerry Lee Lewis

b4 *Fats Domino (Antoine Domino) and Fats Waller*

a5 Warner Brothers

b5 *Mel Blanc*

a6 Suicidal (from Japanese 'suicide pilots' who crash-landed bomb-laden planes)

b6 *Woman's item of clothing, combining a camisole (worn on the top half of the body) and knickers*

a7 *Educating Rita*

b7 *Edward VIII (especially in* Edward and Mrs Simpson*)*

a8 One million tons

b8 *One eighth*

a9 Austro-Hungary

b9 *Belgium*

a10 Laughing gas

b10 *Sodium chloride*

a11 Thomas Hardy

b11 *Henry Williamson*

a12 Indonesia

b12 *South Africa*

Tie-breaker

Q Which four American states border Mexico?

A *California, Arizona, New Mexico and Texas*

No. 119

a1   What is 'real estate'?

b1   *The word 'nervy' has different meanings in Britain and America. What are they?*

a2   In which comedy series on television does Gordon Kaye play Réné?

b2   *On television, in which series did Ronnie Barker play a jailbird?*

a3   'Paperback Writer' and 'Day Tripper' were both hits for which group?

b3   *Which honour did the Beatles receive at Buckingham Palace in 1965?*

a4   In which country is the city of Poznan?

b4   *In which country is the port of Chittagong?*

a5   Which is André Agassi's sport?

b5   *What is Ayrton Senna's sport?*

a6   What or who is an apparatchik?

b6   *Who or what is or was a Beatnik?*

a7   Which 1982 hit film resulted in a catch phrase asking the central character to phone home?

b7   *In which film is there an evil character called 'the Joker'?*

a8   What is the motto of Girl Guides?

b8   *When did we hear the slogan 'Not a penny off the pay, not a minute on the day'?*

a9   In which country is the Ogaden region?

b9   *Name one of the two countries which border Belize.*

a10   A boy violinist (aged 10) became famous in 1927. In adult life, he was still a famous violinist – called . . .?

b10   *As what did Edward Ardizzone mainly achieve fame?*

a11   In which year was the Six-Day War (in the Middle East)?

b11   *In which year did the first facsimile transmission of a picture take place: 1907, 1957, or 1977?*

a12   King Umberto I was shot dead in 1900. Of which country was he king?

b12   *In which country did Marshal Pilsudski seize power in 1926?*

No. 119 Answers

a1 Property consisting of land and houses; houses to be bought/sold
b1 *In Britain: nervous; in America: cheeky*
a2 *'Allo, 'Allo!*
b2 Porridge (Going Straight *showed him after his 'release'*)
a3 The Beatles
b3 *The MBE (they later gave them back as a protest against the Vietnam War)*
a4 Poland
b4 *Bangladesh*
a5 Tennis
b5 *Motor-racing*
a6 A bureaucrat, firmly entrenched in his/her post
b6 *A hippie (term used in the fifties and sixties); person who opts out of traditional values*
a7 *ET – The Extra-Terrestrial*
b7 Batman
a8 Be prepared
b8 *During the General Strike (1926)*
a9 Ethiopia
b9 *Mexico, Guatemala*
a10 Yehudi Menuhin
b10 *Illustrator (children's books) (also an author)*
a11 1967
b11 *1907*
a12 Italy
b12 *Poland*

Tie-breaker

Q In electronics, what does a rectifier rectify?
A *An (alternating) electric current (a rectifier can change alternating current to direct current)*

No. 120

a1 What is a billboard?

b1 *What is a helipad?*

a2 In the sixties, which London street was the centre of the fashion scene?

b2 *What is or was a Vespa?*

a3 In which sport might you use a foil or épée (say: ay-pay)?

b3 *Which game begins with a bully?*

a4 In the film *Doctor Dolittle*, which actor said 'you've got to talk to the animals'?

b4 *Which lanky American comedian starred in the films* Chitty Chitty Bang Bang *and* Some Kind of a Nut?

a5 On television, in which trade is Lovejoy involved?

b5 *On television, who played Callan?*

a6 For what was Harry Houdini famous?

b6 *Who was Lenny Bruce?*

a7 What was a Dakota?

b7 *What kind of ship was the Torrey Canyon?*

a8 In which country was the revolutionary Baader-Meinhof (say: barder-mine-hof) gang active?

b8 *In which country did the revolutionary Red Brigade (or Brigades) operate in the seventies?*

a9 In which city is the Ballymurphy housing estate?

b9 *In which city was or is the Sabra refugee camp?*

a10 What was *The British Gazette*, edited by Winston Churchill?

b10 *Under what name did William Connor start a crusading column in the Daily Mirror?*

a11 In which country is Benghazi?

b11 *In which country is the Kikuyu Reserve?*

a12 What instrument was played by the jazz musician Bix Beiderbecke (say: by-der-beck)?

b12 *And which instrument was played by Jack Teagarden?*

No. 120 Answers

a1   Advertising hoarding (American)
b1   *Site for landing a helicopter (e.g. on a building's roof)*
a2   Carnaby Street
b2   *Motor-scooter*
a3   Fencing
b3   *Hockey*
a4   Rex Harrison
b4   *Dick Van Dyke*
a5   Antiques
b5   *Edward Woodward*
a6   Escaping; escapologist
b6   *American comedian*
a7   Passenger aircraft (Douglas DC-3)
b7   *Oil tanker (went aground off Cornwall, causing pollution)*
a8   West Germany
b8   *Italy*
a9   Belfast
b9   *Beirut*
a10   Daily paper, published during the General Strike (1926)
b10   *Cassandra*
a11   Libya
b11   *Kenya*
a12   Cornet
b12   *Trombone*

Tie-breaker

Q Who were the people of India whom Gandhi called *Harijans*, the children of God?

A *Outcasts; lower-caste people; or 'untouchables'*

No. 121: Famous Buildings

For which building is each of the following places especially famous?

a1 Balmoral
b1 *Osborne, Isle of Wight*
a2 Blackpool
b2 *York*
a3 Framlingham, Suffolk
b3 *Greenwich*
a4 Avebury, Wiltshire
b4 *Fountains, near Ripon, Yorkshire*
a5 Alnwick (say: annick), Northumberland
b5 *Furness, near Barrow, Cumbria*
a6 Blenheim, Oxfordshire
b6 *Haworth, Yorkshire*
a7 Alloway, Ayrshire
b7 *Ayot St Lawrence, Hertfordshire*
a8 Buckfast, Devon
b8 *Harlech, North Wales*
a9 Grasmere, in the Lake District
b9 *St Michael's, Cornwall*
a10 Drax, in Yorkshire
b10 *Sizewell, in Suffolk*
a11 Banbury, Oxfordshire
b11 *Kenilworth, Warwickshire*
a12 Woolwich Reach
b12 *Barton and Hessle*

No. 121 Answers

a1   Castle; private home of the reigning monarch
b1   *Osborne House (Queen Victoria's home)*
a2   Blackpool Tower
b2   *York Minster*
a3   Framlingham Castle
b3   *Royal Naval College; National Maritime Museum*
a4   Stone circle (largest in the world)
b4   *Fountains Abbey (Cistercian)*
a5   Alnwick Castle
b5   *Furness Abbey*
a6   Blenheim Palace (birthplace of Winston Churchill)
b6   *Haworth Parsonage, home of the Brontë sisters*
a7   Burns' Cottage (birthplace of Robert Burns)
b7   *Home of Bernard Shaw*
a8   Buckfast Abbey
b8   *Harlech Castle*
a9   Dove Cottage (home of William Wordsworth)
b9   *St Michael's Mount (castle, monastery)*
a10   Power station
b10   *Nuclear power station*
a11   Banbury Cross (also a castle)
b11   *Kenilworth Castle*
a12   Thames (flood) barrier
b12   *Humber Bridge*

Tie-breaker

Q Which architect designed the controversial new Lloyds building, opened in London in 1986?

A *Richard Rogers*

No. 122

a1 In which country is Alice Springs?

b1 *In which country is the port of Tangiers?*

a2 What is the full name of the Scottish soccer club, 'Hearts'?

b2 *Which sport is played by the Boston Red Sox?*

a3 What is 'featherbedding'?

b3 *What was meant by psychedelic?*

a4 Within which country is the mouth of the River Plate?

b4 *Off the north coast of which country is the White Sea?*

a5 Who is the star of the pop video or film *Moonwalker*?

b5 *What item of clothing is sometimes used to mute a trumpet in a jazz or dance band?*

a6 What is a conurbation?

b6 *Who or what is a cinéaste (say: sin-ay-ast)?*

a7 Who was 'Little Mo'?

b7 *What was Reg Harris's sport?*

a8 In 1957, what was the popular name for the type of flu which hit many people in Britain?

b8 *What tragedy hit Aberfan in 1966?*

a9 Svetlana was the daughter of which Soviet ruler?

b9 *Who died when his boat 'Bluebird' somersaulted at 300 mph?*

a10 Which cartoon rabbit invariably outwits Elmer Fudd?

b10 *Which film cartoon character was supposedly based on 'boop-a-doop' singer Helen Kane?*

a11 On BBC Television, what kind of show was *Monitor*?

b11 *On television, which variety show was introduced by Leonard Sachs?*

a12 In South African politics what are or were 'Bantustans'?

b12 *In which country was the Mujahideen a fighting force?*

No. 122 Answers

a1 Australia
b1 *Morocco*
a2 Heart of Midlothian F. C.
b2 *Baseball*
a3 Giving a group of people an easy time
b3 *Mind-influencing; making the senses seem keener; of patterns and lights which have this effect*
a4 Argentina
b4 *Russia*
a5 Michael Jackson
b5 *A bowler or 'derby'*
a6 A number of towns which have spread to form one built-up area
b6 *Connoisseur of films (or, in France, someone working in the film industry)*
a7 Maureen Connolly (US tennis player)
b7 *Cycling*
a8 Asian flu
b8 *A coal tip buried a village school (116 children were killed)*
a9 Joseph Stalin
b9 *Donald Campbell*
a10 Bugs Bunny
b10 *Betty Boop*
a11 Arts programme
b11 *The Good Old Days*
a12 Supposedly independent homelands
b12 *Afghanistan*

Tie-breaker

Q Which whitish powder results from the action of chlorine on slaked lime?
A *Bleaching powder or chloride of lime (consists mainly of calcium oxychloride)*

No. 123

a1   What is a risotto?

b1   *What is meant by 'raffish'?*

a2   What is a retro-rocket?

b2   *What is the colour of a sodium flare?*

a3   What was the name of the cartoon pirate captain who became a popular children's television character?

b3   *On television, who was Andy Pandy's best friend?*

a4   For what is Woomera in Australia famous?

b4   *In which Northern Ireland county is Crossmaglen?*

a5   To which film was *The Empire Strikes Back* a sequel?

b5   *What is Superman's other name?*

a6   In which ocean are the Galapagos Islands?

b6   *To which country does the Pacific island of Guam belong?*

a7   Which American television situation comedy is set in a bar?

b7   *Who was BBC Television's main commentator on royal events in the fifties and early sixties?*

a8   In which country is the town of Maastricht?

b8   *Of which country is Hyderabad a part?*

a9   Alec and Eric both played cricket for Surrey, Alec being a record-breaking bowler. What was their surname?

b9   *Who was in goal when England won the World Cup in 1966?*

a10   With what was the Plowden Report concerned?

b10   *And what was the Beeching Report about?*

a11   The Colts play football; the Orioles play baseball. In which American city do both teams play?

b11   *What were the British Commonwealth Games originally called?*

a12   Claude Monet (say: mon-ay) is said to have been what kind of painter or artist?

b12   *Which dancer was strangled by her own shawl when it caught in a car wheel?*

No. 123 Answers

a1 Dish made of rice plus meat and/or vegetables
b1 *Happy, wild and not very respectable*
a2 Rocket used to slow down a rocket or aircraft
b2 *Yellow*
a3 Captain Pugwash
b3 *Teddy*
a4 Rocket range, rocket testing
b4 *Armagh*
a5 Star Wars
b5 *Clark Kent*
a6 Pacific
b6 *United States of America*
a7 Cheers
b7 *Richard Dimbleby*
a8 The Netherlands (Holland)
b8 *India*
a9 Bedser
b9 *Gordon Banks*
a10 Primary school education
b10 *British Railways*
a11 Baltimore
b11 *British Empire Games*
a12 Impressionist
b12 *Isadora Duncan*

Tie-breaker

Q One of the two major Russian ballet companies is the Kirov company in St Petersburg. Which is the other?

A *The Bolshoi (in Moscow)*

No. 124

a1 Abbreviations: what is a CD?

b1 *And what is CD?*

a2 In London, what trade is conducted at Billingsgate Market (now held on the Isle of Dogs)?

b2 *And what is sold at Smithfield?*

a3 In film, what kind of creature is Dumbo?

b3 *And what was Rin-Tin-Tin?*

a4 What is Factor Eight?

b4 *What is 'faction'?*

a5 Which British pop star had a hit with 'I Remember You'?

b5 *'Walkin' Back to Happiness' was a hit for which singer/actress?*

a6 Who was the first man to run a mile in under four minutes?

b6 *What pioneer swim did Gertrude Ederle achieve in 1926?*

a7 Of which city in America was Wyatt Earp a marshal?

b7 *In which American city was there a gangland St Valentine's Day massacre?*

a8 Which television detective has been played by John Nettles?

b8 *In which television comedy series did Michael Crawford play Frank Spenser?*

a9 Who wrote the play *A View from the Bridge*?

b9 *Who wrote the play* Educating Rita?

a10 Which Canadian province borders the Pacific Ocean?

b10 *What is Canada's national anthem or 'hymn'?*

a11 Which high office did William Temple take over in 1942?

b11 *And who was Archbishop of Canterbury throughout the eighties?*

a12 Which is the heaviest metal?

b12 *Which is the lightest metal?*

No. 124 Answers

a1 A compact disc
b1 *Civil Defence (accept: Corps Diplomatique)*
a2 Fish
b2 *Meat*
a3 Flying elephant
b3 *German Army dog; star of many silent films*
a4 A substance in blood which helps it to coagulate
b4 *A blend of fact and fiction – especially in a film, television play or novel*
a5 Frank Ifield
b5 *Helen Shapiro*
a6 (Dr Roger) Bannister
b6 *First woman to swim the English Channel*
a7 Dodge City
b7 *Chicago*
a8 Bergerac
b8 *Some Mothers Do 'Ave 'Em*
a9 Arthur Miller
b9 *Willy Russell*
a10 British Columbia
b10 *O, Canada*
a11 Archbishop of Canterbury
b11 *Robert Runcie*
a12 Osmium
b12 *Lithium*

Tie-breaker

Q Can you name the four English counties which border Wales?
A Cheshire; Shropshire (Salop); Hereford and Worcester (one county from 1974); Gloucestershire

---

No. 125

a1 In which country did the Caledonian Railway operate until 1923?

b1 *And in which country did the Cambrian Railway chiefly operate?*

a2 What is a debriefing?

b2 *What is 'double-think'?*

a3 On which sport is Richie Benaud a television commentator?

b3 *On television, on which sport have John Motson and Kenneth Wolstenholme been commentators?*

a4 With which song did Sandie Shaw win the Eurovision Song Contest in 1967?

b4 *And in 1970, who won the contest with 'All Kinds of Everything'?*

a5 What is the DFC?

b5 *What happens to you in the Army if you're 'CB'?*

a6 What name or nickname is given to someone who buys shares in the hope of selling them when the price goes up?

b6 *And what name is given to someone who sells shares in the hope of buying them back at a lower price?*

a7 Where in London is the Royal National Theatre?

b7 *Where is the London home of the Royal Shakespeare Company?*

a8 Which city was host for the 1992 summer Olympic Games?

b8 *For which country did Eusebio (say: u-say-bee-o) play soccer?*

a9 What is damaged by CFCs?

b9 *Which gas is the 'greenhouse' gas?*

a10 Which Chinese-American practitioner of the martial arts starred in Enter the Dragon and Way of the Dragon?

b10 *Which Oriental film detective has been played by Warner Oland, J. Carrol Naish, and once by Peter Ustinov?*

a11 Which television comedy series starred Wendy Craig with Geoffrey Palmer as her dentist-husband?

b11 *In which television comedy series did Michael Williams play opposite Judy Dench?*

a12 In which country is the city of Aleppo?

b12 *And in which country is the city of Casablanca?*

No. 125 Answers

a1   Scotland
b1   *Wales*
a2   Extracting all available information from a returned astronaut, spy, soldier, etc.
b2   *Believing two contradictory ideas at once*
a3   Cricket
b3   *Soccer*
a4   'Puppet on a String'
b4   *Dana*
a5   Distinguished Flying Cross
b5   *You're confined to barracks*
a6   Bull, bullish
b6   *Bear, bearish*
a7   On the South Bank (near Waterloo)
b7   *The Barbican*
a8   Barcelona
b8   *Portugal*
a9   The ozone layer
b9   *Carbon dioxide*
a10   Bruce Lee
b10   *Charlie Chan*
a11   *Butterflies*
b11   A Fine Romance
a12   Syria
b12   *Morocco*

Tie-breaker

Q Who is this lyricist?: 'Gertrude Lawrence appeared in three of my works. Fred Astaire in two. I collaborated with various composers but especially with my brother. As for myself, when I say I got plenty of nothing, it ain't necessarily so.'

A *Ira Gershwin (brother of George, the composer)*

No. 126

a1 For what is Petticoat Lane in London famous?

b1 And for what is Savile Row famous?

a2 Colloquially, who or what is a 'sab'?

b2 What is a clip joint?

a3 In the Eurovision Song Contest who sang 'Boom-Bang-A-Bang'?

b3 And who won the competition with 'Making Your Mind Up'?

a4 What does the drink Bucks Fizz consist of?

b4 And what is a Bloody Mary?

a5 Which television comedy series features Clegg, Compo and Nora Batty?

b5 Which work-shy lad was played by Hywel Bennett in a television comedy series of the same name?

a6 Which large, bearded Gloucestershire cricketer died in 1915?

b6 Which country did Jean (say: jhan) Borotra represent at tennis?

a7 What is BAFTA?

b7 What is the BFI?

a8 On which island is Famagusta?

b8 Between which two countries is the Khyber Pass?

a9 Who was the first ex-grammar school boy to lead the Conservative Party?

b9 Which was Mrs Thatcher's constituency?

a10 Can you name one of the two male stars of the film *Some Like It Hot*?

b10 Which Oriental master criminal was played on the screen by Harry Agar Lyons in the twenties and by Christopher Lee in the sixties?

a11 For what did Dr Albert Schweitzer become famous?

b11 As what did the Irishman W. B. Yeats (say: yates) achieve fame?

a12 What was the title of Erich Maria Remarque's famous novel about the First World War?

b12 And what was the title of R. C. Sherriff's play about the same war?

No. 126 Answers

a1 Its street market
b1 *Tailors' shops*
a2 Saboteur (especially of blood sports)
b2 *Restaurant or nightclub that charges too much (and which may be dishonest in other ways)*
a3 Lulu
b3 *Bucks Fizz*
a4 Champagne and orange juice
b4 *A mixture of vodka and tomato juice (and possibly Worcestershire sauce)*
a5 *Last of the Summer Wine*
b5 *Shelley*
a6 Dr W. G. Grace
b6 *France*
a7 British Academy of Film and Television Arts
b7 *British Film Institute*
a8 Cyprus
b8 *Pakistan and Afghanistan*
a9 Edward Heath
b9 *Finchley*
a10 Tony Curtis, Jack Lemmon
b10 *Fu Manchu*
a11 As a doctor in Equatorial Africa
b11 *As a poet*
a12 *All Quiet on the Western Front*
b12 Journey's End

Tie-breaker

Q Which gas is produced by the action of water on calcium carbide?
A Acetylene (accept: Ethyne)

No. 127

a1   At the end of which London thoroughfare does Buckingham Palace stand?

b1   *And where in London is Nelson's Column?*

a2   In which television serial did we meet Adam Chance and Jill Harvey?

b2   *And in which serial did we meet Stan and Hilda Ogden?*

a3   Which sport would you most likely want to play if you visited Gleneagles?

b3   *In which sport has the Gillette Cup been a trophy?*

a4   Which newspaper cartoon hero saved the world in his first film, when he was played by Buster Crabbe?

b4   *In the world of film, what have the following in common: Nurse, Teacher, Constable, Regardless . . .?*

a5   What is meant by 'Subtopia'?

b5   *What is the literal meaning of the word 'veto'?*

a6   In the Vietnam War, were the Viet Cong fighting with or against the Americans?

b6   *Who was crowned Emperor of Japan in 1928?*

a7   Of which political party was George Brown a colourful member?

b7   *And of which party was Jeremy Thorpe a leader?*

a8   In music, what is the LSO?

b8   *And also in London, what is the LSE?*

a9   Which pop group had a No. 1 hit with 'I'll Never Find Another You'?

b9   *What was the name of Eric Burdon's original group?*

a10   In which country is the Great Bear Lake?

b10   *And in which country is Mount Kilimanjaro?*

a11   Who wrote the play The Royal Hunt of the Sun?

b11   *And who wrote a trio of plays called The Norman Conquests?*

a12   In the world of finance, who issues 'gilts' or 'gilt-edged' securities?

b12   *Which was the first British credit card?*

No. 127 Answers

a1	The Mall
b1	*Trafalgar Square*
a2	*Crossroads*
b2	Coronation Street
a3	Golf
b3	*Cricket*
a4	Flash Gordon
b4	*They are all Carry On films*
a5	Ill-conceived building development; a sprawl of houses, etc.
b5	*I forbid (from the Latin)*
a6	Against (they were Communist forces)
b6	*Hirohito*
a7	Labour
b7	*Liberal*
a8	London Symphony Orchestra
b8	*London School of Economics*
a9	The Seekers
b9	*The Animals*
a10	Canada
b10	*Tanzania*
a11	Peter Shaffer
b11	*Alan Ayckbourn*
a12	The Government
b12	*Barclaycard*

Tie-breaker

Q Which author wrote a book about the art of 'one-upmanship'?
A *Stephen Potter*

No. 128

a1   On television, who played the scarecrow, Worzel Gummidge?

b1   On television, who played Arthur Daley's original 'Minder'?

a2   Which is the home country of golfer Ian Woosnam?

b2   Which ground is headquarters of the Welsh Rugby Union?

a3   In which country is the ski resort of St Moritz?

b3   In which country is the historic city of Granada?

a4   What is broken at Mach 1?

b4   What is the Maghreb?

a5   In which year was John F. Kennedy shot dead?

b5   And in which city did it happen?

a6   Which famous art gallery stands on Millbank in south-west London?

b6   Whereabouts in London is the Science Museum?

a7   What is or was the CEGB?

b7   What is a country's GDP?

a8   Which British comedy actor starred in the film *Dr Strangelove*?

b8   Which television comedian starred in the cinema film A Fish Called Wanda?

a9   'Happy Birthday, Sweet Sixteen' and 'Breaking Up is Hard to Do' were both hits for which male singer?

b9   Which English pop group had hits with 'Needles and Pins', 'Sweets for My Sweet' and 'Don't Throw Your Love Away'?

a10   To whom did the 'Balfour Declaration' promise a homeland?

b10   Born Max Aitken, this Canadian became a newspaper baron – under what name?

a11   Kingsley and Martin are father-and-son authors. Their surname is . . .?

b11   Who wrote the novels Wilt and Blott on the Landscape?

a12   In which country is the Horn of Africa (its most easterly point)?

b12   In which country is Stanleyville?

No. 128 Answers

a1	Jon Pertwee
b1	*Dennis Waterman*
a2	Wales
b2	*Cardiff Arms Park*
a3	Switzerland
b3	*Spain*
a4	Sound barrier
b4	*North-west Africa*
a5	1963
b5	*Dallas, Texas*
a6	The Tate
b6	*Exhibition Road; Kensington; south-west London*
a7	Central Electricity Generating Board
b7	*Gross domestic product (or output)*
a8	Peter Sellers
b8	*John Cleese*
a9	Neil Sedaka
b9	*The Searchers*
a10	The Jewish people (in Palestine)
b10	*Lord Beaverbrook*
a11	Amis
b11	*Tom Sharpe*
a12	Somalia
b12	*Congo*

Tie-breaker

Q Which fly transmits African sleeping sickness?
A *Tsetse fly*

No. 129

a1 In films, what was the first name of the cowboy called Cassidy?

b1 *Which 'cops' were a group of slapstick comedians who appeared in Mack Sennett films?*

a2 In the early sixties, which group of teenagers regularly fought Rockers at seaside resorts?

b2 *Of which major crime was Ronald Biggs convicted?*

a3 Which Sheffield theatre has become famous as a venue for snooker tournaments?

b3 *Which London theatre boasted 'We never closed' during the Second World War?*

a4 Which bandleader was famous for his Tijuana (say: ti-whar-na) Brass?

b4 *What is tequila?*

a5 You might have had the DTs, but what does DT stand for?

b5 *What is ESP?*

a6 Which was Paddy Hopkirk's sport?

b6 *In which sport did Herbert Sutcliffe achieve fame?*

a7 Which pop group issued an album called 'Revolver'?

b7 *And for whom was 'I'd Like to Teach the World to Sing' a hit?*

a8 Of which country is the region of Thrace a part?

b8 *And of which country is the region of Umbria a part?*

a9 What is tinnitus?

b9 *What is neuralgia?*

a10 Which army was commanded by General Bramwell Booth?

b10 *Which high religious office does Basil Hume hold?*

a11 In the world of finance, what are 'securities'?

b11 *What is the difference between libel and slander?*

a12 On radio and the stage, who was comedian Jimmy Jewel's long-time partner?

b12 *Which organist's signature tune was 'I Do Like to Be Beside the Seaside'?*

No. 129 Answers

a1 Hopalong (Cassidy)
b1 *Keystone Kops*
a2 Mods
b2 *The Great Train Robbery*
a3 The Crucible
b3 *The Windmill*
a4 Herb Alpert
b4 *Mexican alcoholic drink*
a5 Delirium tremens ('the shakes')
b5 *Extra-sensory perception*
a6 Rally driving
b6 *Cricket*
a7 The Beatles
b7 *The New Seekers*
a8 Greece
b8 *Italy*
a9 A buzzing or ringing in the ear, heard only by the sufferer
b9 *Pain from a damaged nerve*
a10 Salvation Army
b10 *Archbishop of Westminster; leader of the Roman Catholic Church in England*
a11 Stocks and shares
b11 *Libel is written, slander is spoken*
a12 Ben Warris
b12 *Reg Dixon (at Blackpool)*

Tie-breaker

Q In which sport does gold score 9?
A Archery

No. 130

a1   Of which country is Bavaria a part?

b1   *Of which country is the island of Corfu a part?*

a2   On television, what is the first name of the barrister called Rumpole?

b2   *Which actor plays Alf Garnett on television?*

a3   Which country was captained by Ian Chappell – and in which sport?

b3   *For which country did Johann Cruyff (say: yo-han kroyff) play soccer?*

a4   Whom did Jack Ruby kill live on television in a police car-park?

b4   *Which American leader won the Nobel Peace Prize in 1964?*

a5   Which chemical is found in coffee and tea and is thought to have a powerful action on the heart?

b5   *Is chloroform a gas, a liquid or a salt?*

a6   In which county are the Chislehurst Caves, used as air-raid shelters in the Second World War?

b6   *What was the last item to be freed from rationing after the Second World War?*

a7   Which charge card advertised with the slogan 'That'll do nicely'?

b7   *In financial jargon, what is the 'grey economy' or 'grey market'?*

a8   Where is the official London residence of the Archbishop of Canterbury?

b8   *And what address is the official home in London of the Chancellor of the Exchequer?*

a9   Where would you see an ISBN?

b9   *And which book is sometimes described as the AV?*

a10   Which pop group played 'Apache'?

b10   *And which group played 'Telstar'?*

a11   Which two countries were at war over claims to Kashmir in 1965?

b11   *What two buildings were linked by a 'hot line' in 1963?*

a12   In 1932, Vicki Baum's novel provided film roles for Garbo, the Barrymore brothers and Joan Crawford. What was it called?

b12   *In which 1966 film did David Hemmings play a photographer who thinks he has witnessed a murder?*

No. 130 Answers

a1	Germany
b1	Greece
a2	Horace
b2	*Warren Mitchell*
a3	Australia; cricket
b3	*Holland (the Netherlands)*
a4	Lee Harvey Oswald (who was charged with President Kennedy's murder)
b4	*Martin Luther King*
a5	Caffeine
b5	*A liquid*
a6	Kent
b6	*Meat (including bacon) in 1954*
a7	American Express
b7	*Income, earnings, profit which does not appear in official or public accounts; business done 'on the side'*
a8	Lambeth Palace
b8	*11 Downing Street*
a9	On a book (International Standard Book Number)
b9	*The Bible (Authorized Version)*
a10	The Shadows
b10	*The Tornados*
a11	India and Pakistan
b11	*The Kremlin and the White House*
a12	*Grand Hotel*
b12	Blow-Up

Tie-breaker

Q 'Four Quartets', published during the Second World War, were considered by many to be the most important poems to appear in that period. Who wrote them?

A *T. S. Eliot*

No. 131: More Capitals

Another round of capital cities – and their countries, all of which have been in the news in recent years. Of which country is each of the following the capital city?

a1	Islamabad
b1	*Manila*
a2	Brazzaville
b2	*Luanda*
a3	Sofia
b3	*Bogotá*
a4	Kinshasa
b4	*Lusaka*
a5	Mogadishu
b5	*Quito*
a6	Ventiane
b6	*Dodoma*

And what is the capital city of these countries?

a7	Israel
b7	*South Korea*
a8	Switzerland
b8	*Burma*
a9	Taiwan
b9	*Lithuania*
a10	United Arab Emirates
b10	*Oman*
a11	Georgia
b11	*Estonia*
a12	Senegal
b12	*Papua New Guinea*

No. 131 Answers

a1   Pakistan
b1   *Philippines*
a2   Congo
b2   *Angola*
a3   Bulgaria
b3   *Colombia*
a4   Zaire
b4   *Zambia*
a5   Somalia
b5   *Ecuador*
a6   Laos
b6   *Tanzania*
a7   Jerusalem (not recognized by the United Nations)
b7   *Seoul*
a8   Berne
b8   *Rangoon*
a9   Taipei
b9   *Vilnius*
a10   Abu Dhabi
b10   *Muscat*
a11   Tbilisi (Tiflis)
b11   *Tallinn*
a12   Dakar
b12   *Port Moresby*

Tie-breaker

Q What is the capital of Burkina Faso?
A *Ouagadougou*

No. 132

a1   What or who is an MFH?

b1   What is an MTB?

a2   In golf, what is an Eagle?

b2   What is the Tote?

a3   Which black American with a Mohawk hairstyle starred in television's *The A-Team*?

b3   In the sixties television series, who played Dr Kildare?

a4   Whose jazz band was famous for playing 'Midnight in Moscow'?

b4   And who played 'Stranger on the Shore'?

a5   Who famously said 'Ich bin ein Berliner'?

b5   Who originally said 'Non' to British membership of the Common Market?

a6   Which film by Walt Disney is a visualization of musical classics?

b6   What was the screen name of the intelligent collie dog which began its film career in 1940?

a7   What does a carcinogen cause?

b7   Which germ-killing mould was discovered by accident (by Professor Fleming) in 1928?

a8   After Burgess and Maclean (say: ma-klane), who was the 'Third Man' in the spy ring?

b8   Why did Greville Wynne become famous?

a9   As what did the American Robert Frost achieve fame?

b9   And as what did the Frenchman Francis Poulenc achieve fame?

a10   Which two seas are linked by the Kiel Canal?

b10   Which two English counties border Scotland?

a11   Who wrote the children's novel *Ballet Shoes*?

b11   And who wrote the children's novel Swallows and Amazons?

a12   What happened to Britain's currency in both 1949 and 1967?

b12   What was the major financial change in Britain in 1931?

No. 132 Answers

a1   Master of Foxhounds
b1   *Motor torpedo boat*
a2   A hole completed in two strokes under 'par' or 'bogey'
b2   *Machine (totalizator) which shows amounts bet on a race, and amounts to be paid out*
a3   Mr T
b3   *Richard Chamberlain*
a4   Kenny Ball
b4   *Acker Bilk*
a5   President Kennedy (in Berlin in 1963)
b5   *President de Gaulle (of France)*
a6   *Fantasia*
b6   *Lassie*
a7   Cancer
b7   *Penicillin*
a8   Kim Philby
b8   *He was jailed in Moscow as a spy*
a9   Poet
b9   *Composer*
a10   North Sea, Baltic Sea
b10   *Cumbria and Northumberland*
a11   Noel Streatfeild
b11   *Arthur Ransome*
a12   It was devalued
b12   *Britain abandoned the Gold Standard*

Tie-breaker

Q Which Pete Seeger song did Marlene Dietrich record in 1962?
A 'Where Have All the Flowers Gone?'

No. 133

a1　For what is 'white spirit' mainly used?

b1　*For what is the alloy 'solder' generally used?*

a2　In which sport was His Highness the Aga Khan a sponsor and competitor?

b2　*Which FA Secretary became a Knight in 1949?*

a3　In film classifications, for what does 'PG' stand?

b3　*And away from films, what is a PG?*

a4　Which Radio One disc jockey is famous for a daily 'Our Tune' spot?

b4　*Which disc jockey is famous for the line 'Greetings, pop-pickers'?*

a5　In which country is Gallipoli?

b5　*In which country is Arnhem?*

a6　Which Labour leader died unexpectedly in 1963?

b6　*And who succeeded him?*

a7　Which actor played Henry VIII, Captain Bligh and the Hunchback of Notre Dame?

b7　*What does an actor do if he 'corpses'?*

a8　Can you complete this American quartet: Crosby, Stills, . . .?

b8　*And can you complete this quintet: Dave Dee, Dozy, Beaky, . . .?*

a9　Which important national museum faces onto Great Russell Street in London?

b9　*And which other national museum is in Lambeth Road in south-east London?*

a10　Until 1923, which railway was known as the LNWR?

b10　*And which railway was the LBSCR?*

a11　Who played the female lead in the film Mary Poppins?

b11　*And who wrote the novel Mary Poppins?*

a12　Which British prime minister bought Polaris missiles from America?

b12　*Which Secretary of State for War had to resign in 1963 after a scandal involving call girls?*

No. 133 Answers

a1 To dissolve paint
b1 *Joining metals (including wires)*
a2 Horse-racing
b2 *Sir Stanley Rous*
a3 Parental Guidance
b3 *Paying guest*
a4 Simon Bates
b4 *Alan Freeman*
a5 Turkey
b5 *Netherlands (Holland)*
a6 Hugh Gaitskell
b6 *Harold Wilson*
a7 Charles Laughton
b7 *Breaks into laughter, accidentally*
a8 . . . Nash and Young
b8 *. . . Mick and Tich*
a9 British Museum
b9 *(Imperial) War Museum*
a10 London and North Western Railway
b10 *London, Brighton and South Coast Railway*
a11 Julie Andrews
b11 *P. L. Travers*
a12 Harold Macmillan
b12 *John Profumo*

Tie-breaker

Q The first-ever soccer world cup was played in 1930 in Montevideo. Who won it?
A *Uruguay*

No. 134

a1 What was the NCB?

b1 *In government, what is the FCO?*

a2 In London, what are the Garrick, the Globe and the Savoy?

b2 *And what are the Garrick, the Savage and the Savile?*

a3 Which American band's theme was 'Moonlight Serenade'?

b3 *During the Second World War, for which musical instrument was Sandy Macpherson famous?*

a4 Which French female singer had no regrets when she sang 'Je ne regrette rien'?

b4 *Which pop singer sang 'Living Doll'?*

a5 Viscount Stansgate gave up his peerage to remain an MP. What name did he resume?

b5 *Prime Minister Lord Home (say: hume) was also known as . . .?*

a6 In which European country is the port of Brindisi?

b6 *In which country is the port of Dunkerque (Dunkirk)?*

a7 What did Molesworth, Aldermaston and Greenham have in common?

b7 *Calder Hall opened in 1956. Why was this a newsworthy event?*

a8 Who was made into an international star by her role in the 1930 film *The Blue Angel*?

b8 *Who played the female lead in the film* Dr Zhivago?

a9 Which small Scottish town became the site of a tragic aviation crime towards the end of 1988?

b9 *In which Yugoslav city was there a major earthquake in 1963?*

a10 Which television drama series featured the adventures of a bomb disposal squad?

b10 *In which television series did Jeremy Irons play an Evelyn Waugh hero?*

a11 George Wallace (who tried to defy new race laws) was governor of which American state?

b11 *In America, what was Alcatraz?*

a12 What did American John De Lorean dream of building in Belfast?

b12 *Chris Bonington was the first Briton to conquer the North Face of which mountain?*

No. 134 Answers

a1   National Coal Board
b1   *Foreign and Commonwealth Office*
a2   Theatres
b2   *Clubs; 'gentlemen's clubs'*
a3   Glenn Miller
b3   *Organ; theatre organ*
a4   Edith Piaf
b4   *Cliff Richard*
a5   Tony Benn (Anthony Wedgwood Benn)
b5   *Sir Alec Douglas-Home (say: hume)*
a6   Italy
b6   *France*
a7   All were Cruise (nuclear) missile bases (USAF bases)
b7   *It was the world's first nuclear power station*
a8   Marlene Dietrich
b8   *Julie Christie*
a9   Lockerbie
b9   *Skopje*
a10   *Danger UXB*
b10   Brideshead Revisited
a11   Alabama
b11   *Prison; a jail built on a rocky island*
a12   Luxury sports cars
b12   *The Eiger (say: eye-ger)*

Tie-breaker

Q Which film star's first line in 'talking pictures' was 'Gimme a vhisky with ginger ale on the side – and don't be stingy, baby'?
A *Greta Garbo*

No. 135

a1   In which London park is the Round Pond?

b1   *And in which park is Speakers' Corner?*

a2   In which radio serial do we meet Eddie Grundy?

b2   *In which radio comedy show did we meet Eccles, Bluebottle and Henry Crun?*

a3   Which island was the focus of a 'missile crisis' in 1962?

b3   *Which country installed the missiles?*

a4   Who was the leader who backed down and removed the missiles?

b4   *Which American president then claimed a victory over the Soviet Union?*

a5   Which television satire show in the early sixties annoyed politicians but won huge late Saturday night audiences?

b5   *And who was the compère of the show?*

a6   Which two countries are separated by the Ionian Sea?

b6   *Which two countries are separated by the Kattegat?*

a7   With what is NASA concerned?

b7   *And what is meant by VTOL?*

a8   In a series of cartoons and films, who was Dagwood Bumstead's wife?

b8   *Which was the Beatles' first film?*

a9   In which city were the 1948 Olympics held?

b9   *In which city were the 1900 Olympic Games held?*

a10   What is RSI?

b10   *What is HIV?*

a11   Which pop group sang 'Part of the Union'?

b11   *Once with Faces; later he sang 'Sailing'. Who is this pop star?*

a12   Who became Poet Laureate in 1984?

b12   *Who composed a 'War Requiem' based on poems by Wilfred Owen?*

No. 135 Answers

a1 Kensington Gardens
b1 Hyde Park
a2 The Archers
b2 The Goon Show
a3 Cuba
b3 Soviet Union
a4 Mr Khrushchev (of the USSR)
b4 President Kennedy
a5 *That Was the Week That Was*
b5 David Frost
a6 Italy and Greece
b6 Denmark and Sweden
a7 Space travel (National Aeronautics and Space Administration)
b7 Vertical take-off and landing
a8 Blondie
b8 A Hard Day's Night
a9 London
b9 Paris
a10 Repetitive strain injury (incurred by spending too long at a keyboard)
b10 Human immunodeficiency virus (breakdown of the body's immune system) – the virus that can cause AIDS
a11 The Strawbs
b11 Rod Stewart
a12 Ted Hughes
b12 Benjamin Britten

Tie-breaker

Q Who is this singer?: 'I was born in Austria in 1900 but later settled in New York. I became famous for what was once described as my 'steel-like' voice, and appeared in cabaret'
A *Lotte Lenya*

No. 136

a1 Which was Peter Thomson's sport?

b1 *And what was Douglas Jardine's sport?*

a2 Who topped the pop charts with his 'Long Haired Lover From Liverpool'?

b2 *And in 1988 who topped the Christmas charts with 'Mistletoe and Wine'?*

a3 Which product is advertised by a group of monkeys?

b3 *And which brand of tea bags were famous for their 'little perforations'?*

a4 On television, on which subject have 'Saint' and 'Greavsie' presented programmes?

b4 *And about which subject does Barry Norman broadcast?*

a5 As what did Sir David Low achieve fame?

b5 *How did Yves St Laurent (say: eve san lo'ron) achieve fame?*

a6 In which county is the town of Barrow-in-Furness?

b6 *And in which county was it prior to 1974?*

a7 With which other country did Britain attack Egypt in 1956?

b7 *Which country did the Soviet Union crush while Britain was attacking Egypt?*

a8 Which action provoked the Suez invasion?

b8 *Which Egyptian town did the British bomb heavily during the Suez invasion?*

a9 What sort of displays were given at Hendon in the thirties?

b9 *What was a 'de-mob' suit?*

a10 Which country very roughly now covers the area called Tripolitania at the start of the century?

b10 *At the beginning of the century, which country lay immediately to the north of Greece?*

a11 If you were on a 'Routemaster', how would you be travelling?

b11 *And if you were travelling in an 'Islander', how would you be travelling?*

a12 Peter, Susan, Edmund and Lucy first appeared in which children's story?

b12 *And which kingdom do they visit (to meet Aslan the Lion)?*

No. 136 Answers

a1 Golf
b1 *Cricket*
a2 Jimmy Osmond
b2 *Cliff Richard*
a3 P. G. Tips tea
b3 *Quick Brew tea*
a4 Soccer (association football)
b4 *Films*
a5 (Political) cartoonist
b5 *As a fashion designer*
a6 Cumbria
b6 *Lancashire*
a7 France
b7 *Hungary*
a8 Egypt's nationalization of the Suez Canal
b8 *Port Said*
a9 Aviation (Royal Air Force)
b9 *Suit issued to servicemen when 'demobilized' after the Second World War (i.e. when leaving the army, etc.)*
a10 Libya
b10 *Macedonia (part of the Turkish Empire)*
a11 Bus (London double-decker)
b11 *By aircraft*
a12 The Lion, the Witch and the Wardrobe
b12 *Narnia*

Tie-breaker

Q What 1904 American invention was later to make it possible to build the first tanks?

A *Caterpillar tread/caterpillar-tracked vehicles*

No. 137

a1 At which game or sport has Stephen Hendry been a champion?

b1 *Which sportsman popularized the phrase 'I am the greatest'?*

a2 In films, whose preferred drink is 'a martini – shaken, not stirred'?

b2 *Which was the first James Bond film?*

a3 What make of car are the Nova, Astra and Carlton?

b3 *The Anglia and Sierra are both models of which make of car?*

a4 Which children's television programme featured a dog called Petra?

b4 *The television play* Cathy Come Home *revealed the plight of which group of people?*

a5 Out of which two counties was Tyne and Wear carved in 1974?

b5 *Into which English county was Huntingdonshire absorbed in 1974?*

a6 Were tea bags invented in 1920, 1955 or 1965?

b6 *In the fifties, which drink was dispensed from Gaggia machines?*

a7 Which television comedian was famous for playing a character who said 'Oo, you are awful – but I like you'?

b7 *Which glove puppet was famous for saying 'Boom, boom!' after his own jokes?*

a8 Who became president of the United States when John F. Kennedy was assassinated?

b8 *In America, what post was held by Dean Rusk?*

a9 In 1991, which prime minister was (like his mother) assassinated?

b9 *Of which country has Mrs Bandaranaike been prime minister?*

a10 What nationality was the composer Béla Bartók?

b10 *And what nationality was Percy Grainger, who composed 'Country Gardens'?*

a11 What kind of cell is used in most 'electric eyes' that work automatic doors?

b11 *Where are you most likely to have a Quartz crystal?*

a12 How did Sir Alexander Korda become famous?

b12 *And how did C. P. Scott become well known?*

No. 137 Answers

a1	Snooker
b1	*Muhammad Ali (formerly Cassius Clay)*
a2	James Bond
b2	*Dr No*
a3	Vauxhall
b3	*Ford*
a4	Blue Peter
b4	*The homeless*
a5	Northumberland and Durham
b5	*Cambridgeshire*
a6	1920 (by Joseph Krieger in San Francisco)
b6	*(Frothy) coffee*
a7	Dick Emery
b7	*Basil Brush*
a8	Lyndon B. Johnson
b8	*Secretary of State*
a9	Rajiv Gandhi (in India)
b9	*Sri Lanka*
a10	Hungarian
b10	*Australian*
a11	Photoelectric cell
b11	*In your watch*
a12	As a film producer and director
b12	*As a newspaper editor (of the* Manchester Guardian)

Tie-breaker

Q Who were the four stars of the theatrical revue *Beyond the Fringe*?

A *Alan Bennett, Peter Cook, Jonathan Miller, Dudley Moore*

No. 138

a1   Which domestic item was advertised with the slogan 'Prolongs Active Life'?

b1   *And which item was said to help you work, rest and play?*

a2   In which country is Siberia?

b2   *On which island was the Bay of Pigs invasion?*

a3   In which stories is Mrs Goggins a postmistress?

b3   *Who wrote the children's books* Fantastic Mr Fox *and* The BFG?

a4   In which sport has Kriss Akabusi been a champion?

b4   *Which has been Will Carling's sport?*

a5   What is controlled by a thermostat?

b5   *What does a humidifier add to the air?*

a6   Wardour Street is said to be the London home of which industry?

b6   *Which film comedian has his statue in London's Leicester Square?*

a7   Which American rock singer joined the army in March 1958?

b7   *Which football team lost seven members in a 1958 air crash?*

a8   Sharon's and Tracey's husbands are in prison – in which television comedy series?

b8   *In which television series has Mike Baldwin been a key character?*

a9   In which county is Milton Keynes?

b9   *In which county is Telford?*

a10   In which western did we first hear the song 'Raindrops Keep Fallin' on my Head'?

b10   *Which film features the song 'Bright Eyes'?*

a11   What have the following in common: Swindon, Crewe and Doncaster?

b11   *What have the following in common: Cowley, Longbridge and Dunstable?*

a12   Which political party was the surprise winner of a 1962 by-election in Orpington?

b12   *When the British Labour Government failed in 1931, how was Britain governed?*

No. 138 Answers

a1   PAL dog food
b1   *Mars bars*
a2   Russia
b2   *Cuba*
a3   Postman Pat
b3   *Roald Dahl*
a4   Athletics (track)
b4   *Rugby Union*
a5   The temperature of something (e.g. a room, oven or refrigerator)
b5   *Moisture; water vapour*
a6   Film
b6   *Charlie Chaplin*
a7   Elvis Presley
b7   *Manchester United*
a8   *Birds of a Feather*
b8   Coronation Street
a9   Buckinghamshire
b9   *Shropshire*
a10   *Butch Cassidy and the Sundance Kid*
b10   *Watership Down*
a11   All are 'railway towns'; all have had important locomotive works
b11   *All have major car plants*
a12   Liberal
b12   *By a coalition (the 'National Government')*

Tie-breaker

Q What useful domestic appliance was invented in 1906 by Alva
J. Fisher?
A *Electric washing machine*

No. 139

a1 Which sport is played at Murrayfield?

b1 *For which sport is Newbury in Berkshire well known?*

a2 In which television show did Bob Monkhouse used to say 'Bernie, the bolt!'?

b2 *On television, who introduced The Record Breakers for many years?*

a3 Which ruling duo was known as 'B and K'?

b3 *On which day of the year in 1991 did President Gorbachev resign?*

a4 Which 1970 film, made in the north of England, featured steam trains?

b4 *Which real-life children's author was portrayed on screen by Danny Kaye?*

a5 With which industry has Port Talbot traditionally been associated?

b5 *Which industry is traditionally associated with Kettering?*

a6 Which comedian had the catch phrases 'A good idea, son!' and 'I've arrived and to prove it I'm here'?

b6 *Which Cockney comedian used the phrase 'Aye, aye, that's yer lot'?*

a7 Which vitamin can help people to see in the dark?

b7 *What 'perk' for Britons flying abroad was introduced in 1959?*

a8 According to the song, who 'regrets she's unable to lunch today'?

b8 *Also according to a song, who goes 'out in the midday sun'?*

a9 Which motorway would you use to travel to London from Oxford?

b9 *And which motorway would you use to reach London from Cambridge?*

a10 What did Hans Geiger invent in 1908?

b10 *An inventor gave his name to a type of emergency bridge which could be built quickly. His name was . . .?*

a11 Walter Mondale was vice-president to which American president?

b11 *Nelson A. Rockefeller was vice-president to which American president?*

a12 Which country's move to independence provoked a right-wing secret army (known as the OAS) into action in 1962?

b12 *In which South African township did police shoot 56 people dead in 1960?*

No. 139 Answers

a1 Rugby Union (Edinburgh)
b1 *Racing (horse-racing)*
a2 *The Golden Shot*
b2 *Roy Castle*
a3 Marshall Bulganin (prime minister) and Mr Kruschev (Communist party leader), in the Soviet Union
b3 *Christmas Day (December 25)*
a4 *The Railway Children*
b4 *Hans Christian Andersen*
a5 Steel
b5 *Footwear; shoe-making*
a6 Max Bygraves (on radio in *Educating Archie*)
b6 *Jimmy Wheeler*
a7 Vitamin A
b7 *Duty-free drink*
a8 Miss Otis (by Cole Porter)
b8 *Mad dogs and Englishmen (Noël Coward)*
a9 M40
b9 *M11*
a10 The geiger counter (which detects radiation)
b10 *Bailey (Sir D. Bailey)*
a11 Jimmy Carter
b11 *Gerald Ford*
a12 Algeria
b12 *Sharpeville*

Tie-breaker

Q What item of (often unpopular) street furniture was invented by Carlton Magee and first installed in Oklahoma City in 1935?
A *Parking meters*

No. 140

a1 Which ex-soap star sang 'I Should Be So Lucky'?

b1 *What was the name of the pop duo made up of George Michael and Andrew Ridgeley?*

a2 What is the capital of the American state of Oklahoma?

b2 *Salt Lake City is the capital of which American state?*

a3 Which disc jockey asked, 'How's about that, then, guys and gals?'?

b3 *In which disc jockey's programmes did we regularly hear the voice of a small boy saying "Ello, darlin'!'?*

a4 With which game is John Parrott associated?

b4 *Which is Nick Faldo's sport?*

a5 In which county is Salisbury Plain?

b5 *In which county is Cannock Chase?*

a6 Eddie Valiant appears in a film with which cartoon character?

b6 *In which film does an eccentric scientist help a teenager to travel back to the fifties to meet his parents?*

a7 In its adverts, which soap promised 'a schoolgirl complexion'?

b7 *And which pills were supposedly worth a guinea a box?*

a8 When the Dalai Lama escaped from Tibet, which country gave him sanctuary?

b8 *What was the name of the U-2 pilot shot down over the Soviet Union and imprisoned as a spy?*

a9 What is an enzyme?

b9 *What is a base metal?*

a10 In Sherlock Holmes' *'Final Problem'*, who was described as 'the Napoleon of crime'?

b10 *Which thriller writer (of 170 books, including* The Four Just Men*) died in 1932?*

a11 For which city is Aldergrove the airport?

b11 *And for which city is Dyce the airport?*

a12 Which British prime minister sacked seven members of his Cabinet in what became known as 'the night of the long knives'?

b12 *In Britain, which Labour minister resigned in 1930 and started his own extreme right-wing party?*

No. 140 Answers

a1 Kylie Minogue
b1 *Wham!*
a2 Oklahoma City
b2 *Utah*
a3 Jimmy Savile
b3 *Ed Stewart*
a4 Snooker
b4 *Golf*
a5 Wiltshire
b5 *Staffordshire*
a6 Roger Rabbit
b6 Back to the Future
a7 Palmolive
b7 *Beecham's Pills*
a8 India
b8 *Gary Powers*
a9 A biological catalyst; a substance which speeds up a reaction or digests starch or fats
b9 *A non-precious metal*
a10 (Professor) Moriarty
b10 *Edgar Wallace*
a11 Belfast
b11 *Aberdeen*
a12 Harold Macmillan (1962)
b12 *Sir Oswald Mosley*

Tie-breaker

Q Name the seven dwarfs.
A *Sleepy, Grumpy, Sneezy, Happy, Dopey, Doc and Bashful*

No. 141: Who Wrote That?

Who wrote the following literary works?

a1   *The History of Mr Polly*
b1   Blandings Castle
a2   *Tinker, Tailor, Soldier, Spy*
b2   *The Maigret novels*
a3   *Of Mice and Men*
b3   An Inspector Calls
a4   *Women in Love*
b4   The Moon and Sixpence
a5   *Clayhanger*
b5   Finnegans Wake
a6   *Doctor Zhivago*
b6   The GULAG Archipelago
a7   *Brideshead Revisited*
b7   The Road to Wigan Pier
a8   *The Trial*
b8   A Severed Head
a9   *Goodbye to All That*
b9   A Shropshire Lad
a10   *Mapp and Lucia*
b10   The Forsyte Saga
a11   *Goodbye to Berlin*
b11   Lolita
a12   *Sea Fever and Cargoes*
b12   The Go-Between

No. 141 Answers

a1	H. G. Wells
b1	*P. G. Wodehouse*
a2	John le Carré
b2	*Georges Simenon*
a3	John Steinbeck
b3	*J. B. Priestley*
a4	D. H. Lawrence
b4	*Somerset Maugham*
a5	Arnold Bennett
b5	*James Joyce*
a6	Boris Pasternak
b6	*Alexander Solzhenitsyn*
a7	Evelyn Waugh
b7	*George Orwell*
a8	Franz Kafka
b8	*Iris Murdoch*
a9	Robert Graves
b9	*A. E. Housman*
a10	E. F. Benson
b10	*John Galsworthy*
a11	Christopher Isherwood
b11	*Vladimir Nabokov*
a12	John Masefield
b12	*L. P. Hartley*

Tie-breaker

Q Who wrote the novels *Point Counter Point*, *Chrome Yellow* and *Eyeless in Gaza*?

A Aldous Huxley

No. 142

a1 What make of car are the Polo and the Jetta?

b1 *What make of car are the Civic and the Accord?*

a2 Which comedian used to say, 'Hello, my darlings'?

b2 *Which comedian is associated with such words as 'tattifilarious', 'plumptiousness' – and also had trouble with the Inland Revenue?*

a3 In which sport has Liz McColgan won a gold medal?

b3 *Which snooker star was, for a time, thought to be 'boring'?*

a4 Which Italian story about a wooden puppet became a major Walt Disney film in 1940?

b4 *Which character plays the Sorcerer's Apprentice in the film Fantasia?*

a5 Out of which counties was the county of Avon created in 1974?

b5 *Into which new county was Westmorland absorbed in 1974?*

a6 What invention, linked with the number 33⅓, first went on sale in 1931?

b6 *What useful domestic item was invented by Tefal in Paris in 1955?*

a7 What was the middle name of American Secretary of State Dulles?

b7 *Which American president started a work programme which promised a 'new deal'?*

a8 Which musician composed the 'Enigma Variations'?

b8 *Which pianist became famous for her war-time recitals in the National Gallery?*

a9 Which actress (who starred in the film A Passage to India) has a theatre named after her in Croydon?

b9 *Which new theatre was opened in 1932 with performances of Shakespeare's Henry IV, parts 1 and 2?*

a10 Which two countries signed an 'Entente Cordiale' in 1904?

b10 *In which country was Patrice Lumumba a leader?*

a11 Which tube line on London's Underground can you take to Heathrow Airport?

b11 *On a London Underground map, what colour is the Jubilee line?*

a12 In which radio programme did we regularly hear the announcement, 'We stop the roar of London's traffic . . .'?

b12 *Which radio show introduced us to the Angus Prune tune?*

No. 142 Answers

a1	Volkswagen
b1	*Honda*
a2	Charlie Drake
b2	*Ken Dodd*
a3	Athletics (10,000 metres)
b3	*Steve Davis*
a4	Pinocchio
b4	*Mickey Mouse*
a5	Gloucestershire and Somerset
b5	*Cumbria*
a6	Long-playing records (revolving at 33⅓ rpm)
b6	*Non-stick pans (and other non-stick implements)*
a7	Foster (John Foster Dulles)
b7	*Franklin D. Roosevelt*
a8	(Edward) Elgar
b8	*Dame Myra Hess*
a9	Dame Peggy Ashcroft
b9	*Shakespeare Memorial Theatre, Stratford upon Avon*
a10	Britain and France
b10	*The Congo*
a11	Piccadilly
b11	*Grey (accept: silver)*
a12	*In Town Tonight*
b12	I'm Sorry I'll Read That Again

Tie-breaker

Q Why was Europe at sixes and sevens in 1959?

A *Six countries were in the Common Market (France, Germany, Italy, Belgium, Netherlands and Luxembourg) and seven were in EFTA or the European Free Trade Association (UK, Norway, Sweden, Denmark, Switzerland, Austria and Portugal)*

No. 143

a1   Which satirical television show is dependent on latex rubber?

b1   *Which television character regularly said, 'Silly old moo'?*

a2   In its adverts, which beer promised to work wonders?

b2   *And which one reached parts other ones could not reach?*

a3   Pop singers Chris Lowe and Neil Tennant were (or indeed are) known as . . . what?

b3   *Who was the lead singer of the group Culture Club?*

a4   Which was athlete Herb Elliott's principal track event?

b4   *In which sport did Billy Wright captain England?*

a5   In what is carbon tetrachloride often used?

b5   *What is made from potassium nitrate?*

a6   Who was the male star of the film *Grease*?

b6   *Who played Gandhi in the film of that name?*

a7   Which post in a Tory Cabinet is Selwyn Lloyd best remembered for holding?

b7   *Which Labour politician was nicknamed 'Nye'?*

a8   In which county is Stevenage?

b8   *In which county is Basingstoke?*

a9   Santa Fe is the capital of which American state?

b9   *Of which American state is Lincoln the capital?*

a10   In which George Orwell novel are there a 'Two Minutes Hate', Thought Police and a language called Newspeak?

b10   *In a poem, T. S. Eliot suggests the way the world ends is not with a bang but with a . . . what?*

a11   Which city has railway stations called Interchange and Forster Square?

b11   *In which Yorkshire cathedral city are there railway stations called Kirkgate and Westgate?*

a12   Which important building was destroyed by fire on the night of February 28, 1933?

b12   *In which Northern Ireland town did the IRA kill eleven people on Remembrance Day in 1987?*

No. 143 Answers

a1 *Spitting Image*
b1 *Alf Garnett*
a2 Double Diamond
b2 *Heineken*
a3 The Pet Shop Boys
b3 *Boy George*
a4 The mile (1500 metres)
b4 *Soccer*
a5 Cleaning
b5 *Matches, fireworks*
a6 John Travolta
b6 *Ben Kingsley*
a7 Chancellor of the Exchequer
b7 *Aneurin Bevan*
a8 Hertfordshire
b8 *Hampshire*
a9 New Mexico
b9 *Nebraska*
a10 1984
b10 *Whimper*
a11 Bradford
b11 *Wakefield*
a12 The German Reichstag (say: rike-starg) or parliament building
b12 *Enniskillen*

Tie-breaker

Q Which pop music manager said, 'I want to manage those four boys. It wouldn't take me more than two half-days a week'?
A *Brian Epstein, about the Beatles (he did become their manager)*

No. 144

a1 What make of car are Pandas, Unos (say: u-nose) and Tipos (say: tee-pose)?

b1 *What make of car are the Micra, Sunny and the Primera?*

a2 In which sport did Terry Spinks win an Olympic gold medal?

b2 *Which was heavyweight boxer Ingemar Johansson's home country?*

a3 Weatherfield is the fictional location of which television serial?

b3 *Which television serial is set in the borough of Walford?*

a4 Which part of London saw race riots in 1958 and, later, an annual carnival?

b4 *And also in London in 1958, who 'came out' for the last time?*

a5 Near which town or city is Devonport naval dockyard?

b5 *Off which mainland port lies the area of sea known as Spithead?*

a6 In the films, what is Rambo's first name?

b6 *What is Crocodile Dundee's first name?*

a7 Who composed the piano piece 'Claire de Lune'?

b7 *Which pianist played 'old ones, new ones'?*

a8 George Bush was vice-president to which American president?

b8 *Which famous American dramatist was accused of being 'un-American' during a Communist witch-hunt?*

a9 What is a saline solution?

b9 *What is gun cotton?*

a10 Whom did Von Hindenburg beat in the 1932 German presidential election?

b10 *What was Soviet President Kruschev's first name?*

a11 *Cavalcade* is a play chronicling a family's life from 1899 to 1930. Who wrote it?

b11 *In 1913, who wrote the play* Androcles and the Lion?

a12 In which wartime comedy show did Mona Lott always gloomily announce, 'It's being so cheerful as keeps me going'?

b12 *In which radio panel game did we regularly hear the phrase 'And the next object is . . .'?*

No. 144 Answers

a1	Fiat
b1	*Nissan*
a2	Boxing
b2	*Sweden*
a3	*Coronation Street*
b3	EastEnders
a4	Notting Hill Gate
b4	*Debutantes (the last time young ladies were 'presented' at court)*
a5	Plymouth
b5	*Portsmouth*
a6	John
b6	*Mick*
a7	(Claude) Debussy
b7	*Semprini*
a8	Ronald Reagan
b8	*Arthur Miller*
a9	Liquid containing salt
b9	*An explosive (nitro cellulose)*
a10	Hitler
b10	*Nikita*
a11	Noël Coward
b11	*George Bernard Shaw*
a12	ITMA
b12	Twenty Questions

Tie-breaker

Q Which was Britain's first stretch of motorway?
A *The Preston bypass (now part of the M6)*

No. 145

a1 With which means of transport is the name Westland associated?

b1 *What are (or were) trolley buses?*

a2 As what did Anna Pavlova achieve fame?

b2 *And what kind of food is Pavlova?*

a3 In an advert, which product were you asked to 'tell' from butter?

b3 *And which product promised to make you a little lovelier each day?*

a4 With which country was Britain in disagreement during the so-called 'Cod War'?

b4 *Which subject caused violent scenes during a debate in the House of Commons in 1902?*

a5 Which prime minister regularly holidayed on the Scilly Isles?

b5 *Which Welsh writer lived in Laugharne near Carmarthen?*

a6 In which war film did Michael Caine lead a team of German commandos trying to assassinate Churchill?

b6 *In which film epic did Charlton Heston go chariot-racing?*

a7 Did Liverpool F. C. first win the Cup Final in 1925, 1935, or 1965?

b7 *Which soccer club did Danny Blanchflower captain to success in the League and the Cup Final in 1961?*

a8 Charleston is the capital of which American state?

b8 *Of which American state is St Paul the capital?*

a9 Which heavy, silvery white metal is more precious than gold?

b9 *In what is plutonium used?*

a10 Which female singer had hits with 'You Don't Have to Say You Love Me' and 'Son of a Preacher Man'?

b10 *Which singer had a hit with 'These Boots Are Made for Walkin''?*

a11 In a wartime broadcast, Winston Churchill said to America 'we will finish the job', provided America were to do what?

b11 *According to Dorothy Parker, at whom do men seldom make passes?*

a12 Which cartoonist created the characters Fungus the Bogeyman and the Snowman, and drew a popular 'Father Christmas'?

b12 *When the Noddy books were re-published in 1987, what did gnomes replace?*

No. 145 Answers

a1   Helicopters
b1   *Buses powered by electricity (drawn from overhead wires through roof-mounted trolley poles)*
a2   Ballet dancer (ballet mistress)
b2   *A cake (Pavlova cake)*
a3   Stork margarine
b3   *('Fabulous pink') Camay soap*
a4   Iceland
b4   *Ireland*
a5   Harold Wilson
b5   *Dylan Thomas*
a6   *The Eagle Has Landed*
b6   Ben Hur
a7   1965
b7   *Tottenham Hotspur*
a8   West Virginia
b8   *Minnesota*
a9   Platinum
b9   *Nuclear reactors, atomic weapons*
a10   Dusty Springfield
b10   *Nancy Sinatra*
a11   'Give us the tools'
b11   *Girls who wear glasses*
a12   Raymond Briggs
b12   *Golliwogs*

Tie-breaker

Q Which prime minister said, 'We are not at war with Egypt. We are in an armed conflict'?
A *Sir Anthony Eden*

No. 146

a1   In which county is Clacton-on-Sea?

b1   In which county is the inland resort of Buxton? •

a2   Of which make of car was the E-type a famous model?

b2   What make of car was the Silver Cloud?

a3   Which television policeman often said 'Evening all'?

b3   Which comedian regularly said 'Now there's a funny thing'?

a4   Which soccer club was famously managed by Kenny Dalglish?

b4   Which soccer club has been linked with pop star Elton John?

a5   Alma Ata is the capital of which former Soviet republic?

b5   Kiev is the capital of which former Soviet republic?

a6   Where did Dr Vivian Fuchs lead an expedition in 1958?

b6   Who was the first American to orbit the Earth in space?

a7   In which film musical (starring Grace Kelly) did Bing Crosby and Frank Sinatra sing 'Well Did You Evah?'?

b7   Which American musical is set partly in Deadwood City's Golden Garter saloon?

a8   Which Sunday newspaper was advertised with the slogan 'All human life is there!'?

b8   Britain's first 'colour supplement' was published in 1962 – with which Sunday newspaper?

a9   Ryan O'Neal starred with his daughter in the film *Paper Moon*. What is her name?

b9   Who dragged up to play the lead in the film Tootsie?

a10   In 1971, Anthony Marriott and Alistair Foot wrote a long-running sex farce called . . . what?

b10   Which Terence Rattigan play features a translation by the poet Robert Browning of a Greek text?

a11   What memorable phrase did Commander Tommy Woodrooffe utter several times on radio in 1937 when describing a Spithead naval review?

b11   In which radio comedy did the line 'He's fallen in the water' originate?

a12   Of which country was Sir Roy Welensky prime minister?

b12   Of which country was Imre Nagy (say: naje) prime minister?

No. 146 Answers

a1   Essex
b1   *Derbyshire*
a2   Jaguar
b2   *Rolls-Royce*
a3   Dixon of Dock Green (P. C. George Dixon)
b3   *Max Miller*
a4   Liverpool
b4   *Watford*
a5   Khazakstan
b5   *Ukraine*
a6   Across the Antarctic
b6   *(Lieutenant-Colonel) John Glenn*
a7   *High Society*
b7   *Calamity Jane*
a8   *News of the World*
b8   Sunday Times
a9   Tatum O'Neal
b9   *Dustin Hoffman*
a10   *No Sex Please – We're British*
b10   The Browning Version
a11   'The fleet's lit up' (Many listeners thought he was drunk)
b11   The Goon Show
a12   Central African Federation (accept: Rhodesia)
b12   *Hungary*

Tie-breaker

Q In 1932 a British law was passed which abolished a previously legal punishment for children. What was it?
A *Whipping*

No. 147

a1 According to the adverts, with which cigarette were you never alone?

b1 *And which lager was (or is) 'probably the best lager in the world'?*

a2 What is the ex-West Indian cricketer Sobers' first name?

b2 *Which sport or game does Eric Bristow play?*

a3 In which film does Dick Van Dyke dance with four penguins?

b3 *In which film is the Pushmipullyou?*

a4 In which television series did Jim do battle with Sir Humphrey?

b4 *Which television programme made the one-word answer 'pass' into a catch phrase?*

a5 What is meant by 'synthetic'?

b5 *What is sucrose?*

a6 Which former Conservative leader accused the Conservative party (under Mrs Thatcher) of 'selling the family silver'?

b6 *How many general elections did Mrs Thatcher win as leader of the Conservative party?*

a7 In which county is Sizewell Nuclear Power Station?

b7 *Why has Daventry in the English Midlands become known world-wide?*

a8 Which city has railway stations called New Street and Snow Hill?

b8 *Which town has railway stations called North, South and Pleasure Beach?*

a9 'Get Ready', 'Papa Was a Rolling Stone' and 'The Way You Do the Things You Do' were all hits for which Motown group?

b9 *Part of the television series* The Partridge Family, *he starred on Broadway in* Joseph and the Amazing Technicolor Dreamcoat. *Who is he?*

a10 Which has been the principal industry in the Rhondda (say: rhontha) Valley for much of the century?

b10 *In which county is the industrial town of Middlesborough?*

a11 Of which American state is Jackson the capital?

b11 *Of which American state is Sacramento the capital?*

a12 Which 'Beat generation' American wrote the book *On the Road?*

b12 *Which French novelist wrote* The Outsider?

No. 147 Answers

a1	Strand
b1	*Carlsberg*
a2	Garfield (Garry)
b2	*Darts*
a3	Mary Poppins
b3	*Dr Dolittle*
a4	*Yes, Minister*
b4	*Mastermind*
a5	Not natural; made from chemicals (by humans)
b5	*Pure white sugar (obtained from sugar beet or sugar cane)*
a6	Harold Macmillan
b6	*Three*
a7	Suffolk
b7	*Because of its radio transmission mast ('Daventry calling . . .')*
a8	Birmingham
b8	*Blackpool*
a9	The Temptations
b9	*David Cassidy*
a10	Coal-mining
b10	*Cleveland*
a11	Mississippi
b11	*California*
a12	Jack Kerouac
b12	*Albert Camus*

Tie-breaker

Q Why was the first American to cross the finishing line in the Marathon in the 1904 Olympics disqualified?

A *He took a lift on a lorry for part of the course*

No. 148

a1 Which television star calls her friends 'possum'?

b1 *On which television show is it possible to hear the line, 'And the same question to number two'?*

a2 Which Russian dancer defected to the West in 1961?

b2 *Who was born Jan Ludvik Hock and died in the sea near the Canaries?*

a3 Which Eskimo word (meaning a jacket of skin or cloth, with a fur-lined hood) has come into the English language?

b3 *In Russia, what is a 'dacha'?*

a4 Into which area of maritime water does the River Hamble flow?

b4 *In which county are the Mendip Hills?*

a5 Which piece of music became the official United States anthem in 1931?

b5 *Which American musician composed the ballet 'Billy the Kid'?*

a6 Which motorway goes north from Preston to Scotland?

b6 *Which motorway crosses the Pennine Mountains from north Manchester to Leeds?*

a7 'Nation shall speak peace unto nation' is a motto of which organization?

b7 *In radio's Children's Hour, who always said, 'Good night, children, everywhere!'?*

a8 Which English fast bowler was at the centre of the 'bodyline' controversy in 1933?

b8 *Which bowler took 19 wickets in one test match in 1956?*

a9 What new building material was invented by a French civil engineer in 1904?

b9 *What was the 'Flying Bedstead'?*

a10 What post or title was Hitler given in 1933?

b10 *Who was elected president of France in 1958?*

a11 Which Norwegian playwright wrote the play *Peer Gynt*?

b11 *And which composer wrote incidental music for Peer Gynt?*

a12 Of which European country was Angola a colony?

b12 *In which Tibetan city did the Dalai Lama have his palace?*

No. 148 Answers

a1 Dame Edna Everage (Barry Humphries)
b1 *Blind Date*
a2 (Rudolf) Nureyev
b2 *Robert Maxwell*
a3 Anorak (anoraq, originally)
b3 *Country house; summer home (a privilege of party officials in Communist times)*
a4 Southampton Water
b4 *Somerset*
a5 'The Star-Spangled Banner'
b5 *(Aaron) Copland*
a6 M6
b6 *M62*
a7 BBC
b7 *Uncle Mac (Derek McCulloch)*
a8 Harold Larwood (also Bill Voce)
b8 *Jim Laker*
a9 Pre-stressed concrete (invented by Eugene Freyssinet)
b9 *Early vertical take-off aircraft (Rolls-Royce TMR)*
a10 Chancellor (of the German Reich, or state)
b10 *General de Gaulle*
a11 (Henrik) Ibsen
b11 *(Edvard) Grieg*
a12 Portugal
b12 *Lhasa*

Tie-breaker

Q There are three main classes of food needed by the human body: fats and carbohydrates are two; what is the third?
A *Proteins*

No. 149

a1   On screen, what make of car was Herbie?

b1   In the cartoon films, what kind of creature is Goofy?

a2   In an advert, what was said to be full of 'Eastern Promise'?

b2   According to the advert, which chocolates 'grow on you'?

a3   For what construction is Jodrell Bank in Cheshire famous?

b3   For which industry was Corby in Northamptonshire famous for part of the century?

a4   Which aircraft company builds the TriStar?

b4   What public transport vehicles were manufactured by Leyland, Bristol and Crossley?

a5   About which boxer did Mike Tyson say, 'He should come back. All Americans love beating up poor old Frank'?

b5   In 1991, which boxer went into a long coma after a fight against Chris Eubank?

a6   On television, what was the setting of the soap opera *Compact*?

b6   Tannochbrae was the setting of which television series?

a7   In the story and the film, why did Cruelle de Vil want to steal 101 dalmatians?

b7   Ring of Bright Water principally features which mammals?

a8   Who was the first King of Britain to broadcast?

b8   Which British Royal gave up the Royal Marines in 1987?

a9   'I'm a Believer' and 'Daydream Believer' were hits for which television pop group?

b9   Which pop group sang 'Dedicated Follower of Fashion', 'Sunny Afternoon' and 'Lola'?

a10   When did the last steam train run on London's Underground?: in 1911, 1931, or 1971?

b10   In Europe, was the first motorway opened in 1921, 1935, or 1955?

a11   In which Eastern state was Mr Gomulka a leading politician?

b11   Of which country was King Feisal monarch until 1958?

a12   As bishop of which diocese did David Jenkins become a controversial figure?

b12   By what name or nickname was Lieutenant General John Glubb known when commanding the Arab Legion?

No. 149 Answers

a1 A Volkswagen
b1 *A dog*
a2 Fry's Turkish Delight
b2 *(Cadbury) Roses*
a3 Radio telescope
b3 *Steel*
a4 Lockheed
b4 *Buses*
a5 Frank Bruno
b5 *Michael Watson*
a6 The editorial offices of a women's magazine (called *Compact*)
b6 *Dr Finlay's Casebook*
a7 To make fur coats
b7 *Otters*
a8 King George V
b8 *Prince Andrew*
a9 The Monkees
b9 *The Kinks*
a10 1971
b10 *1921, in Berlin*
a11 Poland
b11 *Iraq*
a12 Durham
b12 *Glubb Pasha*

Tie-breaker

Q In the Second World War, for what was PLUTO an abbreviation?
A *Pipe line under the ocean (actually across the English Channel, supplying oil to Allied forces after D-Day)*

No. 150

a1   With which entertainer is the line 'I'm in charge' associated?

b1   *In the fifties, whose catch phrase was 'I only arsked'?*

a2   Dame Nellie Melba died in 1931. How did she became famous?

b2   *And what food was named after her?*

a3   In which county is the container port of Felixstowe?

b3   *In which county is Leyland, the home of Leyland trucks and buses?*

a4   Which organization advertised itself with the statement 'We're getting there'?

b4   *And which airline advertised itself by promising 'We'll take good care of you'?*

a5   Which human organ can be regulated by an electronic pacemaker?

b5   *When does a doctor use a spatula?*

a6   What make of car were the Hawk and the Super Snipe?

b6   *What make of car were Imps and Huskies?*

a7   From what is polythene made?

b7   *What percentage of 18 carat gold is actually gold?*

a8   Which boy singer sang 'Walking in the Air' in the cartoon film *The Snowman*?

b8   *Which cartoon character said 'I taut I taw a puddy tat'?*

a9   In which city were the 1956 Olympics held – the first to take place south of the Equator?

b9   *Which tennis player's lover or partner was Nancy Lieberman?*

a10   Who created the character Miss Joan Hunter Dunn?

b10   *In Rupert Brooke's poem 'The Old Vicarage, Grantchester', the poet asks if the church clock still stands at . . .what time?*

a11   How did United Nations Secretary-General Dag Hammarskjöld (say: hammer-shold) die?

b11   *Who died in prison and was known as the 'Butcher of Lyons'?*

a12   From which film comes the song 'Have Yourself a Merry Little Christmas'?

b12   *Which Harvey Fierstein musical features a St Tropez (say: san tropay) drag club?*

No. 150 Answers

a1 Bruce Forsyth
b1 *Bernard Bresslaw*
a2 As a singer
b2 *Peach Melba (peach served with ice cream and raspberry juice)*
      and/or Melba toast
a3 Suffolk
b3 *Lancashire*
a4 British Rail
b4 *British Airways*
a5 The heart
b5 *To hold down your tongue, when examining your throat*
a6 Humber
b6 *Hillman*
a7 Oil
b7 *75%*
a8 Aled Jones
b8 *Tweetie Pie*
a9 Melbourne
b9 *Martina Navratilova*
a10 John Betjeman (poet)
b10 *Ten to three*
a11 In an aircrash
b11 *Klaus Barbie*
a12 *Meet Me in St Louis*
b12 La Cage Aux Folles

Tie-breaker

Q Fungicides get rid of fungi. Which pests are attacked with
formicide?
A *Ants*

No. 151: Singles

Which soloist or group had a hit with each of these pop and rock 'singles'?

a1   'Glad All Over'
b1   'Strawberry Fields Forever'
a2   'Hippy Hippy Shake'
b2   'House of the Rising Sun'
a3   'The Sound of Silence'
b3   'Imagine'
a4   'Anticipation'
b4   'Brown Sugar'
a5   'Every Beat of My Heart'
b5   'Reach Out, I'll Be There'
a6   'All or Nothing'
b6   'Don't Stop the Carnival'
a7   'Catch a Falling Star'
b7   'With or Without You'
a8   'Why Do Fools Fall in Love'
b8   'Will You Love Me Tomorrow'
a9   'I Want You Back'
b9   'Pretty Flamingo'
a10 'California Dreamin''
b10 'Maggie May'
a11 'At the Hop'
b11 'Let's Have A Party'
a12 'Annie's Song'
b12 'School's Out'

No. 151 Answers

a1	The Dave Clark Five
b1	*The Beatles*
a2	The Swinging Blue Jeans
b2	*The Animals*
a3	The Bachelors (accept: Simon and Garfunkel)
b3	*John Lennon*
a4	Carly Simon
b4	*The Rolling Stones*
a5	Gladys Knight and the Pips (accept: Rod Stewart)
b5	*The Four Tops*
a6	The Small Faces
b6	*Alan Price*
a7	Perry Como
b7	*U2*
a8	Frankie Lymon and the Teenagers (accept: Diana Ross)
b8	*The Shirelles*
a9	The Jackson Five
b9	*Manfred Mann*
a10	The Mamas and the Papas
b10	*Rod Stewart*
a11	Danny and the Juniors
b11	*Wanda Jackson (accept also Elvis Presley)*
a12	John Denver (accept also James Galway)
b12	*Alice Cooper*

Tie-breaker

Q Which singer presented the history of rock music on a single called 'American Pie'?

A *Don Maclean*

No. 152

a1 With what sort of television programmes is David Attenborough principally associated?

b1 *Which television police series introduced us to Detective Chief Inspector Barlow?*

a2 What was first painted on London's streets in June 1958?

b2 *Which athletic craze kept many people spinning in 1959?*

a3 What is a viscous liquid?

b3 *What is meant by the word 'translucent'?*

a4 In which county is the town of Weymouth?

b4 *In which county is Dartmoor?*

a5 Which unspoilt Spanish seaside village became a famous holiday resort in the late fifties?

b5 *In which city is Gorky Park?*

a6 As what did Augustus John achieve fame?

b6 *Ronald Searle created an infamous girls' school – called . . .?*

a7 In which unexpected place did a 19-year-old West German land a plane in 1987?

b7 *In which country or countries is the airline SAS based?*

a8 1991 was the bicentenary of the death of which famous Austrian composer?

b8 *Which musician composed a symphony 'From the New World'?*

a9 Known as 'Hollywood's mermaid', she starred in *Bathing Beauty* in 1944. Who was she?

b9 *Which child star sang 'On the Good Ship Lollipop'?*

a10 Which Asian country was beset by civil war in 1971?

b10 *And which African country suffered civil war from 1967–1970?*

a11 On which radio show did we hear the catch phrases 'The answer lies in the soil' and 'Thirty-five years'?

b11 *During the Second World War, which two comediennes played the characters Gert and Daisy?*

a12 Which pop song includes the lines, 'Well, it's a one for the money, two for the show'?

b12 *Whose pop song includes the lines, 'Hop on the bus, Gus, don't need to discuss much'?*

No. 152 Answers

a1 Natural history or wildlife programmes
b1 *Z Cars*
a2 Yellow no-parking lines
b2 *The hula hoop*
a3 One that does not flow easily (e.g. oil or treacle)
b3 *Allowing light to pass through (e.g. tissue paper is 'translucent'; it does not mean transparent)*
a4 Dorset
b4 *Devon*
a5 Benidorm
b5 *Moscow*
a6 Painter (especially of portraits)
b6 *St Trinian's*
a7 Red Square, Moscow (Mathias Rust)
b7 *Scandinavia (Denmark, Sweden, Norway)*
a8 Mozart
b8 *Dvorak (say: vor-jak)*
a9 Esther Williams
b9 *Shirley Temple*
a10 Pakistan
b10 *Nigeria*
a11 Beyond Our Ken
b11 *Elsie and Doris Waters*
a12 'Blue Suede Shoes'
b12 *Paul Simon ('50 Ways to Leave Your Lover')*

Tie-breaker

Q What was abandoned in January 1975 after having made only 3 miles progress in 93 years?

A *(Construction of) the Channel Tunnel*

No. 153

a1   Which comedian regularly said, 'It's the way I tell them'?

b1   *Who on television originally uttered the command 'Exterminate'?*

a2   From which town does the anonymous 'Disgusted' traditionally write to newspapers?

b2   *Which Sussex town is famous for its theatre and theatre festival?*

a3   Which seaside resort has been advertised as 'so bracing' (on posters showing a jolly fisherman)?

b3   *What implement was said to 'beat as it sweeps as it cleans'?*

a4   What name is given to a sea-going vessel which has angled wings under the hull to lift it clear of the waves?

b4   *What form of transport is the 'Sea King'?*

a5   From 1956, what Government scheme offered the public promises of £1,000 prizes?

b5   *Which coin was a joey?*

a6   James Hanratty was hanged in 1962 for murder. By what name was the murder widely known?

b6   *Which drug began to be suspected as the cause of many serious defeats in new-born babies from 1958 onwards?*

a7   'I love to go a wandering, my knapsack on my back.' What was the title of Frank Weir's hit song?

b7   *Which singer (later a radio presenter) once topped the charts with 'The Man from Laramie'?*

a8   Which Royal broke his arm playing polo?

b8   *Of which country was Alfonso king until 1931?*

a9   Which musical instrument did Jacqueline du Pré (say: pray) play?

b9   *What was composer Vaughan Williams' first name?*

a10   What is meant by 'protocol'?

b10   *What is a 'seminar'?*

a11   In the film of that name, who played the 'rebel without a cause'?

b11   *Which swash-buckling Hollywood hero played Captain Blood and Robin Hood – and died in 1959?*

a12   In which year was the Berlin Wall erected?

b12   *And in which year was it torn down?*

No. 153 Answers

a1 Frank Carson
b1 *The Daleks (in Dr Who)*
a2 Tunbridge Wells
b2 *Chichester*
a3 Skegness
b3 *Hoover vacuum*
a4 Hydrofoil (accept: jetfoil)
b4 *Helicopter*
a5 Premium Bonds
b5 *A threepenny bit (3d) – pre-decimal coinage*
a6 The A6 Murder
b6 *Thalidomide*
a7 'The Happy Wanderer'
b7 *Jimmy Young*
a8 Prince Charles
b8 *Spain*
a9 Cello
b9 *Ralph*
a10 Diplomatic etiquette; a correct way of doing things (in diplomacy)
b10 *Small class or group meeting (usually at a university, etc.) for discussion or research*
a11 James Dean
b11 *Errol Flynn*
a12 1961
b12 *1989*

Tie-breaker

Q In electronics, what are the two electrodes contained in a diode?
A *A cathode and an anode*

No. 154

a1 What form of transport is the 'One-Eleven'?

b1 *Which country's airline is called Iberia?*

a2 When Germany was divided, was Saxony in West or East Germany?

b2 *And was Bavaria in East or West Germany?*

a3 Cricket: which two counties play in the Roses Match?

b3 *And which two cricketing countries play each other for the F. M. Worrell Trophy?*

a4 Which instrument did the jazz musician Miles Davis play?

b4 *Which kind of music was played on a guitar, washboard and tea-chest?*

a5 Which radio and television personality used to say, 'Stop messing about'?

b5 *Which northern comedian regularly said, 'Right, monkey'?*

a6 What construction was killed off by Parliament in 1907, on grounds of national security?

b6 *With Mrs Thatcher, which French president gave the go-ahead to the Channel Tunnel?*

a7 Which American statue celebrated its 100th birthday in 1986?

b7 *In which American state did Blacks boycott buses in 1955, because of race laws?*

a8 Which puppet characters live on Tracey Island?

b8 *In which park does Yogi Bear live?*

a9 With which New Forest town is Lord Montagu connected?

b9 *In which British city is there an area known as Bogside?*

a10 Lord Rix (formerly Brian Rix) was leading man at which London theatre?

b10 *By what name was the stage revue The Follies of 1907 popularly known?*

a11 As what did Sir Stanley Spencer achieve fame?

b11 *As what did Toscanini become famous?*

a12 About which outdoor activity did A. E. Wainwright produce many guides?

b12 *Who wrote the best-selling book A Year in Provence?*

No. 154 Answers

a1 Passenger aircraft
b1 *Spain*
a2 East Germany (Lower Saxony, another province, was in West Germany)
b2 *West Germany*
a3 Lancashire and Yorkshire
b3 *West Indies and Australia*
a4 Trumpet
b4 *Skiffle*
a5 Kenneth Williams
b5 *Al Read*
a6 The Channel Tunnel
b6 *President Mitterand*
a7 Statue of Liberty
b7 *Alabama*
a8 The Thunderbirds
b8 *Jellystone Park*
a9 Beaulieu (say: bew-lee)
b9 *Londonderry/Derry*
a10 Whitehall Theatre
b10 *'The Ziegfeld Follies' (after Florenz Ziegfeld, the producer)*
a11 Artist
b11 *Conductor*
a12 (Fell) walking
b12 *Peter Mayle*

Tie-breaker

Q In which Marx Brothers' film, made in 1937, did they cause havoc at a race course?
A A Day At the Races

No. 155

a1 What phrase was the rallying cry of German Nazis?

b1 *Which military alliance came into being in Eastern Europe in 1955?*

a2 Which gangster movie features only children?

b2 *How does Dorothy give her classmates a major surprise in the film* Gregory's Girl?

a3 Why did Ruth Ellis hit the headlines in 1955?

b3 *In which city was James Anderton a controversial policeman?*

a4 If you face the sea at Ilfracombe in Devon, are you looking north, south, east or west?

b4 *Which Isle of Wight town is famous for its regatta week?*

a5 As what did Gilbert Harding achieve fame?

b5 *Who was the first director-general of the BBC?*

a6 In the 1932 hit, what had got his hat on and was coming out to play?

b6 *'Twenty tiny fingers, twenty tiny toes' went the popular song – but which group sang it?*

a7 As a result of which novel and film did the line 'I'm going to make him an offer he can't refuse' become popular?

b7 *In a 1946 speech, what did Winston Churchill say had descended across the continent of Europe?*

a8 Jesse Owens held a world record for 25 years. In which event?

b8 *What was Olympic swimmer Linda Ludgrove's best stroke?*

a9 After travelling north through the Channel Tunnel, which is the first town your train is likely to stop at?

b9 *92 died and nearly 200 were injured in Lewisham, south London, in 1957. How?*

a10 From 1933, what was the LPTB?

b10 *What large building became part of the Battersea skyline in 1933?*

a11 Who wrote the books *Another Country* and *The Fire Next Time*?

b11 *Jaroslav Hasek wrote a novel – about a soldier called . . .?*

a12 In which year did various self-governing colonies join together as the Commonwealth of Australia?

b12 *Which country annexed (or took control of) Korea in 1910?*

No. 155 Answers

a1	'Sieg Heil!' (accept: 'Heil, Hitler!')
b1	*The Warsaw Pact*
a2	*Bugsy Malone*
b2	*She gets on the football team*
a3	For murdering her (unfaithful) lover
b3	*Manchester*
a4	North
b4	*Cowes*
a5	Radio and television personality (in quiz shows)
b5	*Sir John Reith (later Lord Reith)*
a6	The sun
b6	*The Stargazers*
a7	*The Godfather*
b7	*An iron curtain*
a8	Long-jump
b8	*Backstroke*
a9	Ashford
b9	*Two trains crashed (in fog)*
a10	London Passenger Transport Board
b10	*Battersea Power Station*
a11	James Baldwin
b11	*Svejk (or Schweik)*
a12	1901
b12	*Japan*

Tie-breaker

Q 'F-numbers' on a camera indicate the size of . . . what?
A *The size of the lens aperture*

No. 156

a1 Which manufacturer used the advertising slogan, 'Don't forget the fruit gums, mum!'?

b1 *About which toothpaste did an advert say, 'You'll wonder where the yellow went'?*

a2 Near which Royal residence is there a forest and a Great Park?

b2 *Kemp Town and Preston Park are both suburbs of which south-coast town?*

a3 What have the following in common: Marston, Mildenhall and Mawgan?

b3 *Which city has railway stations called Parkway and Temple Meads?*

a4 Which sport, principally, is played at Fenner's?

b4 *For which sport is Indianapolis famous?*

a5 Traditionally, which branch of the Christian Church is dominant in Russia?

b5 *Which important religious documents were found in Jordanian caves in 1947?*

a6 In which magazine did the 'Dear Bill' letters appear?

b6 *Which newspaper ran a gossip column called 'William Hickey'?*

a7 What, notably, was founded by Dame Marie Rambert?

b7 *In the thirties, who were Harry Roy, Jack Jackson and Ambrose?*

a8 King Juan (say: huan) Carlos is King of Spain. His wife is Queen . . .?

b8 *Of which country did King Constantine II become ruler in 1964?*

a9 Jet Morgan was the hero of which classic radio 'space' serial?

b9 *To which century (in the future) did Buck Rogers travel?*

a10 Which pop song includes the lines, 'One of 16 Vestal Virgins/Who are leaving for the coast'?

b10 *Who was the singing half of the pop duo Tyrannosaurus Rex?*

a11 In which northern city were the 1952 Olympics?

b11 *In which capital city was the 1900 World Exhibition?*

a12 Who wrote the book *Eminent Victorians*?

b12 *Who wrote a collection called* The Garden Party and other Stories?

No. 156 Answers

a1 Rowntree
b1 *Pepsodent*
a2 Windsor Castle
b2 *Brighton*
a3 All have airfields (mainly military)
b3 *Bristol*
a4 Cricket (Cambridge University)
b4 *Motor-racing*
a5 Orthodox
b5 *Dead Sea Scrolls*
a6 *Private Eye* (supposedly written by Denis Thatcher)
b6 Daily Express
a7 The Rambert Dance Company (ballet company)
b7 *All were bandleaders*
a8 Sophia
b8 Greece
a9 *Journey into Space*
b9 *25th Century*
a10 'A Whiter Shade of Pale'
b10 *Marc Bolan*
a11 Helsinki
b11 *Paris*
a12 Lytton Strachey
b12 *Katherine Mansfield*

Tie-breaker

Q Chromium is never found alone naturally. Which metal is usually found combined with it?

A *Iron*

No. 157

a1   What make of car were the Velox, Victor and Cresta?

b1   *What form of transport is the 'Chinook'?*

a2   What were the 'H line' and the 'A line'?

b2   *What were A, AA, U and X?*

a3   Which was Johnny Leach's sport?

b3   *Which was Patsy Hendren's sport?*

a4   Which comic actor directed the film *Annie Hall*?

b4   *What is the name of the disaster movie in which a small fire gets out of control in a high-rise building?*

a5   By what name is a cluster of towns around Stoke-on-Trent known?

b5   *By what name are the towns of Rochester, Chatham and Gillingham collectively known?*

a6   In which part of which country is Walloon the traditional language?

b6   *In which part of Spain is Catalan the traditional language?*

a7   Which male singer was associated with a babbling brook?

b7   *Who was the other half of the pop duo, Nina and . . .?*

a8   According to *Peter Pan*, what happens every time a child says 'I don't believe in fairies'?

b8   *Which fictional character regularly says 'Oh crikey' and 'Yaroooo!'?*

a9   Which country was ruled this century by King Frederick IX?

b9   *King Michael is claimant of which country's throne?*

a10   In which year did commercial television start in Britain?

b10   *And in which year did the BBC Television Service officially start?*

a11   On the London Underground map, what colour is the Metropolitan line?

b11   *And what colour is the Victoria line?*

a12   Who wrote the novel about university life called *The History Man*?

b12   *Who wrote the series of novels called* Alms for Oblivion?

No. 157 Answers

a1 Vauxhall
b1 *Helicopter*
a2 Fashion styles (in the fifties, created by Christian Dior)
b2 *Film classifications (i.e. age groups allowed to see them)*
a3 Table tennis
b3 *He played cricket*
a4 Woody Allen
b4 *The Towering Inferno*
a5 The Potteries; or the Five Towns
b5 *The Medway towns*
a6 Southern Belgium (a French dialect)
b6 *North-east (Catalonia)*
a7 Donald Peers ('By a Babbling Brook' was his theme song)
b7 *Frederick*
a8 A little fairy falls down dead
b8 *Billy Bunter*
a9 Denmark
b9 *Romania*
a10 1955
b10 *1936*
a11 Purple
b11 *(Light) blue*
a12 Malcolm Bradbury
b12 *Simon Raven*

Tie-breaker

Q Linus Carl Pauling won the Nobel Prize for Chemistry in 1954, for his work on the structure of molecules. Which Nobel Prize did he win in 1962?

A *Nobel Peace Prize (for his efforts to secure a ban on nuclear testing)*

No. 158

a1   What make of car was the Elan?

b1   *What is a Cessna?*

a2   Who sang 'It's So Good' ('C'est si Bon' in French) (say: say see bon) and wanted 'an old-fashioned millionaire'?

b2   *Paisley Park, Minneapolis has been home to which pop star?*

a3   In which country does the *Picnic at Hanging Rock* take place?

b3   *About which war was the film* Platoon?

a4   As what did Annigoni become famous?

b4   *Which district of Paris was often painted by Maurice Utrillo?*

a5   Can you name a soccer club for which Brian Clough played?

b5   *How many runs did Don Bradman score in his last test innings in England?*

a6   Which television show originated the phrases 'Sock it to me', 'Very interesting . . .but stupid' and 'the fickle finger of fate'?

b6   *Which character on television's* The Muppet Show *often said 'Kissy, kissy' when pursuing Kermit?*

a7   Which country suffered the greatest losses (in number of lives) in the First World War?

b7   *And which of the Allies suffered the greatest shipping losses?*

a8   Into which 'new' country was the kingdom of Montenegro incorporated after 1918?

b8   *Of which country did the island of Crete become a part in 1913?*

a9   Which Japanese car company opened a factory near Sunderland in 1986?

b9   *In which British city is the Harland and Wolff shipyard?*

a10   Which was the only British colony on the South American mainland?

b10   *Which South American soccer star claimed (in the World Cup) to have been helped 'by the hand of God'?*

a11   *Bonjour Tristesse* was written by which female French novelist?

b11   *Which German novelist wrote* Death in Venice?

a12   Before the Second World War, Boris III was King of which country?

b12   *Which country was ruled by King Zog from 1928?*

No. 158 Answers

a1	Lotus
b1	*Small aircraft*
a2	Eartha Kitt
b2	*Prince*
a3	Australia
b3	*Vietnam*
a4	Painter (especially of portraits)
b4	*Montmartre*
a5	Middlesborough; Sunderland
b5	*None: he was out for a duck*
a6	Rowan and Martin's Laugh-In
b6	*Miss Piggy*
a7	Germany
b7	*Great Britain (7.8 million tons; next was France which lost .9 million)*
a8	Yugoslavia
b8	*Greece*
a9	Nissan
b9	*Belfast*
a10	British Guiana
b10	*(Diego) Maradona*
a11	Françoise Sagan
b11	*Thomas Mann*
a12	Bulgaria
b12	*Albania*

Tie-breaker

Q In a children's novel, which race of fairy people live under the kitchen floor of an old house in Bedfordshire?

A *The Borrowers – in* The Borrowers *by Mary Norton*

No. 159

a1   Who said of herself, 'The lady's not for turning'?

b1   *And who (after being re-elected in 1984) said, 'You ain't seen nothing yet'?*

a2   Which English holiday resort had the first nude bathing beach?

b2   *And which Kentish holiday resort has an amusement centre called 'Dreamland'?*

a3   Which member of the Royal Family came close to marrying Group Captain Townsend?

b3   *To what did a branch of the Germanic Royal Family Battenberg change its name?*

a4   Which motor-car manufacturer produced a 'Baby' and a 'Seven'?

b4   *What name was given to aircraft which landed on water?*

a5   What is 'software'?

b5   *What is meant by 'toxic'?*

a6   Why did some people wear red-and-green-lensed glasses in 1955?

b6   *How did BBC Radio steal commercial television's thunder on the night the latter started up?*

a7   Of which political party was Herbert Morrison a leading member?

b7   *For which political party was David Icke once a spokesman?*

a8   Which European country occupied Lebanon from 1918?

b8   *Which European country conquered Libya in 1911?*

a9   What was the calling of the singer of the popular song 'Dominique' (say: dom-in-eek-uh)?

b9   *Which pop group sang 'The Winner Takes It All'?*

a10   In 1933, who wrote the book *The Shape of Things to Come*?

b10   *And who wrote the music for the film of the book?*

a11   Which major sporting event did Angela Mortimer win in 1961?

b11   *Bombardier Billy Wells was a British title holder from 1911 to 1919. In which sport?*

a12   In which film (based on John Braine's novel) did Laurence Harvey star with Simone Signoret?

b12   *Who co-starred with Lauren Bacall in the Hollywood classic* The Big Sleep?

No. 159 Answers

a1 Margaret Thatcher
b1 *Ronald Reagan*
a2 Brighton
b2 *Margate*
a3 Princess Margaret
b3 *Mountbatten*
a4 Austin (Baby Austin, Austin 7)
b4 *Flying boats*
a5 Computer programmes, discs and cassettes
b5 *Poisonous*
a6 To help see films in '3-D'
b6 *Grace Archer (a character in the serial The Archers) was killed in a fire*
a7 Labour
b7 *Green Party*
a8 France
b8 *Italy*
a9 Nun (the singing Nun) (Soeur Sourire)
b9 *Abba*
a10 H. G. Wells
b10 *Sir Arthur Bliss*
a11 Ladies Singles, Wimbledon
b11 *Boxing (heavyweight)*
a12 Room at the Top
b12 *Humphrey Bogart*

Tie-breaker

Q Neon in lamps is naturally red. What colour does it become when a few drops of mercury are added?
A *Bright blue*

No. 162

a1   What is the TA?

b1   *Which charity is known as SCF?*

a2   Whose pop album was titled 'The Immaculate Collection'?

b2   *Which singer's best-selling album and CD were called 'But Seriously'?*

a3   In the police and aviation alphabet, A is alpha. What is C?

b3   *In the same alphabet, what is F?*

a4   And I?

b4   *And what is G?*

a5   Which is the home country of the motor-racing driver Ayrton Senna?

b5   *And which is the home country of the tennis player Arthur Ashe?*

a6   What is 'bhangra'?

b6   *And what is 'salsa'?*

a7   For what has Jeff Banks become famous?

b7   *And as what did Geoff Capes become famous?*

a8   From which one town did 200 men march to London in 1936?

b8   *And, also in 1936, who was involved in the 'Battle of Cable Street' in London's East End?*

a9   What was stolen from Westminster Abbey on Christmas Day in 1950?

b9   *And which group claimed they were responsible?*

a10   In which country has Walter Sisulu been a national leader?

b10   *And who became president of South Africa in 1989?*

a11   How did Tory MP Ian Gow die in 1990?

b11   *Eric Heffer MP represented a parliamentary constituency in which English city?*

a12   From which year was the Soviet Union at war with Germany?

b12   *In which year were West and East Germany formally reunified?*

No. 162 Answers

a1	Territorial Army
b1	*Save the Children Fund*
a2	Madonna
b2	*Phil Collins*
a3	Charlie
b3	*Foxtrot*
a4	India
b4	*Golf*
a5	Brazil
b5	*United States of America*
a6	Pop music, derived from traditional Punjabi (Indian) music
b6	*(Latin) (big-band) dance music (popularized by Puerto Ricans in New York)*
a7	Design (clothes, interiors)
b7	*Strongman (shot-putter)*
a8	Jarrow
b8	*Fascists (plus local inhabitants and police)*
a9	The 'Coronation Stone' (or 'Stone of Scone')
b9	*Scottish Nationalists*
a10	South Africa
b10	*F. W. de Klerk*
a11	He was killed by an IRA bomb at his home
b11	*Liverpool*
a12	1941 (–1945)
b12	*1990 (October)*

Tie-breaker

Q In the world of publishing, what are OUP and CUP?
A *The Oxford University Press and Cambridge University Press*

No. 163

a1 In which cartoon strip do Lucy and Linus appear?
b1 *What is the name of the dog in the same cartoons?*
a2 In 1954, Humphrey Bogart starred with Ava Gardner in *The Barefoot . . .* what?
b2 *Which film and musical feature the song 'Tomorrow'?*
a3 Which is Nancy Lopez's sport?
b3 *Which was Mark Spitz's sport?*
a4 What is a manifesto?
b4 *And what is a mandate?*
a5 For what has the American Calvin Klein become famous?
b5 *In which field did Art Blakey achieve fame?*
a6 Which clarinetist was nicknamed 'the King of Swing'?
b6 *Who originally sang about 'lipstick on your collar'?*
a7 Where in southern England was an opera house built in the grounds of a country house, in 1936?
b7 *Where in Buckinghamshire did a country house film studio open in 1936?*
a8 Which two British diplomats disappeared from their posts in 1951 – and were later revealed as spies?
b8 *1931–1935 and 1937–1945 saw which two Eastern nations at war with each other?*
a9 In which part of the world is CARICOM an organization for economic co-operation?
b9 *By what name is the International Bank for Reconstruction and Development popularly known?*
a10 What does the abbreviation TIR mean?
b10 *For what is CFC an abbreviation?*
a11 Of which country did Ion Iliescu become president in 1990?
b11 *Which Irish party leader was at the centre of a telephone tapping scandal in 1992?*
a12 In 1954, which Asian country was divided along the 17th Parallel?
b12 *Which former British colony was invaded by the United States in 1983?*

No. 163 Answers

a1 'Peanuts'

b1 *Snoopy*

a2 . . . Contessa (*The Barefoot Contessa*)

b2 Annie

a3 Golf

b3 *Swimming*

a4 A political party's prospectus; an outline of the proposals it intends to carry out, if elected

b4 *An authority; the right to do something*

a5 Fashion; clothes designing (including sportswear)

b5 *Jazz (jazz drummer)*

a6 Benny Goodman

b6 *Connie Francis*

a7 Glyndebourne, Sussex

b7 *Pinewood (near Iver)*

a8 (Guy) Burgess and (Donald) Maclean

b8 *China and Japan*

a9 The Caribbean; West Indies

b9 *The World Bank*

a10 International Road Transport (Transports Internationaux Routiers)

b10 *Chlorofluorocarbon*

a11 Romania

b11 *(Charles) Haughey*

a12 Vietnam

b12 *Grenada*

Tie-breaker

Q In 1935, what did police do when they spotted a car breaking the speed limit?

A *They sounded a gong on the police car*

No. 164

a1 Of what did the singer have 'a bunch', in the 1950 popular hit?
b1 *Who was 'Momma kissing' in the 1952 popular hit tune?*
a2 Which darts player is nicknamed 'the Crafty Cockney'?
b2 *Which French motor-racing driver is nicknamed 'the Professor'?*
a3 What is a 'gulag'?
b3 *What is a 'putsch'?*
a4 In films and comics, whose assistant is known as 'the boy wonder'?
b4 *In a film, who drives an Ectomobile?*
a5 Who said he needed 'the help and support of the woman I love'?
b5 *In 1934, which British politician claimed 'We have never been so defenceless as now'?*
a6 Which British trade union is known as NALGO?
b6 *And which was the AEU?*
a7 In which country was Jan Smuts a politician?
b7 *Of which country was Prince von Bülow a statesman before the First World War?*
a8 For what has the Italian Giorgio Armani become famous?
b8 *For what has Henri Cartier-Bresson become famous?*
a9 Who has a summer palace or villa at Castel Gandolfo?
b9 *Which is England's tallest building?*
a10 What was 405 and is now 625?
b10 *And what is a 125?*
a11 Where, in England, was an Anglo-Saxon ship-burial treasure found in 1939?
b11 *Which primitive man's skull, discovered in 1911, was proved a fake in 1949?*
a12 What is GATT (say: gatt)?
b12 *What is G7?*

No. 164 Answers

a1   Coconuts ('I've got a lovely bunch of coconuts')
b1   *Santa Claus ('I saw Momma Kissing Santa Claus')*
a2   Eric Bristow
b2   *Alain Prost*
a3   Soviet labour or prison camp
b3   *Violent seizure of political power*
a4   Batman (Robin)
b4   *The Ghostbusters*
a5   King Edward VIII
b5   *Sir Winston Churchill*
a6   National and Local Government Officers Association
b6   *Amalgamated Engineering Union*
a7   South Africa
b7   *Germany*
a8   Fashion designing; clothes
b8   *Photography*
a9   The Pope
b9   *Canary Wharf (in Docklands) (250 metres/800 feet high)*
a10   The number of lines that make up a (British) television picture (it changed with the introduction of colour and a move from VHF to UHF)
b10   *An Inter-City (diesel) (high-speed) train*
a11   Sutton Hoo
b11   *Piltdown Skull*
a12   The General Agreement on Tariffs and Trade (a United Nations organization)
b12   *The Group of Seven (the seven wealthiest nations in the world)*

Tie-breaker

Q What did Bryan Allen achieve in 'Gossamer Albatross' in 1979?
A *First human-powered flight across the English Channel*

No. 165

a1 On screen, what do doctors Venkman, Stantz and Spengler hunt?

b1 *Which 1968 cartoon film featured the songs and voices of the Beatles?*

a2 Known as 'Lady Day', she sang 'Strange Fruit' and 'I Cover the Waterfront'. Who was she?

b2 *Which English rock singer and song writer had the Attractions as a backing group and sang 'My Aim is True'?*

a3 In military terms, which is larger: a battalion or a brigade?

b3 *And which is larger: a corps or a division?*

a4 Of which country was Andreas Papandreou (say: pap-an-dray-oo) prime minister?

b4 *János Kádár was a communist leader in which country?*

a5 Which American track and field athlete won four gold medals in the 1984 Olympics and three in the 1988 contest?

b5 *Which Canadian sprinter was disqualified and suspended after testing positive for steroids at the 1988 Olympics?*

a6 What are SERPS?

b6 *What is SIS?*

a7 Which cartoon character was created by the artist Mary Tourtel in 1920 and later drawn by Alfred Bestall?

b7 *Which newspaper cartoonist created the character Maudie Littlehampton?*

a8 What was the Russian city of Volgograd called until 1961?

b8 *And what was the Russian city of Tsaritsyn renamed in 1925?*

a9 In the thirties, who asked the British people to elect him as a Fascist dictator?

b9 *In which country was Engelbert Dollfuss a political leader?*

a10 In which year did Queen Elizabeth and Prince Philip marry?

b10 *Where was Princess Elizabeth when she became Queen?*

a11 In America, for what is the Pulitzer Prize awarded?

b11 *In America, in what area might you win a 'Tony' (or Antoinette Perry Award)?*

a12 A. J. P. Taylor became famous for what?

b12 *For what did Norman Parkinson become famous?*

No. 165 Answers

a1   Ghosts (in *Ghostbusters*)
b1   *Yellow Submarine*
a2   Billie Holiday
b2   *Elvis Costello*
a3   Brigade
b3   *Corps*
a4   Greece
b4   *Hungary*
a5   Carl Lewis
b5   *Ben Johnson*
a6   (State Earnings-Related) Pension Schemes
b6   *Special Intelligence Service*
a7   Rupert Bear
b7   *Osbert Lancaster*
a8   Stalingrad
b8   *Stalingrad*
a9   Sir Oswald Mosley
b9   *Austria*
a10   1947
b10   *In Kenya (Treetops Hotel, or a game reserve)*
a11   Novels/fiction
b11   *The theatre*
a12   His television programmes; historical lectures on television
b12   *Fashion (and portrait) photography*

Tie-breaker

Q In which year this century did Poland first become an independent republic?

A *1918*

No. 166

a1 In the alphabet used by the police and in aviation, V is Victor, T is Tango. What is Z?

b1 *And what is Y?*

a2 And in the same alphabet, what is W?

b2 *And what is J?*

a3 What is a referendum?

b3 *What is a federation?*

a4 Which blond, left-handed cricketer has played for Leicestershire and Hampshire and has been England's most capped cricketer?

b4 *Which Rhodesian-born cricketer played for Zimbabwe and, from 1991, for England?*

a5 For what is 'wpm' a standard abbreviation?

b5 *In science or mathematics, what is meant by 'ppm'?*

a6 Which singer and record producer, associated with Motown records, had solo hits with 'Cruisin'' and 'Being With You'?

b6 *Which jazz pianist's 'standards' included 'Round Midnight' and 'Blue Monk'?*

a7 In 1989 in Britain, which party surprised many people by winning two million votes in the European elections?

b7 *In Europe, what is the CAP?*

a8 Which American politician did Jacqueline Lee Bouvier marry in 1953?

b8 *As what did William Randolph Hearst become famous?*

a9 Of which country were the Philippines a colony until this century?

b9 *Until 1966, of which country was Botswana (formerly Bechuanaland) a colony?*

a10 Where in Flanders did 400,000 British soldiers die in 1917?

b10 *Off the coast of which country was the naval battle of Jutland fought in 1916?*

a11 Of which country was Manuel Noriega the ruler?

b11 *And on what charges was he arrested by the United States?*

a12 Who said, on losing her job, 'It's a funny old world'?

b12 *Which King of Britain this century said, 'I don't like abroad, I've been there'?*

No. 166 Answers

a1   Zulu
b1   *Yankee*
a2   Whiskey
b2   *Juliet*
a3   A vote by the people on a particular issue
b3   *When two or more countries or states combine under one government, but keep some independence*
a4   David Gower
b4   *Graeme Hick*
a5   Words per minute
b5   *Parts per million*
a6   Smokey Robinson
b6   *Thelonius Monk*
a7   Green Party
b7   *Common Agricultural Policy*
a8   John F. Kennedy
b8   *As a newspaper publisher*
a9   Spain
b9   *Britain/United Kingdom*
a10   Passchendaele
b10   *Denmark*
a11   Panama
b11   *Drug-trafficking*
a12   Mrs Thatcher
b12   *King George V*

Tie-breaker

Q To the military, what is NBC?
A *Nuclear, biological and chemical warfare*

No. 167

a1 Which cartoonist depicted the TUC as a cart-horse?

b1 *Which newspaper cartoonist became famous for drawing a family that included a black-coated Grandma?*

a2 In what field has Helen Mirren become famous?

b2 *For what did Kathleen Ferrier achieve fame?*

a3 For what is IBM an abbreviation?

b3 *When talking of milk, what is UHT?*

a4 Whom did John Wayne play in the frontier film *The Alamo?*

b4 *Which actor played Professor Higgins in the film of* My Fair Lady?

a5 Which is Joe Montana's sport?

b5 *Which is the Austrian Franz Klammer's sport?*

a6 Whose home was Fort Belvedere?

b6 *Why did Rillington Place in London become infamous in 1953?*

a7 Launched in 1938, what was *Picture Post?*

b7 *What is Scuba?*

a8 Who wrote the popular hit tune 'Cheek to Cheek'?

b8 *Alain Boublil was co-writer of a musical called Miss . . .?*

a9 When did rationing end in Britain after the Second World War: 1947, 1950, or 1954?

b9 *In which year did Britain's first North Sea oil flow ashore: 1967, 1971, or 1975?*

a10 Where is the International Court of Justice based?

b10 *In which two cities is the European Parliament based?*

a11 Which Secretary-General of the United Nations later became president of Austria?

b11 *Of which country did Mary Robinson become president in 1990?*

a12 Which building (including a banqueting hall) is the civic headquarters of the City of London)?

b12 *Which building is the official residence of the Lord Mayor of London?*

No. 167 Answers

a1   (David) Low
b1   *Giles*
a2   Acting
b2   *As a singer (contralto)*
a3   International Business Machines
b3   *Ultra heat-treated milk*
a4   Davy Crockett
b4   *Rex Harrison*
a5   US Football
b5   *Ski-ing (downhill races)*
a6   Prince Edward (the Prince of Wales; later King Edward VIII)
b6   *Because of a series of murders (by John Christie)*
a7   A weekly illustrated magazine
b7   *Self-contained underwater breathing apparatus (used by divers)*
a8   Irving Berlin
b8   *. . . Saigon (Miss Saigon)*
a9   1954
b9   *1975*
a10   The Hague (in the Netherlands)
b10   *Luxembourg and Strasbourg*
a11   Kurt Waldheim
b11   *Ireland*
a12   Guildhall
b12   *Mansion House*

Tie-breaker

Q Which two countries joined the European Community in 1985?
A *Portugal and Spain*

No. 168

a1   Which trade union is known as COHSE?

b1   *And which union is USDAW?*

a2   Which war involved Operation Desert Shield?

b2   *By what name was America's Strategic Defense Initiative popularly known?*

a3   *Steamboat Willie* was the first colour cartoon film to feature which character?

b3   *'Ars gratia artis' is the Latin motto of which film studio?*

a4   Who starred in television's *Fall and Rise of Reginald Perrin*?

b4   *Can you name a major children's television series created by Jim Henson, apart from* The Muppet Show?

a5   What is an 'espadrille'?

b5   *What is 'bonsai'?*

a6   In which sport could you compete in the US Open, Australian Open and French Open?

b6   *In which sport is the Suntory Championship held?*

a7   As what did Leopoldo Galtieri become famous?

b7   *To listen to which speaker did 180,000 people pack Wembley Stadium in 1954?*

a8   Which was the musician Paul Tortelier's instrument?

b8   *Which instrument did bebop musician Dizzy Gillespie play?*

a9   What name is given to the night in June 1934 when Hitler had many comrades shot and killed because he said they were plotting against him?

b9   *What political change involved 'coloured' or 'mixed-race' people in South Africa in 1951?*

a10   A proposed extension to which London building was described as 'a monstrous carbuncle' by Prince Charles?

b10   *Of what were the Dome of Discovery and Skylon both a part?*

a11   About what did King Edward VIII say, 'Something must be done'?

b11   *Which member of the Royal Family died a few weeks before Elizabeth II's coronation?*

a12   Of which country did Daniel arap Moi become president in 1978?

b12   *Of which country was Lee Kuan Yew prime minister?*

No. 168 Answers

a1 Confederation of Health Service Employees
b1 *Union of Shop, Distributive and Allied Workers*
a2 The Gulf War (1991)
b2 *Star Wars programme*
a3 Mickey Mouse
b3 *MGM ('Art for art's sake')*
a4 Leonard Rossiter
b4 *Sesame Street or Fraggle Rock*
a5 Shoe (canvas upper, rope sole)
b5 *The art of producing miniature trees*
a6 Tennis
b6 *Golf*
a7 Argentine general (during Falklands War)
b7 *Billy Graham (the evangelist)*
a8 Cello
b8 *Trumpet*
a9 'Night of the Long Knives'
b9 *They lost the right to vote*
a10 National Gallery
b10 *The (1951) Festival of Britain (on London's South Bank)*
a11 Unemployment (in South Wales)
b11 *Queen Mary (widow of George V)*
a12 Kenya
b12 *Singapore*

Tie-breaker

Q In which film festival is the 'Golden Bear' awarded to the best film?
A Berlin

No. 169

a1   In the police and aviation alphabet, how is the letter N identified?

b1   *And how is R identified?*

a2   What part of the body can suffer from glaucoma?

b2   *What part of the body can suffer from dermatitis?*

a3   According to the 1953 popular hit tune, what are 'a girl's best friend'?

b3   *In the thirties pop song, where were the 'red sails'?*

a4   What is the IMF?

b4   *By what name or initials is the British association or organization of employers known?*

a5   What is measured by ASA or ISO numbers?

b5   *In physics, for what is UV an abbreviation?*

a6   Which play opened in London in 1952 – and looked likely to run for quite a long time?

b6   *In 1923, who wrote the play St Joan?*

a7   In what position did Peter Shilton earn his place on England's soccer team (from 1970 to 1990)?

b7   *Specifically, what has been Peter Scudamore's sport?*

a8   Which English composer (who died in 1934) was associated with the Malvern Hills?

b8   *Aged 52 in 1930, he was England's oldest ever test cricketer. Who was he?*

a9   Of which country was Mozambique a colony?

b9   *Until 1960, of which country was Madagascar a colony?*

a10   Which educational toy construction system was invented by Sir Frank Hornby?

b10   *J. Robert Oppenheimer is sometimes called 'the father of the . . .' What?*

a11   What is Iwo Jima?

b11   *What caused an entire island (Eniwetok Atoll) to disappear in 1952?*

a12   Who has been president of the European Commission since 1984?

b12   *Of which country has Ruud Lubbers been prime minister?*

No. 169 Answers

a1 November
b1 *Romeo*
a2 The eye
b2 *The skin*
a3 Diamonds
b3 *'In the sunset' ('Red Sails in the Sunset')*
a4 International Monetary Fund
b4 *CBI (Confederation of British Industry)*
a5 The 'speed' of film
b5 *Ultra-violet*
a6 *The Mousetrap* (by Agatha Christie)
b6 *George Bernard Shaw*
a7 As goalkeeper
b7 *National Hunt racing/steeplechasing*
a8 Sir Edward Elgar
b8 *Wilfred Rhodes*
a9 Portugal
b9 *France*
a10 Meccano (he also manufactured Hornby trains and Dinky Toys)
b10 *. . . atom bomb*
a11 Japanese island (captured by USA in 1945; returned to Japan in 1968)
b11 *America's first hydrogen bomb test*
a12 Jacques Delors
b12 *Netherlands (Holland)*

Tie-breaker

Q Which American tennis player won her first Wimbledon title in 1974 and became the first woman player to win a million dollars in prize money?

A *Chris(tine) Evert*

No. 170

a1   As what did Lee Remick become famous?
b1   *How did Stan Mortensen become famous?*
a2   Which comic strip wing-helmeted character first appeared in France in 1959?
b2   *Which cartoon character shouts 'Yabba dabba do'?*
a3   Which group's album was called 'Rumours'?
b3   *What kind of singer was Hank Williams?*
a4   Which American tennis player became known for grunting while he played?
b4   *Which cricketer has crossed the Alps in the style of Hannibal?*
a5   For what is GCHQ the abbreviation?
b5   *And where is GCHQ?*
a6   Which war was portrayed in the 1915 film *The Birth of a Nation*?
b6   *Of what did the film star Rock Hudson die?*
a7   In which country do the Tigré people live?
b7   *Where do the Tamil people live?*
a8   Who was prime minister of Australia from 1983 to 1991?
b8   *And of which political party was he a member?*
a9   Following the 1986 Chernobyl disaster, which livestock trade was affected in Britain?
b9   *What disaster put the north London town of Harrow in the headlines in 1952?*
a10   Which famous American aviator's baby was kidnapped and murdered in the thirties?
b10   *Which pair of young American gangsters and robbers did the law finally catch up with in 1934?*
a11   The monarchs of which two empires met for the first time in 1908?
b11   *What happened in 1936 for the first time since the year 1399?*
a12   How long did Hitler claim his Reich (or state) would last?
b12   *In which year was the Battle of Arras?*

No. 170 Answers

a1 Film actress
b1 *As a soccer player*
a2 Astérix
b2 *Fred Flintstone*
a3 Fleetwood Mac
b3 *Country and Western*
a4 Jimmy Connors
b4 *Ian Botham*
a5 Government Communications Headquarters
b5 *Cheltenham*
a6 American Civil War
b6 *AIDS*
a7 Ethiopia
b7 *India (the state of Tamil Nadu); also Sri Lanka, Malaysia, Singapore and South Africa*
a8 Bob Hawke
b8 *Labour*
a9 Lamb (movement of sheep restricted)
b9 *A train crash (112 dead; the second worst ever at that time)*
a10 (Charles) Lindbergh
b10 *Bonnie and Clyde (Clyde Barrow; Bonnie Parker)*
a11 Russian and British (Tsar Nicholas II and King Edward VII)
b11 *An English King abdicated*
a12 1,000 years
b12 *1917*

Tie-breaker

Q Who said this about whom?: 'He stands for nothing; he is nothing. He is grey. He has no ideas. I have been totally deceived.'

A *Mrs Thatcher about John Major*

No. 171: The Second World War

a1   What was an 'Axis' power?

b1   *What was a 'siren suit'?*

a2   In which year did Rommel open his North African campaign?

b2   *In the same year, which 'unsinkable' German battleship was sunk?*

a3   Who was nicknamed the 'Desert Fox'?

b3   *What was the nickname of the Thompson sub-machine gun?*

a4   In which country did Vidkun Quisling collaborate with the Nazis?

b4   *What name was given to the French government which collaborated with the Germans?*

a5   In which country is Tobruk?

b5   *In which country is Anzio?*

a6   In which year were the Battles of El Alamein?

b6   *And in which year was the Battle of Arnhem?*

a7   American servicemen were called GIs. For what did GI stand?

b7   *For what did the initials NAAFI stand?*

a8   In which year was the Russian victory at Stalingrad?

b8   *Who said in 1940 that Mr Hitler had 'missed the bus'?*

a9   What were 'Mulberries'?

b9   *What was Changi?*

a10   Whose film parodied Hitler as 'The Great Dictator'?

b10   *Who was Hitler's deputy who flew secretly to Scotland in 1941?*

a11   Whereabouts in Europe did the 'Battle of the Bulge' take place in 1944–5?

b11   *Which city was devastated by the Allies in February 1945?*

a12   Who succeeded Hitler in 1945?

b12   *Which American general was known as 'Blood and Guts'?*

No. 171 Answers

a1   Germany and those countries allied to it
b1   *One-piece overall, dungaree-like garment (made popular by Churchill)*
a2   1941
b2   *'Bismarck'*
a3   (Field Marshal) Rommel
b3   *The tommy gun*
a4   Norway
b4   *Vichy*
a5   Libya
b5   *Italy*
a6   1942
b6   *1944*
a7   Government Issue
b7   *Navy, Army and Air Forces Institutes*
a8   1943
b8   *Neville Chamberlain*
a9   Artificial harbours, used on D-Day
b9   *Japanese prison camp*
a10   Charlie Chaplin's
b10   *Rudolf Hess*
a11   The Ardennes; southern Belgium
b11   *Dresden*
a12   Admiral Dönitz
b12   *General Patton*

Tie-breaker

Q How did (a) Hitler, (b) Mussolini and (c) Goering die?
A *(a) Suicide, by gunshot in the mouth; (b) shot by partisans and then hung by his heels; (c) suicide, by cyanide just before execution*

No. 172

a1   Which singer released the album called 'No Jacket Required'?

b1   *One of the highest-selling albums of all time is 'Brothers in Arms'. Who is it by?*

a2   In the police and aviation alphabet, B is Bravo. What is E?

b2   *In the same alphabet, what is O?*

a3   And what is S?

b3   *And what is L?*

a4   Until 1988, what was the DHSS?

b4   *DPP is an abbreviation for . . .?*

a5   In which sport did Giacomo Agostini hold world titles?

b5   *In which sport has the Australian David Campese held a record?*

a6   Who are the Algonquin people?

b6   *From which country do the Gurkhas come?*

a7   Which natural disaster hit England in January, 1953?

b7   *Which new town is near Gatwick Airport?*

a8   On the salt flats of which American state did Malcolm Campbell set a world speed record in 1935?

b8   *By what name is the Harrier jet aircraft popularly known?*

a9   Of which country was Franz Josef Emperor until 1916?

b9   *Of which country was Victor Emmanuel III King until 1946?*

a10   Who was Secretary-General of the United Nations from 1982 to 1991?

b10   *And what is his nationality?*

a11   The king of which country was assassinated by a Croatian nationalist in France in 1934?

b11   *Which Chinese communist headed 'the Long March' in the thirties?*

a12   As what has Caryl Churchill become famous?

b12   *As what did Linda Evangelista become famous?*

No. 172 Answers

a1   Phil Collins
b1   Dire Straits
a2   Echo
b2   Oscar
a3   Sierra
b3   Lima
a4   Department of Health and Social Security
b4   Director of Public Prosecutions
a5   Motorcycling
b5   Rugby Union (record number of tries scored up to May 1990)
a6   North American Indians (formerly living around the Ottawa River)
b6   Nepal
a7   The East Coast floods
b7   Crawley
a8   Utah
b8   The Jump Jet
a9   Austro-Hungary
b9   Italy
a10   (Javier) Pérez de Cuéllar (say: havier pe-ress de qway-ya)
b10   Peruvian
a11   Yugoslavia
b11   Mao Tse-tung
a12   Playwright/dramatist
b12   As a model

Tie-breaker

Q Of which country did Flavio Cotti become head of state in 1991?
A *Switzerland*

No. 173

a1 'Light My Fire' was which pop group's first hit?

b1 *Which female pop singer starred in the films* Desperately Seeking Susan *and* Dick Tracy?

a2 What medical term is given to the lack of desire to eat?

b2 *What medical term is used to describe word-blindness?*

a3 Which American jockey was UK champion jockey in 1984, 1985 and 1987?

b3 *Which English middle-distance runner started a new career in 1990 as a Conservative politician?*

a4 What have the following in common: Geneva, Reykjavik and Washington, DC?

b4 *What have Trawsfynydd (say: traws-fun-uth) and Wylfa (say: wil-va) in common?*

a5 Who became the effective political leader of Iran in 1989?

b5 *Of which country was Milton Obote (say: O-boh-tay) twice president?*

a6 In which country do the Khmer people live?

b6 *In which country do the Ibo people mainly live?*

a7 What is the RPI?

b7 *What is the NEDC?*

a8 Who starred in the film *The Silence of the Lambs*?

b8 *Which French film maker created the character Monsieur Hulot (say: huw-lo) who appeared in films such as* Mon Oncle?

a9 In the Rupert cartoon strips, what was the name of the elephant?

b9 *And what was the name of the pug dog?*

a10 In 1934, Harry Beck designed what was to become a famous diagrammatic map. What was it of?

b10 *What celebration took place in London's streets on May 6, 1935?*

a11 For what has Eric Hosking become famous?

b11 *As what did Isaac Bashevis Singer achieve fame?*

a12 What is the French name for Bergen (in Belgium), where a First World War battle took place?

b12 *Which country did Mussolini invade in 1935?*

No. 173 Answers

a1 The Doors
b1 *Madonna*
a2 Anorexia
b2 *Dyslexia*
a3 Steve Cauthen
b3 *Sebastian Coe*
a4 They were all meeting places between USA and Soviet leaders (Reagan and Gorbachev)
b4 *Both are nuclear power stations (in Wales)*
a5 (Ali Akbar) Rafsanjani
b5 *Uganda*
a6 Cambodia
b6 *Nigeria*
a7 Retail Price Index
b7 *The National Economic Development Council (or 'Neddie')*
a8 Anthony Hopkins (accept: Jodie Foster)
b8 *Jacques Tati*
a9 Edward Trunk
b9 *Algy Pug*
a10 London's Underground
b10 *King George V's Silver Jubilee*
a11 (Wild-life) photography
b11 *Writer (of novels and short stories)*
a12 Mons
b12 *Abyssinia (Ethiopia)*

Tie-breaker

Q 1994 is the centenary year of London's Promenade Concerts. Who founded the concerts, and in which concert hall were they originally held?

A *Sir Henry Wood; Queen's Hall*

No. 174

a1   Which television cartoon features Ermintrude and Mr Rusty?

b1   *Which space-travelling cartoon's female companion was Dale Arden?*

a2   Militarily speaking, what is 'R and R'?

b2   *In the Gulf War, what was a 'Patriot'?*

a3   In which country do members of parliament have the letters TD after their names?

b3   *For what is SJ an abbreviation?*

a4   Which international sporting team was captained from 1985 by Allan Border?

b4   *Which is the home country of tennis player Stefan Edberg?*

a5   Which American film actress was married to Mickey Rooney, Artie Shaw and Frank Sinatra?

b5   *Which French actress became known as the 'Sex Kitten'?*

a6   By what name is the American index or scale for measuring share prices known?

b6   *And what is the Japanese equivalent?*

a7   From 1934, what did British motorists have to observe?

b7   *In 1951, with which other motor manufacturer did Morris amalgamate?*

a8   Of which party has President Mitterand been a founder member?

b8   *In which country has Menachem Begin been a right-wing leader?*

a9   What medical term describes a shortage of haemoglobin (say: hee-mo-glo-bin), part of the red blood cells?

b9   *What is paraplegia?*

a10   Hindenburg ceased being president of Germany on his death. Was that in 1929, 1934, or 1939?

b10   *In which year did Swiss women first get the vote in federal elections: 1931, 1961, or 1971?*

a11   As what did André Gide (say: an-dray jeed) become famous?

b11   *In which field did Stan Getz become famous?*

a12   Since 1982, King Fahd has been head of state of which country?

b12   *Of which island was Queen Salote once the ruler?*

No. 174 Answers

a1 *The Magic Roundabout*
b1 *Flash Gordon*
a2 'Rest and recuperation'
b2 *(Ground-to-air) missile (used against Iraqi 'Scud' missiles)*
a3 Ireland (Teachta Dála = a member of the Irish parliament)
b3 *Society of Jesus (the Jesuits)*
a4 Australian cricket
b4 *Sweden*
a5 Ava Gardner
b5 *Brigitte Bardot*
a6 Dow Jones
b6 *Nikkei*
a7 Speed limits; also pedestrian crossings
b7 *Austin*
a8 (French) Socialist Party
b8 *Israel*
a9 Anaemia
b9 *Paralysis of the lower limbs*
a10 1934
b10 *1971*
a11 (French) novelist/writer
b11 *Jazz*
a12 Saudi Arabia
b12 *Tonga*

Tie-breaker

Q In 1944, which was the first major French port to fall to the Allies after the Normandy landings?
A *Cherbourg*

No. 175

a1   In which sport might you win the US Triple Crown?

b1   *In which sport can you compete in the US Masters?*

a2   Which British trade union is known as the GMB?

b2   *And which is known as NUPE?*

a3   Which environmental group campaigns to conserve the world's resources?

b3   *And which group campaigns to persuade governments to protect and improve the environment?*

a4   For what has Kenneth Branagh become famous?

b4   *In the world of religion, why did Barbara Harris become well known in 1989?*

a5   What medical term is used to describe the process which imitates the work of the kidneys?

b5   *And what name is given to the treatment of cancer with synthetic chemical drugs?*

a6   Which movement did the author Simone de Beauvoir (say: bo-voir) do much to inspire?

b6   *In 1934, Dale Carnegie published a book called* How to Win Friends and . . . *what?*

a7   Which soccer player spent most of his career with Manchester United, and is the younger brother of Jack?

b7   *Which Belfast sportswoman won the pentathlon gold medal in the Munich (1972) Olympics?*

a8   Muhammad Jinnah was governor general of which country?

b8   *Which country was ruled by Erich Honecker?*

a9   What is the WCC?

b9   *In sport, what is the WBC?*

a10   Where do the Masai people live?

b10   *Who are the Navajo (say: na-va-ho)?*

a11   On which planet is the Great Red Spot?

b11   *Which planet in our solar system was discovered in 1930?*

a12   Who wrote the play *Six Characters in Search of an Author*?

b12   *Who wrote the play* What the Butler Saw?

No. 175 Answers

a1   (Horse) racing
b1   *Golf*
a2   General Municipal Boilermakers
b2   *National Union of Public Employees*
a3   Friends of the Earth
b3   *Greenpeace*
a4   Acting
b4   *First woman to become a bishop*
a5   Dialysis
b5   *Chemotherapy*
a6   Feminism, the Women's Movement
b6   *. . . Influence People*
a7   Bobbie Charlton
b7   *Mary Peters*
a8   Pakistan
b8   *East Germany*
a9   World Council of Churches
b9   *World Boxing Council*
a10   East Africa (Tanzania, Kenya)
b10   *North American Indians (living in Arizona)*
a11   Jupiter
b11   *Pluto*
a12   (Luigi) Pirandello
b12   *Joe Orton*

Tie-breaker

Q Just before the start of the Second World War, MPs (in the House of Commons) shouted, 'Speak for England, Arthur.' Arthur was Arthur Greenwood MP. What was his importance?

A *He was Labour's leader (Neville Chamberlain, the prime minister, appeared reluctant to declare war)*

No. 176

a1 The Bee Gees song 'Stayin' Alive' featured in which film?

b1 *Which film family gives their children meat cleavers to play with, and play a graveyard game called 'Wake the Dead'?*

a2 In the police and aviation alphabet, what is P?

b2 *And in the same alphabet, what is H?*

a3 For which country did Willie John McBride play Rugby Union?

b3 *For which country does Sunil Gavaskar play cricket?*

a4 Which cartoon character turns into shy college student Peter Parker?

b4 *Which cartoon character appeared in a number of films involving Inspector Clouseau (played by Peter Sellers)?*

a5 Did Carl David Anderson become famous for his work in education, modern dance, or physics?

b5 *As what did Edward Gordon Craig become famous?*

a6 In October 1936, who was famously divorced from her husband Ernest at a court in Ipswich?

b6 *Which member of the Royal Family was nicknamed 'Bertie'?*

a7 With what is obstetrics concerned?

b7 *With what is haematology (say: hee-ma-tol-ogy) concerned?*

a8 What was Abu Simbel?

b8 *Which expedition set out to prove that Polynesian islanders must have sailed there from South America?*

a9 What is a 'blue chip' company?

b9 *What name is given to the illegal use of private information when dealing on the Stock Exchange?*

a10 From 1949 to 1963, who was Chancellor of West Germany?

b10 *Which Burmese diplomat was Secretary-General of the United Nations from 1962 to 1971?*

a11 Which agency launched the 'Ariane' rockets?

b11 *Where in America is the Kennedy Space Center?*

a12 In 1902, which famous novelist published The Ambassadors?

b12 *Which English author (and 'poet of the Empire') won the Nobel Prize for Literature in 1907?*

No. 176 Answers

a1 Saturday Night Fever
b1 The Addams family
a2 Papa
b2 Hotel
a3 Ireland
b3 India
a4 Spiderman
b4 The Pink Panther
a5 Physics (Nobel Prize-winner for physics)
b5 Stage designer
a6 Mrs (Wallis) Simpson
b6 King George VI
a7 Pregnancy, childbirth, postnatal care
b7 Disorders of the blood
a8 Temple (flooded by the Aswan Dam project on the Nile)
b8 The Kon-Tiki Expedition
a9 One whose shares are strong and reliable
b9 Insider trading
a10 Dr (Konrad) Adenauer
b10 U Thant
a11 European Space Agency
b11 Cape Canaveral (Florida)
a12 Henry James
b12 Rudyard Kipling

Tie-breaker

Q In 1988, who was voted 'Golfer of the Century'?
A Jack Nicklaus

No. 177

a1 About what does David Bellamy broadcast and campaign?

b1 *How did Margaret Lockwood achieve fame?*

a2 What are enhancers, emulsifiers and stabilizers?

b2 *What international symbol is used to indicate a poisonous or toxic substance?*

a3 In which sport do the San Francisco 49ers compete?

b3 *In which country is Juventus a soccer club?*

a4 Which television police series teamed an American lieutenant (say: loo-ten-ant) with a British (woman) sergeant?

b4 *On television, in which city does the detective Taggart operate?*

a5 What is meant by AWACS?

b5 *In computing, for what does DOS stand?*

a6 In which city was the 'no war over Czechoslovakia' deal signed in 1938?

b6 *Which Polish port did Hitler have his eye on in the weeks leading up to the Second World War?*

a7 Which whale, in particular, is an endangered species?

b7 *And which animal is in danger of being hunted to extinction in East Africa?*

a8 What is Farsi?

b8 *In India, what is an 'ashram'?*

a9 Which is the most popular indoor tourist attraction in London?

b9 *Outside London, what is England's most popular tourist attraction?*

a10 Since 1951, who has been King of Belgium?

b10 *Who became Emperor of Japan in 1989?*

a11 Who wrote the novel *Hotel du Lac*?

b11 *Who wrote the book* Midnight's Children?

a12 In July 1940, which nation sank a large proportion of the French navy?

b12 *In 1940, which country eventually defeated Finland?*

No. 177 Answers

a1   The environment; wild life; natural history
b1   *As an actress (film and stage)*
a2   Food additives
b2   *A skull (and crossbones)*
a3   American football
b3   *Italy*
a4   *Dempsey and Makepeace*
b4   *Glasgow*
a5   Airborne Warning and Control System (long-range surveillance)
b5   *Disc operating system*
a6   Munich
b6   *Danzig (later Gdansk)*
a7   Blue whale
b7   *(African) elephant*
a8   A Persian language (spoken in Iran, Iraq, Afghanistan and parts of the former Soviet Union)
b8   *A place where holy teaching takes place*
a9   Madame Tussaud's Waxworks
b9   *Alton Towers (1990 figures)*
a10   King Baudouin
b10   *Akihito*
a11   Anita Brookner
b11   *Salman Rushdie*
a12   Britain (to prevent it falling into German control)
b12   *Soviet Union (Russia)*

Tie-breaker

Q Which pub game was banned in Glasgow in 1939 as being 'too dangerous'?

A *Darts*

No. 178

a1 As what did 'Big Daddie' achieve fame?

b1 For what is Wayne Sleep famous?

a2 By what name are members of the Unification Church colloquially known?

b2 By what name are members of the Church of Jesus Christ of Latter-Day Saints often known?

a3 Yangon, formerly Rangoon, is capital of Myanmar, formerly . . . what?

b3 Of which European state is the small town or village of Vaduz the capital?

a4 For what did Robert Dougall become a well-known television personality?

b4 Which subject does Patrick Moore broadcast about?

a5 What type of bridge is the famous Forth rail bridge in Scotland?

b5 And what type of bridge is the Humber bridge?

a6 What is Alzheimer's disease?

b6 Rubella is the technical term for which childhood illness?

a7 When is the announcement 'Habemus Papam' (say: hab-ay-mus pa-pam) made?

b7 What has the French phrase 'pied à terre' (say: pya-da-ter) come to mean?

a8 Which war ended in 1939?

b8 On which date in 1939 did Britain declare war on Germany?

a9 Which is the home town of ice-skaters Torvill and Dean?

b9 And which is golfer Wayne Grady's home country?

a10 Of which country has Edith Cresson been prime minister?

b10 Which European country's prime minister was murdered in 1986?

a11 In which African country did South African troops fight Cuban troops?

b11 In which African country did a war of independence against France begin in 1954?

a12 Who wrote the play The Corn is Green?

b12 Who wrote the play Dear Octopus which was a hit during the Second World War?

No. 178 Answers

a1   As a wrestler (on television)
b1   *(Ballet) dancing*
a2   'Moonies'
b2   *Mormons*
a3   Burma
b3   *Liechtenstein*
a4   Newsreading (BBC)
b4   *Astronomy*
a5   Cantilever bridge
b5   *Suspension bridge*
a6   A form of dementia, or memory loss
b6   *German measles*
a7   When a new pope is elected (Latin: 'We have a pope')
b7   *A second home (usually small and in a city)*
a8   Spanish Civil War
b8   *September 3rd*
a9   Nottingham
b9   *Australia*
a10   France
b10   *Sweden (Olaf Palme)*
a11   Angola
b11   *Algeria*
a12   Emlyn Williams
b12   *Dodie Smith*

Tie-breaker

Q What were the first four items of food to be rationed in Britain in 1940?

A *Butter, sugar, bacon and ham (cooked and uncooked)*

No. 179

a1   On television, who originally manipulated Sooty?

b1   *In its early days, which children's television programme was introduced by Valerie Singleton and Christopher Trace?*

a2   Which part of Britain fell to the Nazis in 1940?

b2   *Which French soldier rallied his nation in a radio message just after Paris fell to the Nazis?*

a3   In which sport is the Refuge Assurance League?

b3   *In which sport is the Pilkington Cup a British competition?*

a4   What did the word 'Blitzkrieg' (say: blitz-kreeg) mean?

b4   *In 1940, what nickname was given to the Local Defence Volunteers?*

a5   Which movement or philosophy was started by the Maharishi Mahesh Yogi?

b5   *In 1967, which European country declared itself 'the first atheist state in the world'?*

a6   Which organization (established in 1958) helps Third World development by sending skilled, voluntary workers to such countries?

b6   *In Britain, what kind of school is a CTC?*

a7   In 1944, which Shakespeare play was made into a patriotic film by Laurence Olivier?

b7   *In which film did Merle Oberon co-star with Laurence Olivier?*

a8   As what did Jackson Pollock become famous?

b8   *Which ballerina starred in the film The Red Shoes?*

a9   Which island became part of Canada in 1949?

b9   *Until 1949, by what name was the Kingdom of Jordan known?*

a10   In which year was the United States Air Force established, independent of the other services: 1918, 1941, or 1947?

b10   *What role is performed by America's F-117A Stealth aircraft?*

a11   Of which country was Major General Zia the ruler?

b11   *Of which South American country did Carlos Menem become president in 1989?*

a12   Which famous novel had as its comic hero Jim Dixon?

b12   *Which international prize did William Golding win in 1983?*

No. 179 Answers

a1	Harry Corbett
b1	Blue Peter
a2	Channel Islands
b2	*General de Gaulle*
a3	(County) cricket
b3	*Rugby union*
a4	Lightning war (a sudden, ferocious attack)
b4	*Home Guard (or 'Dad's Army')*
a5	Transcendental Meditation (TM)
b5	*Albania*
a6	VSO (Voluntary Service Overseas)
b6	*City Technology College*
a7	*Henry V*
b7	*Wuthering Heights*
a8	Painting (especially 'action painting' or 'Abstract Expressionism')
b8	*Moira Shearer*
a9	Newfoundland
b9	*Transjordan*
a10	1947 (During the Second World War it was the Army Air Force)
b10	*Bomber*
a11	Bangladesh
b11	*Argentina*
a12	*Lucky Jim* (by Kingsley Amis)
b12	*Nobel Prize for Literature*

Tie-breaker

Q What name was given to the style of architecture popular in the later thirties, and used in the building of many Odeon cinemas and new railway stations?

A *Art deco*

No. 180

a1 In which sport do Kayak fours and Canadian pairs compete?

b1 In which sport might you either snatch or jerk?

a2 In the 1939 popular song, where was the washing to be hung?

b2 Where, in a 1948 pop song, would a 'slow boat' take you?

a3 For what is the chemical aspartame used?

b3 With what is the science of cryogenics concerned?

a4 On television, who hosts the quiz show *A Question of Sport*?

b4 Who was the original host of television's Blankety Blank?

a5 In October 1937, which exhibition or show was held for the first time, at London's Earls Court?

b5 From November 1937, what was Scotland Yard's emergency telephone number?

a6 In the army, what is a formation of two or more brigades called?

b6 Why are minesweepers often built of reinforced plastic?

a7 Which commonwealth country moved its seat of government to a new federal capital in 1927?

b7 In which city was the Massacre of Tiananmen Square in 1989?

a8 In the 1948 film *Oliver Twist*, who played Fagin?

b8 Robert Donat played the lead in a 1939 film about an elderly public schoolmaster. What was the film?

a9 Which British aircraft carrier was launched in 1937?

b9 Which famous Cunard liner made her maiden transatlantic voyage in May, 1936?

a10 In which country did 8,000 people 'disappear' between 1976 and 1983, under a repressive military government?

b10 In which country did the 1956 'Hundred Flowers' movement encourage criticism of the government?

a11 Who wrote the famous (and first) radio play about Jesus Christ, called *The Man Born to be King*?

b11 Which physicist wrote the book A Brief History of Time?

a12 In which country has Prince Sihanouk been a leading political figure?

b12 Which country was ruled between 1986 and 1992 by President Najibullah?

No. 180 Answers

a1 Canoeing
b1 *Weightlifting*
a2 'On the Siegfried Line'
b2 *China ('On a Slow Boat to China')*
a3 As a sweetener (Nutrasweet) in foods and drinks
b3 *Very low temperatures; freezing*
a4 David Coleman
b4 *Terry Wogan*
a5 The Motor Show
b5 *999*
a6 Division
b6 *So they are immune to magnetic mines*
a7 Australia (Canberra)
b7 *Beijing (Peking)*
a8 Alec Guinness
b8 *Goodbye Mr Chips*
a9 'Ark Royal'
b9 *'The Queen Mary'*
a10 Argentina
b10 *China*
a11 Dorothy L. Sayers
b11 *Stephen Hawking*
a12 Cambodia
b12 *Afghanistan*

Tie-breaker

Q After association football, what is the next most popular spectator sport in Britain (measured by numbers attending)?
A *Greyhound racing*

No. 181: Sports Kit

To take part in which sports or games do you officially need the following?

a1   An indoor court, rackets and shuttlecock

b1   *An oval ball, helmets and heavy padding for each player*

a2   A field marked out in the form of a diamond and two teams of nine players

b2   *A large ball, an indoor court with circular hoops and nets at each end and two teams of five players*

a3   Plenty of clubs and balls

b3   *More than one pony*

a4   Map, compass and control cards

b4   *22 balls*

a5   A foil

b5   *Grass and a jack*

a6   A large round ball, a hard court with circular hoops and nets at each end and two teams of seven players

b6   *A round ball, goalposts at each end of the pitch with a net across their lower halves*

a7   Ice and two disc-like stones for each player

b7   *A curved stick for each player, a goal with a crossbar at each end of the pitch and fifteen players a side*

a8   An oval ball and an oval pitch

b8   *A large inflated ball, one net and no bats or rackets*

a9   Small wooden paddles covered with sponge or rubber

b9   *A shale, clay, concrete, grass or wood surface*

a10   A Malibu

b10   *A caman and a leather-covered cork and worsted ball*

a11   Seven players for each team if you play indoors; eleven if you play outside

b11   *Ten players for each team if they are men; twelve if they are women*

a12   A two-wheeled sulky

b12   *A Finn or Windglider*

No. 181 Answers

a1 Badminton
b1 *American football*
a2 Baseball (accept: softball)
b2 *Basketball*
a3 Golf
b3 *Polo*
a4 Orienteering
b4 *Snooker*
a5 Fencing
b5 *Bowls*
a6 Netball
b6 *Gaelic football*
a7 Curling
b7 *Hurling*
a8 Australian football
b8 *Volleyball*
a9 Table tennis
b9 *(Lawn) tennis*
a10 Surfing (it's a surfboard)
b10 *Shinty (the caman is the curved stick used by each player)*
a11 Handball
b11 *Lacrosse*
a12 Harness racing
b12 *Soio (Olympic) yachting*

Tie-breaker

Q What is octopush?
A *Underwater hockey*

No. 182

a1   How did Angela Rippon first become a national figure?
b1   Which chain of shops is associated with the name Anita Roddick?
a2   In which famous Liverpool club did the Beatles once play?
b2   Which Liverpool group sang about 'Lily the Pink'?
a3   In English soccer, the Third Division was formed in 1920. What happened to it a year later?
b3   And what happened to it in 1958?
a4   If you are given a restaurant bill for £17.50 and you want to leave a 10% tip, how much do you leave?
b4   Which is bigger, three hundred thousand or a quarter of a million?
a5   Which envoy of the Archbishop of Canterbury became a hostage in Beirut?
b5   Where did over 1400 pilgrims die in a stampede during 1990?
a6   What is the purpose of an analgesic?
b6   What is a psychosomatic illness?
a7   Where are the headquarters of English Rugby Union?
b7   For what kind of sporting activity has Ruislip (say: rye-slip) in west London become especially well known?
a8   Which French television soap opera (imported to Britain) was set in a quiet Loire town and all about two feuding families?
b8   And which German soap (also imported to Britain) had a medical setting and showed us lots of pine trees and lakes?
a9   Which religious worker won the Nobel Peace Prize in 1979?
b9   In which country was Cardinal Mindszenty a leading religious figure and opponent of Communism?
a10 Who wrote the original series of children's novels about the Wizard of Oz?
b10 Ian Serraillier (say: se-ral-i-ay) wrote a famous children's novel about refugees in the Second World War. What was it called?
a11 In which country is the historical site of the ancient city of Troy?
b11 In which country is the historic site of Luxor?
a12 Of which organization did Oliver Tambo become leader in 1977?
b12 What post did Helmut Schmidt hold from 1974 to 1983?

No. 182 Answers

a1 As a newsreader
b1 *The Body Shop*
a2 The Cavern
b2 *Scaffold*
a3 It divided into Division 3 North and Division 3 South
b3 *The two divisions were re-formed into Divisions 3 and 4*
a4 £1.75
b4 *Three hundred thousand (a quarter of a million = 250,000)*
a5 Terry Waite
b5 *Mecca (in an underground tunnel)*
a6 To relieve pain
b6 *One that is thought to arise from emotional or mental causes*
a7 Twickenham
b7 *Water sports (bathing, water-skiing, sailing on Ruislip Lido)*
a8 Châteauvallon
b8 Schwarzwaldklinik (Black Forest Clinic)
a9 Mother Teresa (of Calcutta)
b9 *Hungary*
a10 Lyman Frank Baum
b10 *The Silver Sword*
a11 Turkey
b11 *Egypt*
a12 ANC (African National Congress)
b12 *Chancellor (premier) of West Germany*

Tie-breaker

Q By what name did the case of murderer George Joseph Smith become known, on account of his drowning his newly married wives?

A *The Brides in the Bath case*

No. 183

a1   For what did John Curry become well-known?

b1   *How has Anthony Sher become famous?*

a2   Which popular entertainer sang the lyrics: 'Did you think I would leave you dying when there's room on my horse for two'?

b2   *From which Christmas hit came the words 'Are you hanging up a stocking on your wall/it's time that Santa has a ball'?*

a3   For what do the initials HMV stand?

b3   *For what do the letters CD stand, as seen on some cars?*

a4   Which fruit became available in Britain in 1946 for the first time for many years?

b4   *What means of urgent communication was abolished by British Telecom in 1981?*

a5   To which country are the platypus, wombat and emu unique?

b5   *What was discovered in caves at Lascaux (say: las-ko) in France in 1940?*

a6   In which year did Queen Victoria die?

b6   *In which month and year was Queen Elizabeth's coronation?*

a7   Which is Ian Baker-Finch's sport?

b7   *In which sport is Dickie Bird a leading figure?*

a8   What is the unit of currency in Portugal?

b8   *And what is it in Spain?*

a9   Which character did child actor Jack Wild play in the film *Oliver!*?

b9   *In which film is the ballad 'Some Day My Prince Will Come'?*

a10   Which holy city came under British control in 1917 after over 700 years under Islamic control?

b10   *Why is Medina a holy city for Muslims?*

a11   Who wrote the plays *Roots* and *Chicken Soup With Barley*?

b11   *Who wrote the score of the musical* The Desert Song?

a12   The sinking of which ship in 1915 infuriated America?

b12   *And where did the tragedy occur?*

No. 183 Answers

a1	Ice-skating
b1	*As an actor*
a2	Rolf Harris ('Two Little Boys')
b2	*'Merry Christmas Everybody' by Slade*
a3	His Master's Voice
b3	*Corps (say: cor) diplomatique*
a4	Bananas
b4	*Telegrams*
a5	Australia
b5	*Prehistoric paintings or carvings*
a6	1901
b6	*June, 1953*
a7	Golf
b7	*Cricket (umpire)*
a8	The escudo
b8	*The peseta*
a9	The Artful Dodger
b9	*Snow White and the Seven Dwarfs*
a10	Jerusalem
b10	*It was the home of the prophet of Islam, Muhammad*
a11	Arnold Wesker
b11	*Sigmund Romberg*
a12	'Lusitania'
b12	*Off the coast of Ireland (off Kinsale)*

Tie-breaker

Q Besides John Major, who were the contenders for the leadership of the Conservative party in November, 1990?

A *Michael Heseltine and Douglas Hurd*

No. 184

a1   What is a junta (say: hunta)?

b1   *What is a mantra?*

a2   Besides cricket, in which area has the Australian Kerry Packer become well known?

b2   *How did Clive Ponting make the headlines in 1985?*

a3   The New Zealand Rugby Union team is known as the All Blacks. By what name are the New Zealand Rugby League tourists known?

b3   *In which sport would you compete for the Natwest Cup?*

a4   In which musical are the characters Potiphar's wife and Pharaoh?

b4   *In which musical are the characters Aunt Eller and Curly?*

a5   Which illness is treated by doses of quinine?

b5   *And in which common drink can quinine be found?*

a6   By population, which is the largest metropolitan area in Asia?

b6   *After London, which is the largest metropolitan area (by population) in Europe?*

a7   Of which country was Edvard Shevardnadze a leading statesman in the eighties?

b7   *Of which country was Hans Dietrich (say: dee-trisch) Genscher a long-serving foreign minister?*

a8   In which radio serial was someone always worried about Jim?

b8   *Which radio serial, set in London, replaced The Dales in 1969?*

a9   Near which famous American city are Berkeley, Oakland and Richmond?

b9   *In which American city is the district called Arlington?*

a10   'You're Dancing on My Heart' was the signature tune of which dance bandleader – famous for his 'slow, slow, quick-quick, slow'?

b10   *What was Bing Crosby's signature tune?*

a11   What has been named after the English logician John Venn (1834–1923)?

b11   *What are ordinal numbers?*

a12   Which affair caused the resignations of Bob Haldeman and John D. Ehrlichman?

b12   *The wife of a black South African leader, she has herself been a political and controversial figure. Who is she?*

No. 184 Answers

a1 The military rulers of a country, after seizing power
b1 A word or words repeated during meditation
a2 Television (channel boss) and publisher (of newspapers)
b2 (As a civil servant,) he broke the Official Secrets Act (by giving information to MPs about the Falklands War)
a3 The Kiwis
b3 Cricket
a4 Joseph and the Amazing Technicolor Dreamcoat
b4 Oklahoma!
a5 Malaria (and other fevers)
b5 (Indian) tonic water
a6 Tokyo
b6 Paris
a7 Soviet Union
b7 East Germany (German Federal Republic)
a8 Mrs Dale was worried, in *Mrs Dale's Diary* and (later) *The Dales*
b8 Waggoner's Walk
a9 San Francisco
b9 Washington
a10 Victor Silvester
b10 'Where the Blue of the Night'
a11 Venn diagrams (in mathematics: to show the relationship between sets)
b11 First, second, third, fourth, etc. (numbers which indicate order)
a12 The Watergate Affair (in America, 1973)
b12 Winnie Mandela

Tie-breaker

Q In space, what are sometimes described as 'dirty snowballs'?
A Comets

No. 185

a1   Why has Nigel Kennedy become well known?

b1   *How did Tony Greig (say: gregg) become well known?*

a2   As what has Judy Blume become famous?

b2   *Which Bank of England clerk wrote a children's classic (about animals on a river bank) in 1908?*

a3   In 1937, where did you have to go for 'a week's holiday for a week's wage'?

b3   *According to the adverts, what did Phyllosan do?*

a4   To which country do the Faeroe Islands belong?

b4   *To which country do the islands of Lesbos and Rhodes belong?*

a5   What was Ronan Point?

b5   *Which controversial 385-foot high office block was built in central London in 1966 and was then not used for some time?*

a6   Who was West Germany's soccer captain when they won the 1974 World Cup?

b6   *And who was Liverpool F. C.'s captain in the 1974 Cup Final?*

a7   In 1966, who had a hit with 'You Don't Have to Say You Love Me'?

b7   *In 1969, who sang about a 'Boy Named Sue'?*

a8   Which country was governed as a military dictatorship under Antonio Salazar from 1928 to 1968?

b8   *Of which country was P. W. Botha prime minister from 1978?*

a9   In which film did Judy Garland sing 'The Trolley Song'?

b9   *Which American film 'sex goddess' starred in Hell's Angels and Riffraff – and died at the age of 26?*

a10   The sum of the interior angles of a triangle is 180 degrees. What is the sum of the interior angles of a quadrilateral?

b10   *And of a pentagon?*

a11   In which town did the Germans sign the unconditional surrender at the end of the Second World War?

b11   *And who, on behalf of the Allies, received that surrender?*

a12   For which element is the chemical symbol Si?

b12   *And for which is it Ra?*

No. 185 Answers

a1	For his violin playing (and 'punk' style)
b1	*As a cricketer*
a2	As a writer (of novels for young teenagers, especially girls)
b2	*Kenneth Grahame (The Wind in the Willows)*
a3	Butlins (holiday camp)
b3	*'Fortifies the over-forties'*
a4	Denmark
b4	*Greece*
a5	A tower block of flats (which collapsed in 1968)
b5	*Centrepoint*
a6	Franz Beckenbauer
b6	*Emlyn Hughes*
a7	Dusty Springfield
b7	*Johnny Cash*
a8	Portugal
b8	*South Africa*
a9	*Meet Me in St Louis*
b9	*Jean Harlow*
a10	360 degrees
b10	*540 degrees*
a11	Rheims (say: Ranse)
b11	*General Eisenhower*
a12	Silicon
b12	*Radium*

Tie-breaker

Q Besides Liberia, which was the only independent country in Africa in 1911?

A *Ethiopia (Abyssinia)*

No. 186

a1   In which television 'soap' do or did we see Nellie Mangel?

b1   And in which soap has Dot Cotton also been something of a 'sour puss'?

a2   What is the unit of currency in Greece?

b2   And what is it in the Netherlands?

a3   In soccer, which Spanish club won the European Cup for the first five years of the competition?

b3   In which sport do the Cincinnati Reds compete?

a4   Ian Macleod was once Chancellor of the Exchequer. Of which party was he a member?

b4   When Yugoslavia became a federal republic in 1945, who became its leader?

a5   In 1971, who sang 'Chirpy Chirpy Cheep Cheep'?

b5   About which means of transport did the Mixtures have a chart hit?

a6   Introduced from 1941 onwards, what were the earliest group of antibiotic drugs?

b6   In the field of medicine, what is a placebo (say: pla-see-bo)?

a7   Which secular movement in Britain was, for some time, led by a Roman Catholic priest, Bruce Kent?

b7   Hope Street runs between an Anglican cathedral and a Roman Catholic cathedral in which English city?

a8   Who wrote the novel *Prester John*?

b8   Who wrote the satirical novel Scoop?

a9   In which two continents is the Muslim religion most influential?

b9   And in which large country is Hinduism the primary influence?

a10   Which two countries fought each other in a Gulf War which began in the early eighties?

b10   Which two countries signed a joint 'Pact of Steel' in 1939?

a11   Who was William Holman Hunt (who died in 1910)?

b11   Who was Marie Tempest?

a12   Which European country has a coast line on the Black Sea and includes the Transylvanian Alps?

b12   Which Canadian province has a Pacific Ocean coastline?

No. 186 Answers

a1	*Neighbours*
b1	EastEnders
a2	The drachma
b2	*The guilder*
a3	Real (say: ray-al) Madrid
b3	*Baseball*
a4	Conservative
b4	*Tito*
a5	Middle of the Road
b5	*Bicycle ('The Pushbike Song')*
a6	Penicillin
b6	*A harmless substance or pill; the person taking it believes it will cure a problem or illness*
a7	CND (Campaign for Nuclear Disarmament)
b7	*Liverpool*
a8	John Buchan
b8	*Evelyn Waugh*
a9	Asia, Africa
b9	*India*
a10	Iran, Iraq
b10	*Germany, Italy*
a11	Artist ('the last of the Pre-Raphaelites')
b11	*Famous actress*
a12	Romania
b12	*British Columbia*

Tie-breaker

Q Which new novel sold a million copies in America in 1936?
A Gone With the Wind *(by Margaret Mitchell)*

No. 187

a1   What is probate?

b1   *What is parole?*

a2   Of which Canadian province is Labrador a part?

b2   *On to which lake or sea does the city of Chicago face?*

a3   In a film, what was the name of the biggest dog in the world?

b3   *In which Walt Disney film do two dogs dine out in an Italian restaurant?*

a4   For which sport has Ty Cobb become well known?

b4   *For what has Jim (or James) Clark become famous?*

a5   In which Palace of Justice were Nazi leaders put on trial in 1945?

b5   *What was the name of Hitler's mistress (and, for the last day of his life, his wife)?*

a6   From which hit came the words 'When the Moon is in the seventh house, and Jupiter aligns with Mars'?

b6   *From which hit came the words 'Well, it's one for the money, two for the show, three to get ready, now go cat go'?*

a7   For which area is 061 the STD telephone code?

b7   *And for which city is 031 the code?*

a8   For which poisonous element is the chemical symbol As?

b8   *And for which is it Fe?*

a9   In which year was England's first official Rugby Union tour abroad: 1902, 1947, or 1963?

b9   *In soccer, what is the Inter-Cities Fairs Cup now called?*

a10   Until its recent civil war, which Mediterranean country was the financial centre of the Middle East?

b10   *Which country borders Norway at its extreme north-eastern tip?*

a11   Who wrote the play *A Streetcar Named Desire*?

b11   *Which Arthur Miller play is about Willy Loman?*

a12   Of which country did Jim Bolger become prime minister in 1990?

b12   *Of which country was Gro Harlem Brundtland elected prime minister in 1986 and 1990?*

No. 187 Answers

a1 The formal proof of a will
b1 *Conditional release of a prisoner*
a2 Newfoundland
b2 *Lake Michigan*
a3 Digby
b3 *Lady and the Tramp*
a4 Baseball
b4 *Motor-racing*
a5 Nuremberg
b5 *Eva Braun*
a6 'Aquarius' (by Fifth Dimension)
b6 *'Blue Suede Shoes' (by Elvis Presley)*
a7 (Greater) Manchester
b7 *Edinburgh*
a8 Arsenic
b8 *Iron*
a9 1963
b9 *UEFA Cup*
a10 Lebanon
b10 *Russia*
a11 Tennessee Williams
b11 *Death of a Salesman*
a12 New Zealand
b12 *Norway*

Tie-breaker

Q What was remarkable about the result of the 1910 British
general election?

A *It resulted in a tie (Both Liberals and Conservatives winning
272 seats) (42 Labour MPs and 84 Irish Nationalists agreed to
support the Conservatives)*

No. 188

a1   Which was David Broome's sport?

b1   *Which is Curtis Strange's sport?*

a2   Who belongs to Equity?

b2   *In France, what is Le Figaro?*

a3   In Scotland, with which industry has Bilston Glen been associated?

b3   *And what was Ravenscraig's principal industry?*

a4   Which country includes the holiday resort of Acapulco?

b4   *Which African country includes the Great Rift Valley, Lake Nakuru and the port of Mombasa?*

a5   Back in 1956, which female singer sang 'Lay Down Your Arms'?

b5   *Which American bandleader was particularly associated with the tune 'The Peanut Vendor'?*

a6   What is the unit of currency in Malta?

b6   *And in Morocco?*

a7   In the late forties, which popular 'special agent' appeared in a daily radio serial?

b7   *In which BBC comedy radio show did Bebe Daniels appear with the rest of her family?*

a8   What name did Wilhelm Roentgen (who died in 1923) give to the short electromagnetic waves he discovered earlier in his life?

b8   *In 1912, Sir Frederick Gowland Hopkins discovered substances we now know are a vital part of our diet. What are they?*

a9   Which London Underground station was the title of a hit by the New Vaudeville Band?

b9   *Which comedian used his own song 'Confidentially' as his signature tune?*

a10   In 1983, which Cabinet member had to resign after an affair with his secretary?

b10   *In which riots in 1968 was Daniel Cohn-Bendit a leader?*

a11   As what did John Piper achieve fame?

b11   *Why did Gustav Mahler (died 1911) become famous?*

a12   Of which country was Turgut Ozal the prime minister from 1983?

b12   *Of which country was Bettino Craxi prime minister from 1983?*

No. 188 Answers

a1 Showjumping (horse-riding)
b1 *Golf*
a2 Actors (it's their trade union)
b2 *Daily newspaper*
a3 Mining/coal
b3 *Steel*
a4 Mexico
b4 *Kenya*
a5 Anne Shelton
b5 *Stan Kenton*
a6 The Maltese lira (accept: pound)
b6 *The dirham*
a7 Dick Barton
b7 *Life with the Lyons*
a8 X-rays
b8 *Vitamins*
a9 Finchley Central
b9 *Reg Dixon*
a10 Cecil Parkinson
b10 *Paris student riots*
a11 As a painter/artist
b11 *He was a composer*
a12 Turkey
b12 *Italy*

Tie-breaker

Q Which English county was the first to plan 'comprehensive schools' (in 1948)?
A *Middlesex*

No. 189

a1 Who was Olive Oyl?

b1 Can you complete this pop song title: 'Gilly-Gilly-Ossenfeffer . . .'?

a2 What did Britain suffer from particularly in February 1947?

b2 And in the summer of 1976?

a3 In a computer, what is a 'buffer'?

b3 In space, what is 'Mir'?

a4 Which sport is said to have the most active participants in Britain?

b4 Which game (or variation of a game) was invented in Scotland in 1924 – and played in Middlesex two years later?

a5 In the film *The Prince and the Showgirl*, Marilyn Monroe played the showgirl. Who was her prince?

b5 In the film Blue Skies, which two male singers were 'Puttin' on the Ritz'?

a6 What is HDTV?

b6 In a teletext system, how is information sent to a receiver?

a7 By population, which is the largest city in India?

b7 By population, which is the largest city (that is, metropolitan area) in China?

a8 From which musical come the songs 'Luck Be a Lady' and 'A Bushel and a Peck'?

b8 Which musical tells the story of a Scottish village that appears only once each century?

a9 In the world of finance, what is a dividend?

b9 How many sheets of paper are there in a ream?

a10 Besides Germany, which country invaded Poland in September 1939?

b10 Which German port and industrial city was severely bombed by British bombers in August 1943?

a11 As what did Ravi Shankar become well known?

b11 Why did the Nawab of Pataudi become famous?

a12 Which Labour Chancellor of the Exchequer had to resign in 1947 because he told a journalist what would be in his Budget speech?

b12 And who simply said about the incident, 'Pity. Never could keep his mouth shut'?

No. 189 Answers

a1 Popeye's girlfriend
b1 '. . Katzenellen-Bogen-By-the-Sea'
a2 Heavy snowstorms; freezing temperatures
b2 *A major drought*
a3 Temporary memory (or any electronic protective device)
b3 *Soviet space station*
a4 Angling
b4 *Rugby union sevens (seven-a-side rugby)*
a5 Laurence Olivier
b5 *Bing Crosby and Fred Astaire*
a6 High-definition television (television with much clearer pictures)
b6 *It is broadcast with an ordinary television signal (in the view data system, it is sent via the telephone network)*
a7 Calcutta
b7 *Shanghai*
a8 *Guys and Dolls*
b8 Brigadoon
a9 The part of the profits of a company paid to shareholders (usually annually)
b9 *480*
a10 Soviet Union (Russia)
b10 *Hamburg*
a11 As an (Indian) musician (sitar player)
b11 *He was an international Indian cricketer (in the thirties)*
a12 Hugh Dalton
b12 *Clement Attlee (Prime Minister)*

Tie-breaker

Q Sandra (played by Nerys Hughes) and Carol (played by Elizabeth Estensen) were the main characters in which television comedy series?

A The Liver Birds

390

No. 190

a1 In which television serial was David Hunter a famously dull character?

b1 *And which television serial included the characters Sister Carole Young, Dr Chris Anderson, and Alan Dawson?*

a2 Who was Edith Cavell?

b2 *Who was Sybil Thorndike?*

a3 In law, what is a 'decree nisi' (say: ni-si)?

b3 *What is extradition?*

a4 In which sport would you compete for the Thomas Cup?

b4 *In which British sport is the Challenge Cup a national competition?*

a5 Which group had a hit with 'Ob La Di, Ob La Da'?

b5 *Which pop group had a hit with 'Marrakesh Express'?*

a6 What is the unit of currency in Chile?

b6 *And what is it in Israel?*

a7 Who wrote *Keep the Aspidistra Flying?*

b7 *How did the novelist Virginia Woolf die?*

a8 When did Admiral Sandy Woodward make the headlines?

b8 *Which British Foreign Secretary resigned over Argentina's invasion of the Falklands?*

a9 Which Australian city is close to Botany Bay?

b9 *And which Australian city is neighbour to Fremantle?*

a10 Which Mediterranean country includes part of the Atlas Mountains, Barbary Coast and the port of Oran?

b10 *Which country includes the Patagonian plateau and the estuary of the river Plate?*

a11 In which country could you travel by the 'Blue Train' or by the 'Orange Express'?

b11 *Of which people is Chief Buthelezi (say: boo-ta-lay-zi) a leader?*

a12 If statics is the branch of physics concerned with objects at rest, which branch is concerned with moving objects?

b12 *What is viscosity?*

No. 190 Answers

a1	*Crossroads*
b1	Emergency – Ward Ten
a2	British nurse, executed by the Germans
b2	*Famous actress (played Joan of Arc in G. B. Shaw's play, St Joan)*
a3	A conditional order of divorce
b3	*The surrender of a person by a state or country to another country (where the person is 'wanted', possibly for legal reasons)*
a4	Badminton
b4	*Rugby league*
a5	Marmalade (accept: The Bedrocks)
b5	*Crosby Stills and Nash*
a6	The peso
b6	*The shekel*
a7	George Orwell
b7	*By drowning (believed to be suicide)*
a8	During the Falklands War (1982) (He was the Task Force commander)
b8	*Lord Carrington*
a9	Sydney
b9	*Perth*
a10	Algeria
b10	*Argentina*
a11	South Africa
b11	*Zulu; Kwa Zulu black 'homeland' (in South Africa)*
a12	Dynamics
b12	*The resistance of a liquid to flow*

Tie-breaker

Q What are tectonic plates?

A *The continental 'plates' which are slowly moving and so cause 'continental drift' (that is, they cause the continents to move very slowly in relation to each other)*

No. 191: Brand Names

The following are all brand names of products that have been on sale during the twentieth century. What is each product?

a1   Dansette
b1   *Tide*
a2   Tibs
b2   *Baby Belling*
a3   Wincarnis
b3   *Euthymol*
a4   Lilliput
b4   *Mullard*
a5   Cerebos
b5   *Bemax*
a6   Procea
b6   *Eno's*
a7   Virol
b7   *Jelloids*
a8   Abdullah
b8   *John Bull*
a9   Lexicon
b9   *Parlophone*
a10   Triang
b10   *Zubes*
a11   Spirella
b11   *Symington*
a12   Vidor
b12   *Three Castles*

No. 191 Answers

a1	Record-player
b1	*Washing powder*
a2	Cat food
b2	*(Small) cooker*
a3	Health drink
b3	*Toothpaste (or powder)*
a4	Magazine (men's)
b4	*Wireless (or radio) and television sets and valves*
a5	Salt
b5	*Vitamin supplement (wheatgerm)*
a6	Bread
b6	*'Fruit Salts' (laxative)*
a7	'Nutritious supplementary food' for children (malt extract)
b7	*Iron pills*
a8	Cigarettes
b8	*Weekly magazine*
a9	Card game (not unlike Scrabble)
b9	*Gramophone records*
a10	Toys (especially toy cars and trains)
b10	*Throat pastilles*
a11	Corsets
b11	*Soups*
a12	Batteries
b12	*Cigarettes*

Tie-breaker

Q What was 'The Nugget'?
A *A polish for shoes and other leather goods*

No. 192

a1 Which child actress was seen in the films *Pollyanna* and *Whistle Down the Wind*?

b1 In *The Wizard of Oz*, what was the name of Dorothy's dog?

a2 In London, which distinctive tower building was opened in 1964 – complete with a revolving restaurant at the top?

b2 Which new, modernist building was designed for London Zoo by Lord Snowdon and opened in 1965?

a3 Which Australian state is immediately north of New South Wales?

b3 Marlborough, Nelson and Westland are all provincial (or statistical) areas in which country?

a4 Which year was the Russian revolution?

b4 During the Second World War, in which year was Rome liberated?

a5 Of which novel and play is Billy Fisher the untruthful hero?

b5 Which Irish writer created the character Molly Bloom?

a6 From which hit come the lyrics 'The weather here has been as nice as it can be, although it doesn't really matter much to me'?

b6 Which pop hit includes the lyrics, 'My folks were always putting him down, they said he came from the wrong side of town'?

a7 In which sport have Rex Williams, Norman Dagley and Mike Russell been recent world champions?

b7 Which two sports did Fred Titmus and Denis Compton both play?

a8 For which metal is the chemical symbol Zn?

b8 And for which is it Pb?

a9 Who wrote the plays *Habeas Corpus* and *Forty Years On*?

b9 Which relative of a prime minister wrote the plays *The Chiltern Hundreds* and *Lloyd George Knew My Father*?

a10 In the world of finance, what is APR?

b10 What is the aim of monetarism?

a11 For what have Michael Clark, Twyla Tharp and Merce Cunningham become famous?

b11 How did Harry Tate and 'Little Tich' become famous?

a12 In which city did the United Nations General Assembly hold its first meeting (in 1946)?

b12 Whose visit to Britain in 1982 was a 'first' for 450 years?

No. 192 Answers

a1 Hayley Mills
b1 *Toto*
a2 Post Office Tower (now Telecom Tower)
b2 *The Aviary*
a3 Queensland
b3 *New Zealand*
a4 1917
b4 *1944*
a5 *Billy Liar*
b5 *James Joyce*
a6 'It Might As Well Rain Until September' (by Carole King)
b6 *'Leader of the Pack' (by The Shangri-las)*
a7 Billiards
b7 *Cricket and soccer*
a8 Zinc
b8 *Lead*
a9 Alan Bennett
b9 *William Douglas-Home*
a10 Annual percentage rate (the rate of interest you pay on borrowed money)
b10 *Reduction of inflation*
a11 Dance/choreographers
b11 *As music hall artists*
a12 London
b12 *The Pope*

Tie-breaker

Q In a golf tournament, what is the maximum number of clubs that may be carried in your bag?

A *Fourteen*

No. 193

a1 In which television serial has Fred Feast been Fred Gee?

b1 *Who played Felicity Kendall's 'husband' in the television series The Good Life?*

a2 According to the war time slogan, what did 'careless talk' cost?

b2 *In post-war austerity Britain, there were a number of slogans. 'Export or die' was one; another was 'Work or . . .' What?*

a3 Which is London's principal opera house?

b3 *In England in 1916, which prehistoric monument was sold at auction for £6,000?*

a4 Which two countries border Tunisia?

b4 *Which two countries lie to the south of Bulgaria?*

a5 In what sort of setting did most of Angela Brazil's novels take place?

b5 *Which famous fictional schoolboy was invented by Anthony Buckeridge?*

a6 Which female vocalist sang 'This Ole House'?

b6 *In 1962, who had a hit with 'I Can't Stop Loving You'?*

a7 In which sport do the Chicago Bears compete?

b7 *In which country is PSV Eindhoven a soccer team?*

a8 In which country did General Pinochet (say: pi-no-shay) lead a coup in 1973?

b8 *On which island did General Grivas wage a guerrilla war?*

a9 For what is thermal imaging used?

b9 *And what is a seismic (say: size-mick) wave?*

a10 In what was the armistice signed at the end of the First World War?

b10 *Which American general commanded American forces at the end of the Second World War in the Far East (and received Japan's surrender)*

a11 As what has A. S. Byatt become famous?

b11 *As what did Paul Klee become famous?*

a12 What is the unit of currency in Finland?

b12 *And in the Greek part of Cyprus?*

No. 193 Answers

a1	*Coronation Street*
b1	*Richard Briers*
a2	Lives ('Careless talk costs lives')
b2	*Want*
a3	Royal Opera House, Covent Garden
b3	*Stonehenge*
a4	Algeria and Libya
b4	*Greece and Turkey*
a5	In girls' boarding schools
b5	*Jennings*
a6	Rosemary Clooney
b6	*Ray Charles*
a7	American football
b7	*Netherlands (Holland)*
a8	Chile
b8	*Cyprus*
a9	To help see or photograph objects in the dark (also used by doctors to locate diseased cells)
b9	*A wave of energy or vibrations that spread out from the centre of an earthquake*
a10	In a railway carriage (in the forest of Compiègne)
b10	*General MacArthur*
a11	Novelist
b11	*Painter/artist*
a12	The markka
b12	*The Cyprus pound*

Tie-breaker

Q Which chemical element is common to diamonds, soot and coal?

A *Carbon*

No. 194

a1 The 1943 film *Lassie Come Home* featured an 11-year-old girl. She is still an actress – called . . .?

b1 *In the film* Fantastic Voyage *(about a miniaturized submarine's trip inside a human body), which actress played the only female member of the submarine's crew?*

a2 Who was Gorgeous Gussie?

b2 *What is athlete Florence Griffith-Joyner's usual nickname?*

a3 For which British city is 041 the STD telephone code?

b3 *And for which area is 051 the code?*

a4 Lee Hazlewood sang 'Did You Ever' with which female singer?

b4 *Which pop personality sang 'Everyone's Gone to the Moon'?*

a5 What were once called the Home, Light and Third?

b5 *What is the difference between freehold and leasehold?*

a6 In which war was the Tet offensive?

b6 *In which year did the Common Market officially come into being?*

a7 In 1911, which British physicist discovered the atomic nucleus?

b7 *In physics, which theory (that energy is absorbed or radiated discontinuously) was first stated in 1900?*

a8 Where was the British battleship 'Royal Oak' sunk in the first weeks of the Second World War?

b8 *And of what was Operation Dynamo official name?*

a9 Which Asian country includes the Hindu Kush mountain range, part of the Khyber Pass, and the Panshir Valley?

b9 *Which republic comprises 13,677 tropical islands (including Bali, Timor and Moluccas)?*

a10 With which means of transport has the village of Cardington been especially associated?

b10 *Which motor-racing circuit is near Towcester (say: toaster) in Northamptonshire?*

a11 Who wrote the novel *Goodbye to Berlin*?

b11 *Who wrote the novels* No Highway *and* A Town Like Alice?

a12 For what has Norman Thelwell (or 'Thelwell' as he simply signs himself) become well known?

b12 *As what has Thomas Keneally become famous?*

No. 194 Answers

a1	Elizabeth Taylor
b1	*Raquel Welch*
a2	(American) tennis player – with distinctive panties (Gussie Moran)
b2	*Flo-Jo*
a3	Glasgow
b3	*Merseyside (accept: Liverpool)*
a4	Nancy Sinatra
b4	*Jonathan King*
a5	BBC radio networks (until 1967)
b5	*Freehold is absolute ownership, leasehold is ownership for a specified period*
a6	Vietnam
b6	*1957*
a7	(Ernest) Rutherford
b7	*Quantum Theory*
a8	In her home base (Scapa Flow)
b8	*Evacuation of Dunkirk*
a9	Afghanistan
b9	*Indonesia*
a10	Airships (R101 was built here)
b10	*Silverstone*
a11	Christopher Isherwood
b11	*Nevil Shute*
a12	His cartoons (particularly of pony club members)
b12	*Novelist*

Tie-breaker

Q 'I saw something nasty in the woodshed' is a frequent claim made by a character called Aunt Ada Doom. In which novel does she appear (and make her claim)?

A Cold Comfort Farm *(by Stella Gibbons)*

No. 195

a1   On television, who was Catweazle?

b1   *In Royal circles, who was 'Crawfie'?*

a2   Which popular hit refers to 'Father MacKenzie writing the words of a sermon that no one will hear'?

b2   *And which includes the line 'I felt the knife in my hand and she laughed no more'?*

a3   Why has Bill Giles become a well-known face on television?

b3   *Why did Mike Yarwood become a popular television entertainer?*

a4   Where is the Sea of Tranquillity?

b4   *And where is the giant volcano, Olympus Mons?*

a5   In 1953, what form of possibly dangerous footwear for women became popular?

b5   *Which British prime minister first said, 'A week is a long time in politics'?*

a6   In which Caribbean island are Spanish Town and Montego Bay?

b6   *Which country comprises over 1,000 islands and contains Mount Fuji and Mount Aso?*

a7   Which report (in 1942) outlined the idea of the Welfare State?

b7   *Which organization was formed in 1945 to promote Arab unity?*

a8   Of which American city is Long Beach a part?

b8   *Fort Worth is neighbour to which American city?*

a9   Colonel Harry Llewellyn won a gold medal in the 1952 Olympics. What was the name of his famous horse?

b9   *In 1967, which two soccer teams were involved in the first ever all London Cup Final?*

a10   'Depart, I say, and let us have done with you. In the name of God, go!' To whom were those words addressed?

b10   *What was 'Lease-Lend'?*

a11   What is the unit of currency in Hungary?

b11   *And what is it in China?*

a12   Who wrote a play called *Way Upstream*, which had a Thames cruiser floating on stage?

b12   *A 1981 musical is named after a New York thoroughfare (and theatre): what's it called?*

No. 195 Answers

a1 A wizard in a children's television serial (played by Geoffrey Bayldon)

b1 *Nanny to the Princesses Elizabeth and Margaret*

a2 'Eleanor Rigby' (by The Beatles)

b2 *'Delilah' (by Tom Jones)*

a3 He's a regular weather forecaster

b3 *Because of his 'impressions' ('show biz' and political)*

a4 On the Moon (near side)

b4 *On the planet Mars*

a5 Stiletto heels

b5 *Harold Wilson*

a6 Jamaica

b6 *Japan*

a7 The Beveridge Report

b7 *The Arab League*

a8 Los Angeles

b8 *Dallas*

a9 'Foxhunter'

b9 *Chelsea and Tottenham Hotspur (Spurs won 2–1)*

a10 Neville Chamberlain (in the House of Commons)

b10 *Free loan of American military equipment to Britain during the Second World War*

a11 The forint

b11 *The yuan*

a12 Alan Ayckbourn

b12 *42nd Street*

Tie-breaker

Q A Fahrenheit thermometer shows the temperature of a room to be 68°. What temperature would a Celsius (or Centigrade) thermometer show in the same room?

A 20°

No. 196

a1　How does the Alexander Technique aim to improve your health?

b1　*Medically speaking, what is IVF?*

a2　In Britain, why was 12 May 1937 a significant date?

b2　*In February 1939, who or what was the cause of bomb blasts at two of London's Underground stations?*

a3　In which sport did Geoff Duke win a world championship title four times in five years?

b3　*Paul Schockemöhle (say: shock-a-muller) was a champion in which sport?*

a4　Which British naval base fell to the Japanese in February 1942?

b4　*Half a million were built by the motor industry towards the end of the Second World War – and each had two bedrooms, a bathroom and lavatory. What were they?*

a5　What is the unit of currency in Austria?

b5　*And in Denmark?*

a6　Cornwall's cathedral was completed in 1910. Where is it?

b6　*Which natural gas has been found to seep into houses in Devon and Cornwall, and is thought to increase the risk of cancer?*

a7　For which gas is the chemical symbol He (say: aitch-ee)?

b7　*And for which is it Ne?*

a8　Who wrote the musical Lock Up Your Daughters?

b8　*Which was the musician Artur Schnabel's instrument?*

a9　The first record on BBC Radio 1 in 1967 was by the group the Move. What was it?

b9　*Which song did Pearl Carr and Teddy Johnson sing in the 1959 Eurovision Song Contest?*

a10　How was Hitler greeted when he invaded Austria in 1938?

b10　*The Sudetenland was once under German control. Of which country was it a part between the World Wars?*

a11　For what has David Mamet become well known?

b11　*Who was Augustus John?*

a12　Jessie Matthews sang 'Dancing on the Ceiling' in which film?

b12　*Richard Addinsell wrote a concerto for the film Dangerous Moonlight – called . . .?*

No. 196 Answers

a1 By correcting bad posture (and breathing and muscular tension)
b1 *In vitro fertilization ('test-tube' fertilization)*
a2 Coronation of King George VI
b2 *The IRA*
a3 Motor-cycling (500 cc)
b3 *Showjumping*
a4 Singapore
b4 *'Pre-fabs' ('Pre-fabricated' houses)*
a5 The schilling
b5 *The kroner*
a6 Truro
b6 *Radon*
a7 Helium
b7 *Neon*
a8 Lionel Bart
b8 *Piano*
a9 'Flowers in the Rain'
b9 *'Sing Little Birdie'*
a10 By cheering, enthusiastic crowds (99% voted in favour of his 'Anschluss')
b10 *Czechoslovakia*
a11 Playwright (American)
b11 *Painter (1878–1961)*
a12 Evergreen
b12 *The 'Warsaw' Concerto*

Tie-breaker

Q Which famous dam, completed in 1959, controls the waters of the river Zambezi?
A *Kariba Dam*

No. 197

a1   For what has Andy Irvine become famous?

b1   *For what has Roy Lichtenstein become famous?*

a2   Which television series was based (very loosely) on a Walter Scott novel, and starred Roger Moore?

b2   *In which television comedy series did we meet Joey, Adrian and 'our Aveline'?*

a3   Who had pop hits with 'Friendly Persuasion' and 'Love Letters in the Sand'?

b3   *Which popular singing group sang 'Whispering Grass'?*

a4   What was *Reynolds News*?

b4   *What is the Fosbury Flop?*

a5   Erich Segal wrote a sentimental romantic novel in 1970, which was equally successful when filmed. What was it?

b5   *William Peter Blatty wrote a controversial and best-selling novel in 1971 – later filmed. What was it?*

a6   At which disaster did the liner 'Carpathia' play a vital role?

b6   *What deadly mission was carried out by an American bomber aircraft called 'Enola Gay'?*

a7   In which country is Kruger National Park?

b7   *What is linked by the Bosporus Bridge?*

a8   By what title has the ruler of Kuwait been generally known?

b8   *Which post did Boutros Boutros Ghali take up in 1992?*

a9   Where is the region known as Kurdistan?

b9   *Ajaccio is the capital of which island?*

a10   What is the unit of currency in Brazil?

b10   *And what is it in Albania?*

a11   In cycling, what is a 'criterium'?

b11   *Which sport or ball game needs the largest pitch (excluding golf)?*

a12   Which law of physics states that energy can neither be destroyed nor created?

b12   *The Kelvin is the basic scientific unit for measuring . . . what?*

No. 197 Answers

a1 Rugby union player
b1 *Pop art/artist*
a2 Ivanhoe
b2 Bread
a3 Pat Boone
b3 *The Ink Spots*
a4 A (radical) Sunday newspaper
b4 *A style of high-jumping (it involves crossing the bar backwards)*
a5 *Love Story*
b5 The Exorcist
a6 The sinking of the Titanic (it was the first 'rescue' ship on the scene)
b6 *It dropped the atomic bomb on Hiroshima*
a7 South Africa
b7 *European and Asian Turkey (Europe and Asia)*
a8 Emir
b8 *Secretary-General of the United Nations*
a9 Northern and western Iran (and northern Iraq)
b9 *Corsica*
a10 The cruzado
b10 *The lek*
a11 Races round a town or city centre (on closed roads)
b11 *Polo*
a12 (First) law of thermodynamics
b12 *Temperature*

Tie-breaker

Q In which move in the game of chess may a player move two pieces at once?

A *Castling (when moving a castle and the king at once)*

No. 198

a1 Which is golfer Tom Watson's home country?

b1 *Which is snooker player Dennis Taylor's home country?*

a2 In which film do some astronauts (led by Charlton Heston) think they are on another planet but actually are still on Earth?

b2 *What was the name of the modern, almost soundless film made by Mel Brooks?*

a3 Which pop group had hits with 'Donna' and 'Rubber Bullets'?

b3 *Which male pianist had an early hit with 'You're a Lady'?*

a4 What does a cereologist study?

b4 *What is computer hacking?*

a5 Who was elected president of France in 1945?

b5 *In 1991, who said, 'It's time to pay up for Mumsie'?*

a6 In 1983, whose diaries (later shown to be fakes) were serialized in a German magazine and a British newspaper?

b6 *What was Lord Haw-Haw's real name?*

a7 When India was divided into India and Pakistan in 1947, which northern state was the major disputed area?

b7 *In 1979, where in America was there a serious nuclear accident?*

a8 Which humorous British writer was denounced for broadcasting from Germany to America in 1941?

b8 *Who wrote the crime novel Death of an Expert Witness?*

a9 As what did Sir Edwin Lutyens achieve fame?

b9 *Why did Carl Nielsen become famous?*

a10 The Isaac Newton telescope is at the new home of the Royal Greenwich Observatory. In which Sussex village is it situated?

b10 *Which English town has theatres called the Swan and The Other Place?*

a11 Which Czech composer (who died in 1928) was influenced by folk music and wrote operas including The Cunning Little Vixen?

b11 *Who was the Russian pianist and composer who died in 1943 and is particularly remembered for his piano concertos?*

a12 The formula to find the circumference of a circle is $2\pi r$ (say: 2-pie-r). What is the formula to find the surface area of a sphere?

b12 *And what is the formula to find the volume of a cylinder?*

No. 198 Answers

a1   United States of America
b1   *Northern Ireland*
a2   *Planet of the Apes*
b2   Silent Movie
a3   10cc
b3   *Peter Skellern*
a4   Crop circles
b4   *Unauthorized access to someone else's computer*
a5   General de Gaulle
b5   *Mark Thatcher, fund-raising on behalf of his mother*
a6   Hitler
b6   *William Joyce*
a7   Kashmir
b7   *Three Mile Island (Harrisburg, Pennsylvania)*
a8   P. G. Wodehouse
b8   *P. D. James*
a9   Architect
b9   *He was a composer*
a10   Herstmonceux (say: hurst-mon-soo)
b10   *Stratford-upon-Avon*
a11   (Leos) Janácek (say: yan-a-check)
b11   *(Sergei) Rachmaninov*
a12 $4\pi r^2$ (r = radius) (π = say: pi)
b12   *$\pi r^2 h$ (where h = height)*

Tie-breaker

Q Who said, 'I am a Bear of Very Little Brain and long words
    Bother me'?
A *Winnie-the-Pooh (in the book of that name, by A. A. Milne)*

No. 199

a1   What is the next line in the old hit 'A – you're adorable'?

b1   *Which pop hit includes the line, 'Ground control to Major Tom, take your protein pills and put your helmet on'?*

a2   Which industry has developed since 1950 at Fawley, near Southampton?

b2   *Which suspension bridge, opened in 1966, carries the M4 motorway?*

a3   In Scotland, legally speaking, what is a provost?

b3   *What is an Act of Parliament called before it receives the Royal Assent?*

a4   Which disc jockey became known on television as Captain Kremmen?

b4   *On which sport has Peter Alliss been a television commentator?*

a5   Until 1974, Belize was known as British . . .?

b5   *Which is the only Hindu Kingdom in the world?*

a6   For which element is the chemical symbol Mg?

b6   *And for which gas is the chemical symbol Kr?*

a7   What is the everyday name for the non-prescription drug, acetylsalicylic acid?

b7   *What is the general purpose of 'beta-blocker' drugs?*

a8   What is Ronald Reagan's middle name?

b8   *Who was the Soviet leader from 1977 to 1982?*

a9   Which sporting event did Mrs Helen Wills Moody win eight times (Miss Helen Wills before marriage)?

b9   *Ann Jones represented England at tennis and which other sport?*

a10   What is the unit of currency in Saudi Arabia?

b10   *And what is it in Kenya?*

a11   As what did Eugène Ionesco become famous?

b11   *Who became Governor of Hong Kong in 1992?*

a12   'How beastly the bourgeois is . . .' wrote a famous (even notorious) novelist and poet who died in 1930. Who was he?

b12   *'The minority is sometimes right; the majority is always wrong.' Who was the long-living Irish dramatist (who died in 1950) who wrote this?*

No. 199 Answers

a1 'B – you're so beautiful'
b1 *'Space Oddity' (by David Bowie)*
a2 Oil refining
b2 *Severn Bridge*
a3 Chief magistrate of a Scottish burgh (approximately equivalent to an English mayor)
b3 *A Bill*
a4 Kenny Everett
b4 *Golf*
a5 British Honduras
b5 *Nepal*
a6 Magnesium
b6 *Krypton*
a7 Aspirin
b7 *To combat raised blood-pressure, to treat angina, etc.*
a8 Wilson (Ronald Wilson Reagan)
b8 *(Leonid) Brezhnev*
a9 Wimbledon ladies singles
b9 *Table tennis*
a10 The riyal
b10 *The (Kenyan) shilling*
a11 Playwright
b11 *Chris Patten*
a12 D. H. Lawrence
b12 *G. B. Shaw*

Tie-breaker

Q Remembered in an anniversary celebrated in 1992, what did the 'Santa Maria', 'Nina' and 'Pinta' have in common?

A *They were the three ships that made up the fleet of Christopher Columbus on his voyage to find the Indies*

No. 200: Answers to Follow

Despite all the discoveries of the twentieth century, there are still many things we do not know about ourselves and about the world we live in. One day, we may find the answers to some of these questions. Others may always remain mysteries. As the last round of questions in this book, here are 25 questions to which we do not know the answers – at least, at the time of writing!

You may like to discuss what could be the answer to the questions – or whether (and how) we might discover the answers!

a1   We know what happens when we blush, but *why* do people go red when they are embarrassed?

b1   *How can baldness be cured?*

a2   How do homing pigeons find their way home?

b2   *How do migrating birds navigate?*

a3   Where did the Moon come from?

b3   *Why did dinosaurs become extinct?*

a4   Why do we have an appendix?

b4   *Why do some people have freckles?*

a5   Why are zebras striped? (NB: As they live on open, grassy plains, their stripes are not for camouflage!)

b5   *Why were white horses carved on some hillsides in southern England?*

a6   What is the centre of the Earth like?

b6   *Are there really unidentified flying objects?*

a7   When was Shakespeare born? (April 26, 1564 was the day he was baptized)

b7   *Did Robin Hood exist?*

a8   Why are more male babies born during war time? (There were distinct increases in the number of boy babies born during the two World Wars and during the Boer War)

b8   *What actually causes the process of birth to start?*

a9   Is there such a thing as re-incarnation?

b9   *Can some people 'see' into the future?*

a10   Why does some people's hair turn grey?

b10   *How do we remember things?*

a11 Who really first discovered America?
b11 Is there a lost continent of Atlantis?
a12 How can we cure the common cold (or prevent it)?
b12 Why do we dream?

Answers to follow!

Tie-breaker

Q How did the world begin – and why?
A ???

By the same author:

The Questionmaster's Quizbook

For anyone involved in organizing amateur quizzes – in social clubs and village halls, or in pubs, hospitals, or schools – here is an indispensable companion and reference source.

The unique features of this bumper collection include:

- 200 quizzes of 24 graded questions each (plus a tie-breaker), arranged in order of increasing difficulty and suitable for two teams of 3, 4, or 6 contestants.
- Full answers and acceptable alternatives
- Pronunciation guides for tricky words
- General knowledge and special thematic quizzes
- Suggestions and advice on running a quiz

With 5000 questions – compiled and verified by the former question-setter of such popular quiz shows as *Top of the Form, Square One* and *Sale of the Century,* and conveniently arranged in a ready-to-use format – *The Questionmaster's Quizbook* will also provide many hours of family entertainment, as well as giving prospective quiz contestants a useful means of testing their general knowledge before the big day!

How To Develop A Super Power Memory

Harry Lorayne

There is no such thing as a poor memory – only a trained or untrained one. This book proves it by showing with what speed and ease anyone can accomplish seemingly amazing memory feats.

'I don't care how poor you may think your memory is now! I believe that you have a memory 10 to 20 times more powerful than you realize today!'

Harry Lorayne's unique system of memory builders provides a quick and easy remedy for forgetfulness. Read Chapter 5 today and you will learn how to recall twenty important facts that you have never been able to memorize before. Tomorrow you will be able to plan your entire day in your mind – no longer will you need to rely on reminders, notes or other paper crutches!

Allow Harry Lorayne to share his secret with you, and you can build yourself a fabulous memory from scratch. Here at last is your chance to gain the super-powered, filing cabinet memory you've always dreamed about!

Double Your Learning Power

Geoffrey Dudley

Do you often forget the very things you want to remember – names of people you have just met, important addresses, useful contacts, telephone numbers? Are you embarrassed in business and social life by your inability to recall facts that should be on the tip of your tongue? If so, then you will realize that forgetfulness is an exasperating habit.

Yet inside your head you are equipped with an instrument which has a potential for remembering far more remarkable than the most advanced computer. All you need to do is learn how to fully tap its resources.

Here, at last, is a book to help you. After detailed research into modern scientific experiments Geoffrey Dudley reveals what psychologists have discovered about the process of learning and suggests practical ways of using this knowledge to your advantage.

THE QUESTIONMASTER'S QUIZ BOOK	0 7225 2239 8	£5.99	☐
HOW TO DEVELOP A SUPER POWER MEMORY	0 7225 1316 X	£4.99	☐
DOUBLE YOUR LEARNING POWER	0 7225 1211 2	£3.50	☐
SECRETS OF MIND POWER	0 7225 2512 5	£4.99	☐
THE MILLIONAIRE'S BOOK OF QUOTATIONS	0 7225 2499 4	£5.99	☐
TOTAL RECALL	0 7225 1505 7	£5.99	☐
WHAT TO SAY WHEN YOU TALK TO YOUR SELF	0 7225 2511 7	£4.99	☐

All these books are available from your local bookseller or can be ordered direct from the publishers.

To order direct just tick the titles you want and fill in the form below:

Name: _____

Address: _____

_____

_____ Postcode: _____

Send to: Thorsons Mail Order, Dept 32D, HarperCollins*Publishers*, Westerhill Road, Bishopbriggs, Glasgow G64 2QT.
Please enclose a cheque or postal order or your authority to debit your Visa/Access account —

Credit card no: _____

Expiry date: _____

Signature: _____

— up to the value of the cover price plus:

UK & BFPO: Add £1.00 for the first book and 25p for each additional book ordered.

Overseas orders including Eire: Please add £2.95 service charge. Books will be sent by surface mail but quotes for airmail despatches will be given on request.

24 HOUR TELEPHONE ORDERING SERVICE FOR ACCESS/VISA CARDHOLDERS — TEL: **041 772 2281.**